Also by Rick Bayless

Mexican Everyday (with Deann Groen Bayless)

Rick and Lanie's Excellent Kitchen Adventures
(with Lanie Bayless and Deann Groen Bayless)

Mexico—One Plate at a Time
(with JeanMarie Brownson and Deann Groen Bayless)

Salsas That Cook
(with JeanMarie Brownson and Deann Groen Bayless)

Rick Bayless's Mexican Kitchen
(with Deann Groen Bayless and JeanMarie Brownson)

Authentic Mexican (with Deann Groen Bayless)

RICK BAYLESS
WITH DEANN GROEN BAYLESS

FIESTA AT RICK'S

FABULOUS FOOD FOR GREAT TIMES WITH FRIENDS

PHOTOGRAPHS BY PAUL ELLEDGE

W. W. NORTON & COMPANY | NEW YORK LONDON

For information about permission to reproduce selections from this book,
write to Permissions, W. W. Norton & Company, Inc.,
500 Fifth Avenue, New York, NY 10110

For information about special discounts for bulk purchases, please contact
W. W. Norton Special Sales at specialsales@wwnorton.com or 800-233-4830

Manufacturing by Courier Kendallville
Book design by Barbara deWilde
Production manager: Anna Oler

Library of Congress Cataloging-in-Publication Data

Bayless, Rick.
    Fiesta at Rick's : fabulous food for great times with friends / Rick Bayless
with Deann Groen Bayless ; photographs by Paul Elledge.—1st ed.
       p. cm.
       Includes index.
       ISBN 978-0-393-05899-4 (hardcover)
1. Cookery, Mexican. 2. Entertaining. 3. Menus. I. Bayless, Deann Groen.
II. Title.
    TX716.M4B292 2010
    641.5972—dc22

                                                    2010013128

W. W. Norton & Company, Inc.
500 Fifth Avenue, New York, N.Y. 10110
www.wwnorton.com

W. W. Norton & Company Ltd.
Castle House, 75/76 Wells Street, London W1T 3QT

2 3 4 5 6 7 8 9 0

*To DB and LB
for giving me
so many reasons
to celebrate*

Contents

STEAMING TAMALES

Acknowledgments

This book has had a long gestation, from its inception over 30 years ago when Deann and I got married. Deann searched the farmer's market across from her apartment for flowers to grace the church, our mothers, the dining tables, the three-tier wedding cake I made. I cooked for days: *mole poblano*, a tortilla casserole called *budín azteca*, cactus and jícama salads. It was a day of love and celebration, of food like our Ann Arbor friends and far-flung families had never tasted, of sparkling *cremant de bourgonne*, red wine and good beer.

Without Deann, I doubt I'd ever have been open to learning the art of honest-to-goodness fiesta. I owe her a great debt of gratitude for this book's inspiration, plus a lot of thoughtful council, unwavering support, patience and great editing during its creation.

When Lanie came into our family 19 years ago, all I wanted to do was celebrate: from the "picnic" of vending machine chili and corned beef hash Deann and I shared, snuggled with her in a bed moments after her birth at Illinois Masonic birthing center, to baptism, birthdays, holidays, grammar school graduation, quinceañera, high-school graduation. She's inspired me to throw every ounce of my being into creating special, delicious moments when time expands to embrace all of creation.

Maria Guarnaschelli has been my editor for nearly a quarter of a century. Who knows what spark she saw in the clumsy manuscript for *Authentic Mexican* that I submitted to her. But she figured out how to fan it into a full fire, and for that I'll be ever grateful. The way she weighs every word and thought has sharpened my communication skills more than she'll ever know. And she is supported by the staff at W. W. Norton—the designers, copy editors, proofreaders, support staff, promoters, visionaries—especially Melanie Tortoroli, Anna Oler, Barbara deWilde, Nancy Palmquist, Susan Sanfrey, Ingsu Liu, Sue Carlson, Louise Brockett, and Rebecca

Carlisle. They are just what every author wants: an incredibly professional group, always at the ready to make the manuscript better and better.

Doe Coover, literary agent and dear friend, is a trusted shepherd without whom you wouldn't be holding this volume in your hands.

I count my blessings that every day in my "Frontera world" I have the opportunity to work with amazingly smart, dedicated and talented people. Jen Fite has grown with us for many years, from her original position as restaurant host all the way to handling all our public relations, negotiating and producing appearances, juggling schedules—in truth, doing that magical anything and everything necessary to keep my life from flying into a thousand pieces. Andrew McCaughan, my assistant for several years, always brings fresh energy to our team, along with the sensibilities of a natural artist and photographer, enthusiasm for great food and hard work, and the ability to laugh under pressure. Fabi James, who's like Lanie's older sister, offers such love and care that without her the Frontera world would not be the same. And Deb Silberstein tested and tested and retested all the recipes in this book, working out my vagaries and hair-brain ideas for translating restaurant techniques for home cooks, putting up with my single-mindedness and wild-eyed enthusiasm for cooking enough to feed a whole houseful. Deb and I did all the preparations for the individual food photos in the book; Kirsten West and I did all the styling for them. Brian Enyart (chef de cuisine at Topolobampo) and Richard James (chef de cuisine at Frontera) never failed with well-seasoned culinary advice; and together with Carlos Alferez (partner–general manager), they buoy me with steady support, allowing me the freedom to pursue many satisfying endeavors.

Paul Elledge, supported by James Exley and Brian Schilling, really brings this book to life with his photos—honest and brilliant, just like a great fiesta. His individual food shots exude the same heart and soul he's become so famous for when he shoots people. Bravo!

Paul took the party shots while we were filming the sixth and seventh seasons of my Public Television series *Mexico—One Plate at a Time*. I would like to express my sincere appreciation to our television crew for creating such beauty: Chris Gyoury, our longtime director (we miss you!); Scott Dummler and George Elder from Luminair; partners with me and Deann in Frontera Media Productions (Manny Valdes, JeanMarie Brownson, Greg Keller); our indefatigable kitchen staff (Shannon Kinsella, Floria Hernandez, Jaime Sotelo, Lorena Martinez); imaginative stylists (Holly Todd, Cate Sullivan, Roxann Ault); supertalented garden manager (Bill Shores) and guest wranglers (Stacy Dixon, Conchita Valdes). And, as always, I am grateful to our television show's long-term principle sponsors (Bohemia Mexican beer, FiveStar ranges); we are honored to be associated with such incredibly high-quality products.

Introduction

I grew up in a party family. Big family parties presided over by my red-headed, gown-wearing, pie-baking southern grandmother, who understood that great food on the table was a beacon that drew our family closer. And I grew up with big parties thrown by other folks, too—Oklahoma barbeques mostly, for which my family's catering business made the ribs, baked beans, deviled eggs and slaw. Though they were joyous events, at least for the most part, I didn't understand the full potential of "party" until I moved to Mexico and discovered "fiesta."

And what I discovered is this: "Party" is to "fiesta" as "lunch" is to "Thanksgiving dinner." Just think about it: Lunch satisfies nutritional needs, just as Thanksgiving dinner does. But our Thanksgiving meal offers several other satisfactions, as well. By its sheer magnitude, Thanksgiving dinner leads us to marvel at its heartening bounty, at the beauty of natural ingredients and handmade preparations. It makes us feel buoyed by our role as participants in a world that's larger than ourselves, in a cultural tradition that brings together past and present, local and national. And of course, it leads to our feeling nurtured by the mere physical presence of those with whom we share a history—those we care about and who care about us.

I got a hint of real fiesta in my early twenties when I made my first climb up the stair-etched hill to Restaurante Arroyo in the southern Mexico City suburb of Tlalpan. It was a Sunday—the place truly comes alive on Sunday—and the only entrance was through the dirt-floor kitchen. On one side, I could see the huge central Mexican-style *barbacoa* pits packed with roasting lambs in maguey leaves. On the other, cistern-size copper cauldrons of meaty-smelling pork lard stood ready to slow-cook whole hog *carnitas* or flash-fry crunchy sheets of *chicharrón* as big as a fourth grader. Gallon-size lava rock mortars held chunky guacamole, tangy tomatillo salsa and robust *salsa borracha*. Over the next several hours, that kitchen would welcome several thousand folks, big groups of friends or family or family friends, all celebrating, all commemorating something.

The aroma of fresh-baking corn tortillas mixed with the earthy *barbacoa*. And with the pork and fresh cilantro, the stinging dried chiles and blasting mariachis and bougainvillea-colored tissue paper cutouts that adorned the rafters by the tens of thousands. There's no ramp up at Arroyo: Even before your first sip of tequila or *cerveza*, you've become part of a joyous, comfortable, wacky-fun fiesta.

That's because Restaurante Arroyo offers more than just a great meal. Having been welcomed into the kitchen—brought face-to-face with all those aromatic celebration specialties—you're launched toward a mouthwatering experience that's comfortable and clearly out of the ordinary. By the time you've reached one of the rustic dining rooms, saturated with classic Mexican color and song and dance, you've opened yourself up to yet-undiscovered possibilities. And the first mouthful of *barbacoa* or *carnitas*, wrapped in a warm tortilla and daubed with guacamole or drizzled with salsa, cinches it for you. Those flavors eaten in this place with these people provide the conduit to a perfect moment that transcends all that is everyday.

That is fiesta. And what comes from the kitchen is instrumental in creating it.

Fiesta at Rick's may seem an unexpected book for me to have written following on the heels of *Mexican Everyday*, my ode to a satisfying and healthy life through simple, fresh-from-scratch cooking. While there are dishes in this new book that don't require a lot of time to make, a good number of them do involve forethought or dedication. And once you've invested the planning and care, I think you'll agree that the end results taste pretty luxurious, pretty rich and satisfying.

After many years of throwing and participating in parties here and in Mexico, I feel certain about this one conviction of mine: Planning, crafting and splurging are essential building blocks of a real fiesta. Which, of course, is a conviction that's out of sync with what most of us believe about modern life. Luxuriously rich foods are bad for us, we've been told, and we should avoid them. And, certainly, we have little time for anything that's not "quick and easy."

So should fiesta go to the cultural dust bin, along with Easter bonnets and croquet? Should our holidays continue to evolve toward shopping opportunities, focusing less and less on food, family and friends? I think that would be a tragic loss. In fact, ultimately so unsatisfying, so unsustainable that I believe our culture will either crash and burn or swing naturally back to an honest respect for food and its pivotal role in bringing folks together in celebration.

As humans, we have basic needs, and history has shown us that creating fiestas is one of them. We need to break the rhythms of our everyday lives, to plan and anticipate all the potential that a fiesta embraces. We need to invest time in crafting a rich fiesta experience for those we care about. We need to experience those moments when time stands still. Moments when we're filled with exhilaration, joy, some sense of transcendence. Moments reached through the conduit of great food and drink.

And about the bad, rich food? Just remember two things about what the nutritionists tell us. First, the science of nutrition is very young, and, often, what's good one year is bad the next, or vice versa. If I were you, I wouldn't put as much stock in nutrition science as in centuries of (pre-industrial) cultural development. Before our current era of topsy-turvy industrial progress—an era in which we do less physical work and have an overabundance of food at hand, most of it processed in ways our bodies are unaccustomed to—cultures had, over centuries, developed pretty adequate ways of nourishing themselves, both physically and spiritually. Perhaps we need to trust those older approaches as much as—maybe even more than—what nutrition science is telling us.

And second, remember that nutritionists craft simple messages for maximum impact. If they've deemed a food deleterious, it won't likely creep onto the beneficial list . . . even sometimes, even on special occasions. Yet that's exactly where it should be. Because, if we eat a *wide variety* of good food—fresh stuff in reasonable portions—there's a perfect time for *everything*. For the simple pleasure of a fall apple and for the over-the-top chocolate fudge cake.

So, *Fiesta at Rick's* is my companion volume to *Mexican Everyday*—the occasional, celebratory, luxurious yang to the everyday, homey, simple yin. Both are healthy, both are necessary. And it's my hope that both enrich your lives with abundant pleasure.

FIESTA AT RICK'S

Guacamoles, Nibbles and Libations

The real point is just to hang out, isn't it—to listen to some music, have something to eat, something to drink. Tell stories, laugh a lot, loosen into a state of happy relaxation. Maybe the get-together is a "drop by for drinks" kind or the prelude to a restaurant visit or a progressive meal from one location to another, or maybe it's an afternoon deal that ends with a festive cake.

As you're probably already aware, Mexico is great at food for those occasions. And we should just start with the obvious: guacamole. It's become an icon of party food. But guacamole isn't—certainly doesn't have to be—just one recipe. Start with some mashed avocado seasoned with a squirt of lime, a sprinkle of salt, a little cilantro, and then let your imagination take hold. Think fruit, think nuts, think bacon. (I can't help but think bacon.) As the regional cooks of Mexico have proven, guacamole is one of the most adaptable dishes in the kitchen. So follow their lead and adapt it as you see fit.

I don't know if you've had the opportunity to wander the streets of a Mexican town or scour a local market there, but at practically every turn you bump into little portable street stalls with heaps of nuts and nut mixtures, typically seasoned with salt or chile or lime—or all three, plus some garlic thrown in for good measure. Sometimes they're little wooden tables set with plastic-clad "pillars" stuffed full of the vendor's offerings; sometimes the goods are in glass or plastic barrels; I've even seen wondrous nut displays in specially made wheelbarrows. Roasted garbanzos and fava beans are typically part of the mix, as well. And glazed nuts. With all that diversity, I'm inspired to use Mexican market ingredients to create new spicings for the nuts I love so much. In my opinion, having a tin of spiced nuts on hand turns a drink into something much more memorable.

Of course, margaritas are as celebrated as guacamole when it comes to what people love at a get-together. And we all know that there are many varieties. But I'd argue that there are options beyond what you may have

already tried, beyond the fruity, sweet, blended concoctions. Mixed with Champagne or blended with cucumber or made with mezcal, a margarita shows great new possibilities. And why not take inspiration from the nearby Caribbean islands, and adopt the refreshing mojito, just to see how perfectly its limey brightness grooves with the flavors of the Mexican kitchen. Or make it with a silver tequila, or with muddled fruit like watermelon or with a light, citrusy beer like Tecate—I've seen lots of faces light up through my years of party throwing, just from the mention of an unexpected margarita or mojito flavor combo.

And then there are the homemade Mexican soft drinks, the glass barrels of Crayon-colored liquids that punctuate street corners and sit on bars in traditional restaurants in nearly every inhabited square kilometer of the country. I never think of the half-century-old Restaurante Arroyo south of Mexico City without picturing the transparent vessels of *aguas frescas*, as these fresh-made soft drinks are called: milky-looking guava, ruby *jamaica*, bright-red watermelon, russet *tamarindo*—all magic with the restaurant's famous lamb *barbacoa* and pasilla-infused *salsa borracha*. Everyone glides right into a festive mood with the rustic food, the great drinks, the classic music, the earthy surroundings.

The rich colors and vibrant flavors of Mexico's *aguas frescas* are the epitome of refreshment . . . and can be spun into some pretty dazzling cocktails with a modicum of creativity. Tamarind with apple juice and dark beer makes a mean Mexican version of a Snakebite. *Jamaica*, the ruby-red infusion made from a hibiscus relative, does a stunning job standing in for cranberry in a Cosmo. I've even added splashes of silver tequila and sparkling water to Rick's Favorite Summer Soft Drink on page 71 and created a spontaneous—and, I have to admit, pretty cool—cocktail. Give it a whirl.

BACON-AND-TOMATO GUACAMOLE (PAGE 26)

Bacon-and-Tomato Guacamole
Guacamole de Tocino y Jitomate

MAKES ABOUT 3 CUPS, SERVING 8 TO 10 AS A NIBBLE

5 strips medium-thick bacon (full-flavored smoky bacon is great here)

3 medium-large (about 1¼ pounds) ripe avocados

½ medium white onion, chopped into ¼-inch pieces

2 or 3 canned chipotle chiles *en adobo* to taste, removed from the canning sauce, stemmed, slit open, seeds scraped out and finely chopped

1 medium-large round, ripe tomato, cored and chopped into ¼-inch pieces

¼ cup (loosely packed) coarsely chopped fresh cilantro (thick bottom stems cut off), plus a little extra for garnish

Salt

1 or 2 tablespoons fresh lime juice

This is kind of a no-brainer, bacon, lettuce and tomato being such a beloved sandwich combo, especially when there's a good smear of mayo. This guacamole is in the same vein, except that the tangy, creamy mayo is replaced by avocado and lime. Come to think of it, the avocado, along with a little cilantro, brings the lettuce-green to the picture as well. It's a perfect Mexican-American fusion of smoky, bright, creamy, fresh and satisfying.

If the tomato is really ripe and juicy, I'd cut it in half widthwise (across its "equator"), then gently squeeze out the jelly-like seeds from each half. That'll keep the guacamole from becoming runny. And to ensure crisp bacon texture, don't stir it in until just before serving.

In a large (10-inch) skillet, cook the slices of bacon in a single layer over medium heat, turning them occasionally, until crispy and browned, about 10 minutes. Drain on paper towels, then coarsely crumble.

Cut around each avocado, from stem to blossom end and back again, then twist the two halves apart. Dislodge the pit. Scoop the flesh from the skin into a large bowl. Using an old-fashioned potato masher or a large fork or spoon, mash the avocados into a coarse puree.

Scoop the onion into a small strainer and rinse under cold water. Shake off the excess water and transfer to the bowl, along with the chipotle chiles, tomatoes, cilantro (save out a little for garnish if you wish) and about ²/₃ of the bacon. Gently stir to combine all of the ingredients. Taste and season with salt, usually about ¹/₂ teaspoon, and enough lime juice to add a little sparkle.

Cover with plastic wrap directly on the surface of the guacamole and refrigerate until you're ready to serve. Scoop the guacamole into a serving dish, sprinkle with the remaining bacon (and cilantro if you have it), and you're ready to serve.

Toasted Pumpkin Seed Guacamole
Guacamole de Pepita Tostada

MAKES ABOUT 3 CUPS, SERVING 8 TO 10 AS A NIBBLE

3   medium-large (about 1¼ pounds) ripe avocados

½   small red onion, chopped into ¼-inch pieces

½ to 1 fresh serrano chile, stemmed, seeded and finely chopped

2   tablespoons (loosely packed) chopped fresh cilantro, plus a few leaves for garnish

About 2 tablespoons fresh lime juice

¾   cup hulled, toasted, salted pumpkin seeds, plus a few extra for garnish

Salt

Because avocado flavor has a natural affinity with nuttiness (the wild ancestor of our avocados has a very nutty flavor), the native-Mexican pumpkin seed would seem a natural guacamole add-in, wouldn't it? But no one I know adds it, in spite of the fact that it layers a wonderful earthy bass-note flavor onto the avocado's light creaminess. Toasted Pumpkin Seed Guacamole is especially good dipped up with slices of crunchy-raw jícama, cucumber and radish.

Nowadays, toasted salted pumpkin seeds are available in most well-stocked grocery stores. If all you can find are untoasted hulled seeds (those still-in-the-white-hull pumpkin seeds available in Mexican groceries aren't at all right for this preparation), you'll have to toast them yourself: Scoop the pumpkin seeds into a large dry skillet and set over medium heat. When the first seed pops, stir constantly until the vast majority have popped from flat to oval and are lightly browned, about 5 minutes from when the first one pops. Slide onto a plate to cool.

Cut around each avocado from stem to blossom end and back up again, then twist the halves apart. Dislodge the pit. Scoop the avocado flesh into a large bowl. Coarsely mash the avocado with a large fork or potato masher. Scoop the onion into a small strainer and rinse under cold water. Shake off the excess water and mix into the avocado along with the serrano, cilantro and lime juice.

Scoop the pumpkin seeds into a food processor and pulse until finely ground. Scrape down the sides of the processor bowl, then run the processor until the seeds are a chunky-looking paste. Mix the paste into the avocado mixture. Taste and season with salt, usually about $1/2$ teaspoon. If not using immediately, cover with plastic wrap pressed directly on the surface of the guacamole and refrigerate—best if served within a couple of hours.

When you're ready to serve, scoop the guacamole into a decorative bowl and garnish with a sprinkling of pumpkin seeds and cilantro leaves.

Mango Guacamole
Guacamole de Mango

MAKES ABOUT 3 CUPS, SERVING 8 TO 10 AS A NIBBLE

3   medium-large (about 1¼ pounds) ripe avocados

½   small red onion, chopped into ¼-inch pieces

½ to 1 fresh serrano chile, stemmed, seeded and finely chopped

2   tablespoons (loosely packed) chopped fresh cilantro, plus a few leaves for garnish

1   tablespoon fresh lime juice

1   large ripe mango, peeled, flesh cut from the pit and cut into ¼-inch pieces

    Salt

One of my summer favorites: two tropical flavors—creamy avocados and juicy, fragrant mangos—with the sweet crunch of red onion and just enough sparkly lime and cilantro. Other than procuring ripe avocados and mango, there's almost nothing to this preparation.

Cut around each avocado from stem to blossom end and back up again, then twist the halves apart. Dislodge the pit. Scoop the avocado flesh into a large bowl. Coarsely mash the avocado with a large fork or potato masher. Scoop the onion into a small strainer and rinse under cold water. Shake off the excess water and mix into the avocado along with serrano, cilantro, lime juice and $^2/_3$ of the diced mango. Taste and season with salt, usually about $^3/_4$ teaspoon. If not using immediately, cover with plastic wrap pressed directly on the surface of the guacamole and refrigerate—best if served within a couple of hours.

When you're ready to serve, scoop the guacamole into a serving bowl and garnish with the remaining diced mango and a few cilantro leaves if you're so inclined. Serve with tortilla chips or slices of cucumber or jícama.

MANGO GUACAMOLE

Yucatecan Guacamole
Aguacate Machacado

MAKES ABOUT 3 CUPS, SERVING 8 TO 10 AS A NIBBLE

3 Hass or 2 Florida/Caribbean–type (about 1¼ pounds) ripe avocados

1 small red onion, chopped into ¼-inch pieces

1 medium round, ripe tomato, cored and chopped into ¼-inch pieces (squeeze out the seeds for a more refined dish)

2 garlic cloves, peeled and very finely chopped

½ cup (loosely packed) chopped fresh cilantro (thick bottom stems cut off), plus a few sprigs for garnish

1 or 2 fresh habanero chile(s), stemmed, seeded and very finely chopped, plus an extra one for garnish

About 2 tablespoons fresh sour orange (or lime) juice

Salt

1 to 2 tablespoons olive oil if using Florida-style avocados (optional)

Lettuce leaves for lining your serving bowl, if you wish

They haven't traditionally made guacamole in the Yucatan because the local avocados are the large, hard-skin, sweet-tasting, low-fat avocados—the ones most people call Florida/Caribbean avocados. They're great in salads and smoothies and desserts . . . but mash them? They lack the oil content to make a thick creamy guacamole.

Until fairly recently, when transportation became easier and tourist demand for guacamole grew stronger, a simple avocado mash called aguacate machacado was all you could find—and not all that often. Flavored typically with a little habanero, cilantro and sour orange juice, it certainly smacked of Yucatan's distinctive, bright flavors. I say, do the same thing, but use Mexico's west coast avocados—the creamy Hass avocados that are so popular in the States—and add a little tomato, a handful of red onion, maybe even a little olive oil, especially if you're using Caribbean avocados.

Cut around each avocado from stem to blossom end and back up again, then twist the two halves apart. Dislodge the pit, then scoop the avocado flesh into a bowl. Scoop the onion into a small strainer and rinse under cold water. Shake off the excess and add to the avocado along with the tomato, garlic, cilantro and habanero(s). Use a large fork or a potato masher to work all of the ingredients into a coarse mash. Season with the sour orange (or lime) and salt, usually about 1 teaspoon. Gently stir in the oil, if you like. If not using immediately, cover with plastic wrap pressed directly on the surface of the guacamole and refrigerate until you're ready to serve (which, for the best quality, shouldn't be more than an hour or so).

If you're using them, line a decorative bowl with lettuce leaves, then scoop the mixture into it. Sprinkle on a little chopped cilantro and top with an extra habanero to let your guests know what to expect.

Guacamole Basics

AVOCADOS—RIPENESS AND VARIETIES: To make good guacamole, you need ripe avocados. Because avocados don't ripen on the tree, they can be cooled immediately upon picking and held in a state of "suspended animation" until someone needs ripe ones. That's when the produce vendors warm them to room temperature, triggering the ripening process. Ripening can take a week or more; trapping (or increasing) the ethylene gas they naturally emit during ripening can speed the process . . . but too much ethylene gas can lead to unevenly ripe, oddly mushy avocados. Just as too cold a refrigeration temperature for a ripe avocado can lead to brownish flesh. All this technical stuff should help you understand any less-than-optimal avocado experiences you may have had.

If you bring home still-firm avocados from your local grocery, leave them at room temperature until soft. Placing them in a paper bag or fruit-ripening container will speed the process . . . but not much.

When the bulbous end of the avocado yields to firm pressure, the avocado is ready to use; if you have to push hard to get the flesh to yield, the avocado will turn out guacamole that's flavorless and unpleasantly chunky, not creamy.

There are many different varieties of avocados—each with its own texture and flavor—but what we typically see in the United States is the dark, pebbly-skin Hass avocado. It has a nice flavor (though not as interesting as some lesser-known varieties); it darkens (oxidizes) less quickly than certain ones; when ripe, it holds for a week or so in the *warmest* part of your refrigerator (ripe avocados held in too cold a spot will turn brown); and it has a rich, creamy texture.

CONSISTENCY: Tastes differ, but I've found that most people enjoy coarse-textured guacamole with good-size pieces of avocado. Not only is the texture of the guacamole satisfying—no pablum, no puree—but it shows your guacamole is the real deal, nothing from a frozen pouch.

FLAVORING: In Mexico, some cooks coarsely mash avocados, season them with salt—maybe a little garlic—and call the result "guacamole." While I think that's a good start, I'd add a few more flavorings before I'd use the "guacamole" label. I'd add cilantro and a little chopped raw white onion (rinse it under cold water for the cleanest, brightest flavor), plus some chopped green chile if I wasn't planning the guacamole to be a foil for spicier dishes.

And lime? Most of my Mexican friends think Americans lean too heavily on lime when seasoning guacamole, covering the richness of the avocado. But a little lime, I contend, brightens all the flavors.

Once you've got your base, you can add tomatoes (even tomatillos), change white onion for red, add citrus or tropical (or even dried) fruit, stir in smoked fish or nuts, choose from a wide variety of chiles. The possibilities are endless, because avocados are remarkably congenial.

PRESENTATION: My most FAQ: how do you keep guacamole from turning brown? Answer: you can't . . . but you can slow it down. Use Hass avocados, add lime to your guacamole, cover the finished mixture with plastic *directly on its surface*, and keep it cold—even when you serve. Warm, uncovered, limeless guacamole turns dark quickly. I've never found the pit trick to do anything more than annoy my guests.

ROASTED GARLIC GUACAMOLE (PAGE 79)

Grilled Garlic and Orange Guacamole
Guacamole de Ajo Asado y Naranja
MAKES ABOUT 3 CUPS, SERVING 8 TO 10 AS A NIBBLE

6   garlic cloves, unpeeled

1   jalapeño or 2 serrano chile(s), stemmed

1   small red onion, sliced ¼-inch thick

    A little vegetable oil

3   medium-large (about 1¼ pounds) ripe avocados

¼   cup (loosely packed) coarsely chopped fresh cilantro (thick bottom stems cut off)

2   small oranges

1 to 2 tablespoons fresh lime juice

    Salt

¼   cup toasted sliced almonds (optional)

Avocados seem to luxuriate in smoky flavors, from bacon and smoked fish to grilled onions. And grilled garlic and grilled green chiles. Which takes us to this simple guacamole whose garlic, chile and onion all feel the sear of the grill—preferably one fired by charcoal or wood for the most distinctive flavor. For a counterpoint of bright freshness, there are bits of orange, a squeeze of lime, a little cilantro. And a few sliced almonds to add toasty nuttiness to all that charming richness.

1. *Grill the garlic, chile and onion.* Turn on a gas grill or light a charcoal grill and let the coals burn until medium-hot and covered with white ash. Lay the garlic and chile(s) on a perforated grill pan. (A perforated grill pan isn't necessary, but the garlic and chiles tend to slip through the grates on most grills.) Lightly brush both sides of the onion slices with oil and lay them on the grill pan. Set the pan on the grill grates and cook, turning everything until soft and lightly browned, about 15 minutes. (You'll want to remove any pieces that brown more quickly than others.)

Scoop the onion and chile(s) onto a cutting board, chop into small pieces, then scoop into a large bowl. Remove the charred papery skin from the garlic. With the side of a knife or in a mortar, work the garlic into a coarse paste. Add to the onion and chile(s).

2. *Finish the guacamole.* Cut around each avocado from stem to blossom end and back up again, then twist the halves apart. Dislodge the pit. Scoop the avocado flesh into the bowl and add the cilantro. Using an old-fashioned potato masher, large fork or back of a large spoon, coarsely mash everything together.

Cut sections (supremes) from the oranges: Cut the stem and blossom ends off the oranges, stand the oranges on a cutting board and, working close to the flesh, cut away the rind and all the white pith. With a sharp, thin knife, cut out the orange segments from between the white membranes that divide them. Slice the supremes in half and stir into the avocado mixture.

Taste and season with the lime juice and salt, usually about ¾ teaspoon. Scoop into a serving bowl, cover with plastic wrap directly on the surface of the guacamole and refrigerate until you're ready to serve (which, for best results, needs to be within a couple of hours). Just before serving, sprinkle with the toasted almonds, if you're using them, and set before your guests.

Toasted Almond Guacamole with Apricots
Guacamole de Almendra con Chabacano

MAKES ABOUT 3 CUPS, SERVING 8 TO 10 AS A NIBBLE

3   medium-large (about 1¼ pounds) ripe avocados

10 to 15 dried apricots, chopped into small pieces (a scant ½ cup)

3   tablespoons almond butter (available at well-stocked grocery stores)

Hot green chile(s) to taste (roughly 1 serrano or ½ jalapeño), stemmed, seeded (if you wish) and finely chopped

2   tablespoons fresh lime juice, plus a little more if needed

2 to 3 tablespoons (loosely packed) chopped fresh cilantro

Salt

¼   cup toasted sliced almonds (optional)

When you taste the thin-skin wild avocados—they look a little like fresh mission figs—the flavor of nuts and herbs hits you before the green creaminess we typically associate with the common, pebbly-skin Hass avocado. But if you add a nutty flavor to Hass avocados using a little almond butter, the result is remarkable. Once I've gone that far, a little chopped dried apricot always seems the next logical step in flavor combinations.

If you can't find almond butter, toast blanched almonds in a 325-degree oven until they are aromatic, cool them, then grind them as smooth as possible in a food processor (a small processor works best for this quantity). Or, if you buy almond butter and it's stiff, zap it in the microwave for a few seconds, then stir until smooth and spreadable. The addition of a little water may be in order.

Cut around each avocado from stem to blossom end and back up again, then twist the halves apart. Dislodge the pit, then scoop the avocado flesh into a large bowl. Coarsely mash the avocado with a large fork or potato masher. Mix in the apricots, almond butter, chopped chile(s), lime juice and the minimum amount of chopped cilantro. Taste and season with salt, usually about 1 teaspoon, plus more cilantro and lime if you think appropriate. If not using immediately, cover with plastic directly on the surface of the guacamole and refrigerate—best if served within a few hours. When you are ready to serve, scoop into a serving bowl and garnish with sliced almonds if you wish.

Sun-Dried Tomato Guacamole
Guacamole Tomate Deshidratado

MAKES ABOUT 3 CUPS, SERVING 8 TO 10 AS A NIBBLE

Of course, when good tomatoes aren't available, you could just leave them out of guacamole . . . except that I'd miss that gentle sweetness/tartness they add. So when I've gotta have tomato-flecked guacamole, and it's winter, and the fresh tomatoes are awful (and I won't settle for tomatillo guacamole or pumpkin seed guacamole or roasted garlic guacamole), this is what I make. It's essentially my no-holds-barred summer guacamole with sun-dried tomatoes replacing the fresh ones, and the addition of a few little cubes of crunchy jícama for freshness. Not summer, but not bad at all.

The best sun-dried tomatoes to use here are the pliable kind, the ones with a texture similar to that of a dried apricot. (Oil-packed ones are okay, but not my favorite.) In most of my local groceries, they're carrying little packages of pliable sun-dried tomatoes hung up in the produce department. There's a smoked version that's dynamite for this guacamole.

3 medium-large (about 1¼ pounds) ripe avocados

½ medium white onion, chopped into ¼-inch pieces (about ⅓ cup)

Fresh hot green chile(s) to taste (usually 2 serranos or 1 jalapeño), stemmed, seeded (if you wish) and finely chopped

¼ cup soft sun-dried tomatoes, chopped into ¼-inch pieces (patted dry on paper towels if oil-packed)

¼ cup (loosely packed) chopped fresh cilantro (thick bottom stems cut off), plus a little extra for garnish

Salt

1 or 2 tablespoons fresh lime juice

A little Mexican *queso fresco* or other fresh garnishing cheese like feta or salted farmer's cheese, for garnish (optional)

Cut around each avocado, from stem to blossom end and back again, then twist the two halves apart. Dislodge the pit and scoop the avocado flesh into a bowl. Using an old-fashioned potato masher or a large fork or spoon, mash the avocados into a coarse puree. Scoop the onion into a small strainer and rinse under cold water. Shake off the excess water and mix into the avocado, along with the chile(s), tomatoes and cilantro. Taste and season with salt and lime juice—the guacamole usually takes about 1 teaspoon of salt; lime juice is a matter of personal preference.

Cover with plastic wrap directly on the surface of the guacamole and refrigerate until you're ready to serve (for best results, this needs to be within a couple of hours). Scoop the guacamole into a serving dish, sprinkle with a little chopped cilantro and *queso fresco* (if you're using it) and you're ready to serve.

Oaxacan-Style Peanuts with chile and garlic
Cacahuates Oaxaqueños con chile y ajo

MAKES A GENEROUS 4 CUPS, ENOUGH FOR 12 TO 15 AS A NIBBLE

1 tablespoon olive or vegetable oil

4 dried árbol chiles, stemmed and torn into 1-inch pieces

8 garlic cloves, peeled and halved

24 ounces (about 4 generous cups) toasted Spanish peanuts (the ones with the skins still on)

Salt

This is the Oaxacan snack—found in street vendor carts, on restaurant tables, in kitchen cupboards, on bar tops. Spanish peanuts—with their pungent, dark-tasting thin skins still clinging—fried in an oily skillet with garlic cloves and árbol chile. And sprinkled with salt, of course. It's a gutsy snack that offers surprises like the occasional piece of chile or garlic clove or even those peanut skins clinging to your oily fingers. All adding up to a pretty pleasurable experience.

Working Ahead: The peanuts can be made a week or so ahead and kept in an airtight container.

In a very large (12-inch) skillet, combine the oil, árbols and garlic. Set over medium heat and stir until the garlic is softened and the chiles are toasty smelling, about 3 minutes. Add the peanuts, lower the heat to medium-low and stir nearly constantly until the peanuts are richly aromatic, about 10 minutes. Sprinkle generously with salt (usually about ½ teaspoon). Cool and set out for your guests to enjoy.

Chipotle-Roasted Almonds
Almendras Enchipotladas

MAKES 4 CUPS

2 canned chipotle chiles

2 tablespoons *adobo* (tomato-y sauce in the can of chiles)

2 tablespoons fresh lime juice

2 tablespoons ketchup

¼ cup dark brown sugar

½ teaspoon salt

4 cups (1¼ pounds) toasted blanched almonds

Wanting a sweet-spicy nibble to set out for guests, I concocted this sweet chipotle glaze for almonds (though it works just as well on peanuts and other nuts). And you're reading the list of ingredients right: I used ketchup as the medium to work the chiles, lime and brown sugar together into one pretty fine coating that's easy to distribute evenly. When the nuts are ready to remove from the oven, they will no longer feel sticky—but they won't be crisp. That'll happen as they cool off. If the almonds you buy are blanched (peeled) but not toasted, spread them on a rimmed baking sheet and bake in a 325-degree oven until they're aromatic and lightly browned, 10 to 15 minutes.

Working Ahead: The cooled nuts can be stored in an airtight container for 4 or 5 days. If we need to keep them longer, we avoid their becoming sticky by storing them in a sealed container with moisture-absorbing limestone (available from companies that supply equipment and ingredients for candy and pastry making).

Heat the oven to 350 degrees. Scoop the chipotles, *adobo*, lime juice, ketchup, sugar and salt into a blender and process to a smooth puree. Pour into a large bowl along with the almonds and toss until the nuts are evenly coated. Line a rimmed baking sheet with parchment paper and evenly spread the nuts on it. Bake until they are fragrant and no long moist, about 30 minutes, stirring occasionally. Cool the almonds on the sheet pan, then scoop into a serving bowl and set out for all to enjoy.

GARLICKY HABANERO MACADAMIA NUTS (*FOREGROUND*; PAGE 38)
AND CHIPOTLE-ROASTED ALMONDS (PAGE 36)

Garlicky Habanero Macadamia Nuts
Macadamias al Chile Habanero y Ajo

MAKES ABOUT 3 CUPS, ENOUGH FOR 9 TO 12 AS A NIBBLE

6   garlic cloves, unpeeled

1 to 2 fresh habanero chile(s),
    stemmed

2   tablespoons olive oil

1   tablespoon honey

1   teaspoon salt

3   cups (about 1 pound) roasted
    macadamia nuts

Most North Americans think habanero = fire. I think habanero = aroma of tropical fruit and flowers . . . plus some pretty searing heat. By roasting habaneros (along with garlic) and blending them into seasoning, we've already mitigated their heat without doing too much damage to that beautifully aromatic flavor. Adding a touch of honey soothes the heat to a very manageable glow.

Still scared about using habaneros? Try using two or three serrano (or two small jalapeño) chiles instead. And if your macadamia nuts come salted, cut the salt in the seasoning by half.

Working Ahead: *The nuts can be made a week or more ahead. Store in an airtight container.*

1. *Make the flavoring.* Turn on the oven to 350 degrees. In a dry skillet, roast the unpeeled garlic and chiles over medium heat, turning them regularly until soft and blotchy-blackened in spots, about 10 minutes for the habanero, 10 to 15 minutes for the garlic. When the garlic is handleable, peel off the papery skin. In a mortar or small food processor, combine the garlic and habanero. Pound or process to as smooth a mixture as possible. Add the oil, honey and salt and pound or process to incorporate thoroughly.

2. *Mix and bake.* In a large bowl, combine the macadamias and flavoring, stirring to thoroughly coat the nuts. Spread the nuts on a rimmed baking sheet and bake—stirring occasionally—until the nuts are toasty smelling and the flavorings have formed a shiny, dryish coating, about 20 minutes. Cool.

Chilied Peanuts and Pumpkin Seeds
Cacahuates y Pepitas Enchilados
MAKES 3 CUPS, ENOUGH FOR 9 TO 12 AS A NIBBLE

2   cups roasted peanuts (preferably without salt)

2   tablespoons fresh lime juice

2   teaspoons ancho (or guajillo) chile powder (available from national companies like McCormick, Mexican groceries and Internet sites), plus a little árbol chile powder if you like it spicy

     Salt

1   cup hulled, raw pumpkin seeds

You can buy tangy chilied peanuts from street vendors all over Mexico. The vendors will likely have salted toasted pumpkin seeds, too, which I like to mix with the peanuts. A very good (and quite good for you) snack—so good, in fact, that we've set a bowl of the stuff on every table in Frontera Grill for nearly two decades. Some of you will find it easier to buy toasted salted pumpkin seeds; simply buy 5 ounces (1 cup), skip the toasting/salting step and mix them into the cooled baked peanuts.

Working Ahead: If you start with fresh (preferably vacuum-sealed) peanuts and pumpkin seeds, the finished mixture will keep for several weeks in a tightly closed container. For longer storage, keep them in the freezer (I'd vacuum-seal them with a Food Saver or the like if one is available).

Turn on the oven to 250 degrees and position a rack in the middle. In a medium bowl, toss the peanuts with the lime juice until all the nuts have been moistened. Sprinkle evenly with chile powder, then toss until the chile evenly coats the nuts. Spread the nuts into a shallow layer on a rimmed baking sheet. Slide into the oven and bake for 20 to 30 minutes, until the chile has formed a light crust on the nuts. Remove from the oven and sprinkle generously with salt, usually about 1 teaspoon.

In a large skillet over medium heat, toast the pumpkin seeds: Spread the seeds into the skillet and, when the first one pops, stir constantly until all have popped from flat to oval, about 5 minutes. Scoop on top of the peanuts, toss the two together, allow to cool, then scoop the mixture into a serving bowl.

TOASTED PUMPKIN SEEDS

Garlicky Black Pepper Tortilla Chips
Totopos al Ajo con Pimienta Negra

MAKES ENOUGH CHIPS FOR 8 TO 9 AS A SNACK

½ cup light vegetable oil (grapeseed oil works beautifully here)

6 large garlic cloves, peeled and finely chopped or pressed through a garlic press

½ teaspoon freshly ground black pepper, plus more for sprinkling on the chips

1 9- or 10-ounce bag tortilla chips (preferably the thicker, home-style ones from a local tortilleria)

When you're looking for a very quick snack to set out with drinks (and, perhaps, other nibbles), this would be my recommendation: buy some good tortilla chips, lightly brush them with a little garlic oil, bake them, sprinkle with black pepper and serve. You'll wake your guests up to how special a tortilla chip is, and how to savor it.

Working Ahead: *Because these are so simple to make and taste remarkably better right out of the oven, I suggest you make the garlic oil ahead (it will keep for a couple of days at room temperature, several weeks in the refrigerator) and bake the chips just before serving. If that won't work for you, bake them as close to serving time as is workable, popping them back in the oven for a quick re-warm if possible when guests arrive.*

Heat the oven to 325 degrees and position the rack in the middle. In a small saucepan, combine the vegetable oil, garlic and pepper. Set over medium-low heat and cook until the garlic browns slightly, about 10 minutes. Remove from the heat.

Strain the mixture through a fine-mesh strainer into a small bowl; discard the solids.

Place the chips in a large bowl. Use a brush to "paint" the oil onto the chips. (Store the leftover oil in a sealed container and use it for salad dressings or on potatoes destined for roasting.) Spread the chips onto a rimmed baking sheet. Bake the chips until hot and aromatic, about 10 minutes. Sprinkle with fresh pepper and scoop into a serving bowl or basket.

Green Chile Crackers
Galletas Verdes

MAKES 60 TO 70 LONG CRACKERS (ABOUT 1 X 4 INCHES)

Fresh hot green chile(s) to taste (roughly 2 serranos or 1 jalapeño), stemmed

½ medium bunch of cilantro, roughly chopped (thick bottom stems cut off)

⅓ cup olive oil

⅓ cup plus 1 tablespoon water

1 tablespoon sugar

2 teaspoons salt

2 cups all-purpose flour

Coarse salt for sprinkling on the crackers

Who doesn't love crackers as part of pre-dinner snacks or tapas-style meals? With ceviches, dips, cheeses, seafood cocktails, they're pretty much a given. And though nowadays you can buy some really fine handmade crackers in good grocery stores, you might find the right moment to create a unique offering yourself. These Green Chile Crackers (as well as the Red Chile Crackers alternative that follows) are special—and, in my opinion, worth the effort.

Working Ahead: These crackers can be made a week or so ahead and kept in an airtight container.

1. **Make the dough.** In a blender or mini food processor, combine the chile(s), cilantro, oil, water, sugar and salt. Process to as smooth a puree as possible. Pour into a large bowl or a full-size food processor. Add the flour. If working by hand, mix the chile mixture into the flour, then knead the dough in the bowl or on your work surface until completely smooth; if using a food processor, pulse to combine the flour and chile mixture, then run the processor until everything comes together into a smooth-looking ball, about 20 seconds. Wrap the dough in plastic and let stand in the refrigerator for at least 2 hours (or, for even better results, overnight).

2. **Roll and bake the crackers.** Heat the oven to 400 degrees. Lightly and evenly flour your work surface. Cut the dough into 4 equal pieces. Roll each piece into a very thin rectangle about 11 x 8 inches (it'll be about $1/16$ inch thick). Cut into whatever shapes suit your fancy—we like 1 x 4-inch rectangles or triangles in the Frontera/Topolobampo kitchen. Line a baking sheet with parchment paper or a silicone baking mat. Lay on the crackers—they can be placed close together, though they shouldn't touch. Lightly brush each cracker with water and immediately sprinkle with a little coarse salt. Bake until lightly browned and crisp, about 17 minutes. Cool.

To Make Red Chile Crackers: Substitute 2 tablespoons smoked paprika and ½ teaspoon powdered chipotle chile for the green chile(s) and cilantro. Pulse the paprika and chipotle directly in the food processor with the sugar, salt and flour, then add ½ cup plus 1 tablespoon water and the oil. Process until everything comes together into a smooth-looking ball. Let rest in the refrigerator, then roll out the dough and bake the crackers as described above.

Savory Sesame-Pepita "Cookies"
Galletas Saladas de Ajonjolí y Pepitas

MAKES 6 TO 7 DOZEN LITTLE SAVORY "COOKIES," SERVING 15 TO 20 AS A NIBBLE

1½ cups toasted, salted pumpkin seeds (*pepitas*)

1½ cups all-purpose flour

½ cup tahini (sesame paste)

¼ cup dark brown sugar

6   tablespoons milk

1½ teaspoons salt

4   ounces (1 stick) very cold unsalted butter, cubed

With the sandy texture of good shortbread and the nutty intensity of toasted pumpkin seeds and sesame, these little "cookies" will stop conversation when you set them out for friends. For added texture and flavor, feel free to stir a handful of sesame seeds into the mixture.

Working Ahead: These can be made a week or so ahead and stored in an airtight container. If you want to restore their original sparkle, spread them on a baking sheet and heat them for 10 minutes at 350 degrees before serving.

Heat the oven to 350 degrees. In a food processor, pulse the pumpkin seeds until coarsely ground (usually five 1-second pulses). Over the pumpkin seeds, evenly distribute the flour, tahini, brown sugar, milk, salt and cubed butter (in that order). Pulse eight times (1-second pulses). Everything should be evenly mixed together (with tiny pieces of butter still visible), though the mixture won't form a cohesive mass.

Line a rimmed baking sheet with parchment paper or a silicone baking mat. Using a teaspoon or tiny ice cream scoop, scoop out small amounts of dough (about 1 teaspoon), form them into rough-looking balls and lay them on the baking sheet (they can nearly touch). Bake for about 25 minutes, until lightly browned and crisp. Cool, then scoop into a serving bowl for your guests.

TOPOLO MARGARITA (PAGE 49)

The "Original" Margarita
La Margarita Original
MAKES ONE 5-OUNCE MARGARITA

A lime half for moistening the glass rim

Coarse (kosher) salt

Ice cubes (you'll need about ¾ cup—small ones are best)

3 tablespoons (1½ ounces) fresh-squeezed lime juice, preferably from ripe *limones criollos* (yellow-ripe Key limes)

3 tablespoons (1½ ounces) Cointreau orange liqueur (essential here for its concentrated flavor and sweetness)

3 tablespoons (1½ ounces) 100% agave silver tequila (some of our favorites in this style margarita are El Tesoro, El Milagro and Oro Azul)

This is the cocktail we call the Blue Agave Margarita, because it perfectly focuses the bright complexity of 100% agave blanco tequila with equal additions of bracing fresh-squeezed lime juice and the aromatic-orange sweetness of Cointreau. Shaken and served up, it's a pure, strong and satisfying drink for those who are over the sweet slushy sweet-and-sour-mix margaritas.

Like most margaritas, this one features the salt crusting on the edge of the glass, of course, salt being the ingredient that heightens and integrates all the flavors. Before those of you who always opt for saltless margaritas cringe, I'll tell you that drinking all the salt from a margarita's rim would ravage my tongue, too. But an entirely saltless margarita leaves the tequila's flavor potential unrealized—think about how much more potato-y a baked potato tastes when you sprinkle it with salt. So you salt-shy margarita drinkers have two choices for what I'd consider the perfect margarita: brush off some salt from one side of your salt-crusted glass—the side where you'll be drinking— and sprinkle it over the margarita, or skip the salt-crusting and shake up the margarita mixture with a good pinch of salt.

Salt has long been understood to bring out tequila's full flavor, even before the invention of the margarita. Back when tequila was only drunk neat, salt and ripe Key lime were always served alongside. Then, when "tequila" met "cocktail"—when tequila was domesticated for mixed company crowds—the salt and lime stayed, simply sweetened with citrus liqueur.

This recipe is written for a single serving because that's how I think of this margarita: made one (well, up to three) at a time, the lime squeezed in front of my guests, the three equal portions measured and shaken—all part of the margarita-concocting show. If the margarita is too tart for you, feel free to sweeten the mix with a little Simple Syrup (page 53).

Moisten the rim of a 6-ounce martini glass with the cut side of the lime half. Spread coarse salt on a small plate, then upend the glass into the salt to crust the rim. Half fill a cocktail shaker with ice, then measure in the lime, Cointreau and tequila. Shake for about 15 seconds. (This is longer than you may think: 15 seconds is how long it takes for the perfect amount of ice to melt into the drink.) Strain into the prepared glass.

Fresh-Squeezed Lime Juice

The honest truth is that the flavor of lime juice squeezed moments before it's savored soars above any substitutes. But let's face it: buying the bottles of what's called "fresh-squeezed" in the grocery store is certainly attractive. What you need to know is that (1) anything pasteurized is not going to taste like fresh; (2) citrus juice reacts with air (just like an avocado or banana), losing a lot of the characteristics we associate with fresh-fresh-fresh; and (3) not all "fresh-squeezed" citrus juice is squeezed in the same way. One machine cuts the fruits and presses them much as you would at home; another one punctures and presses, cutting through the aromatic skin and bitter pith. If you've ever wondered why the "fresh-squeezed" lemonade from the grocery store tastes bitter and bland, it's usually because a puncturing machine was used to extract the juice and it sat in the store's refrigerated case for several days.

Most of what we know as "lime" is a hybrid lime either called Persian or Tahitian—large, "lime" green, nicely acidic, nicely flavorful. The lime preferred in Mexico is called *limón criollo*, or native lime, which is the same thing as what we call a Key lime. It is slightly more acidic and considerably more aromatic, but *only* if you let it ripen to *yellow*. Yes, Key limes ripen to yellow, even though that messes with what many of us think of as a law of nature: lemons are yellow, limes are green. So, for the full Mexican experience, buy some Key limes, let them ripen to yellow, juice them with a Mexican lime juicer and you'll understand what all the fuss is about.

When juicing limes at home, here are some quantity guidelines. Just remember that limes that feel heavy and have a little give to them are typically the thin-skin ones and will yield the most juice.

● 1 average-size standard lime will yield about 2 tablespoons juice

● 1 pound of average-size standard limes typically contains 5 to 6 limes and yields about ¾ cup of juice

● 1 cup of lime juice typically takes 7 to 8 average-size standard limes

● 1 Key lime yields about 2 teaspoons juice, so it takes about 24 limes to yield a cup

Champagne Margarita
Margarita de Champaña

MAKES EIGHT 6-OUNCE DRINKS

The finely grated zest (colored rind only) from 1 lime

1 cup fresh lime juice

1 cup Cointreau

1 cup 100% agave silver tequila (some of our favorites right now are Cazadores, Herradura and Tres Generaciones)

Superfine sugar, if needed for added sweetness

A lime half for moistening the glass rims

Coarse (kosher) salt

1 bottle chilled brut Champagne or other sparkling white wine

I love Champagne with a steely tang that brings all my taste buds alive, that makes anyone's mood a good one, that makes me hungry for a few salty nuts or full-bore cheese or practically any rich mouthful. Same goes—at least for me—when it comes to margaritas: tangy is enlivening, sweet really isn't.

And, if you put the two together—a bracing Champagne and a limey margarita—you've got what I'd consider the best of both sides of the Atlantic. And you have to admit that serving Champagne Margaritas, at a brunch or before a beautiful, multicourse dinner party a la mexicana, certainly sounds like the right thing to do.

Serve these in typical 6-ounce Champagne flutes, and, as with several other of my drinks, Cointreau (rather than Triple Sec) brings everything into harmony.

1. *Make the margarita mixture.* In a pitcher, combine the lime zest, lime juice, Cointreau and tequila. Taste the mixture: if you like the bracing flavor (it will be quite tart), leave the mixture as is; if it's too tart for you, stir in a little superfine sugar. Cover and refrigerate until chilled, about 1 hour.

2. *Serve.* Strain the mixture to remove the zest. Moisten the rims of eight 6-ounce Champagne glasses with the cut side of the lime half. Spread coarse salt on a small plate, then upend the glasses into the salt to crust the rims. Fill each glass halfway with the margarita (it'll take a generous ⅓ cup). Slowly fill the rest of the way with Champagne or sparkling wine, and hand to one of your lucky guests.

(*CLOCKWISE FROM TOP LEFT*) BLOOD ORANGE
MARGARITA (PAGE 48), CHAMPAGNE MARGARITA
(PAGE 46) AND SUMMER MARGARITA (PAGE 50)

Blood Orange Margarita
Margarita de Naranja Rosa

MAKES NINE 6-OUNCE COCKTAILS

⅔ cup fresh lime juice

¼ cup sugar

1 cup 100% agave silver tequila (some good choices for this drink are Tres Generaciones and El Milagro)

½ cup Cointreau

2 cups fresh blood orange juice (you'll need about 6 juicy blood oranges)

A lime half for moistening the glass rims

Coarse (kosher) salt

Ice cubes (you'll need about 6 cups—small ones are best)

If by some alchemical process you were able to infuse the perfect sweet-tart orange juice with the stunning color—and satisfying deep-red flavor—of Bing cherries, you'd have this beautiful, silky-textured margarita. It can be so smooth and gorgeous and easy to drink that you might be understanding the word "downfall" from a different perspective. Cointreau (not Triple Sec) is a necessary ingredient here, focusing the orange flavor in just the right way.

1. *Make the margarita mixture.* In a large pitcher, stir together the lime juice, sugar and ¾ cup water until the sugar has dissolved. Mix in the tequila, Cointreau and blood orange juice. Cover and refrigerate until chilled, about 1 hour.

2. *Shake and serve.* Moisten the rims of three 6-ounce martini glasses with the cut side of a lime half. Spread coarse salt on a small plate, then upend the glasses into the salt to crust the rims. Fill a cocktail shaker about ¾ full of ice and measure in 1½ cups of the margarita mixture for three drinks. Cover and shake for about 15 seconds to thoroughly chill the mixture. Strain into the prepared glasses and hand to your guests. When you're ready, finish the remaining margaritas in the same way.

Topolo Margarita
Margarita Estilo Topolobampo
MAKES ABOUT TWELVE 6-OUNCE DRINKS

1½ cups fresh lime juice

¾ cup sugar

2¼ cups 100% agave *añejo* tequila (our favorite for this margarita is Tres Generaciones)

½ cup Torres Orange Liqueur

A lime half for moistening the glass rims

Coarse (kosher) salt

Ice cubes (you'll need 6 to 7 cups—small ones are best)

Though I'd steadfastly defend Topolobampo's two-decades-old reputation as one of Chicago's (if not the country's) premier fine-dining restaurants, I'm savvy enough to know that its reputation isn't due unequivocally to the food we serve. No, these margaritas have carried a fair amount of influence. They're smooth as silk, a trait that can encourage an almost seamless transition from one to the next. But be aware that their smoothness comes as much from the specific ingredients we use as it does from the recipe. Torres Orange Liqueur offers a flavor that's perfectly between the simple orangey lightness of Triple Sec (or the sweeter Cointreau) and the heavier, brandy-like Grand Marnier. A soft, well-balanced, agave-bursting añejo tequila and a good splash of fresh lime juice tip the scale flawlessly back in balance. This is definitely a drink to remember, a drink for special moments.

In an average-size cocktail shaker, you can shake three 6-ounce drinks at a time.

1. *Make limeade.* In a pitcher, stir together the lime juice, sugar and 2 cups water until the sugar has dissolved. Cover and refrigerate until chilled, about 1 hour.

2. *Shake and serve.* Add the tequila and orange liqueur to the pitcher to finish the margarita mixture. Moisten the rims of three 6-ounce martini glasses with the cut side of a lime half. Spread coarse salt on a small plate, then upend the glasses into the salt to crust the rims. Fill a cocktail shaker about ¾ full of ice and measure in 1½ cups of the margarita for three drinks. Cover and shake for about 15 seconds (time is important to get the right balance of flavor in the margarita). Strain into the prepared glasses and hand to your guests. When you're ready, finish the remaining margaritas in the same way.

Summer Margarita
Margarita Veraniega
MAKES NINE 6-OUNCE MARGARITAS

3   cups thin-sliced, peeled, seeded cucumber: you'll need 1 large 16-ounce (European) cucumber or 2 standard 8-ounce (6-inch-long) cucumbers

1½ cups 100% agave silver tequila (we like El Milagro or Cazadores in this drink)

1   cup fresh lime juice

1   cup Simple Syrup (page 53)

A lime half for moistening the glass rim

Coarse (kosher) salt

Ice cubes (you'll need 6 or 7 cups—small ones are best)

Cucumber slices, for garnish

Most people stumble on the first ingredient of these incredibly delicious margaritas. Cucumbers in a margarita? Sounds like creativity gone awry to some, while those thinking outside the box imagine the refreshing, melon-like flavor that cucumber can offer to sweetened lime and tequila. No orange liqueur here to dull the crisp freshness.

1. *Make the margarita mixture.* In a blender, combine the cucumber, tequila, lime juice and simple syrup. Blend until the mixture is as smooth as you can get it. Strain into a pitcher, cover and refrigerate until chilled, about 1 hour.

2. *Shake and serve.* Moisten the rims of three 6-ounce martini glasses with the cut side of the lime half. Spread coarse salt on a small plate, then upend the glasses into the salt to crust the rims. Fill a cocktail shaker ¾ full with ice, then measure in 1½ cups of the margarita mixture. Cover and shake for 10 to 15 seconds. Strain into the prepared glasses. Garnish with cucumber slices (I usually cut a slit in each slice and impale one on the side of each glass). When you're ready, finish another round of margaritas in the same way.

Mezcal Margarita
Margarita de Mezcal

MAKES EIGHT 6-OUNCE MARGARITAS

⅔ cup fresh lime juice

¼ cup sugar

1 cup mezcal (I love all the single-village Del Maguey mezcals)

⅓ cup brandy (an inexpensive brandy is fine here)

1 teaspoon Peychaud bitters

A lime half for moistening the glass rims

Coarse (kosher) salt

Ice cubes (you'll need a generous quart—small ones are best)

To say that this is my favorite margarita will be incomprehensible to many. I mean, when you read the ingredients, it's hard to imagine how they'll taste together. And how can I even call it a margarita, a few might wonder, if it's made from mezcal, rather than tequila? And a few more will certainly question what in the world made me reach for a bottle of Peychaud bitters and brandy when I was putting it together?

Here's the rundown: really good mezcals—the ones that are artisan-crafted in Oaxaca—are glorious on the tongue. Rich, complex, smoky, tangy, exotic. They're so remarkably good, in fact, that I'd like to introduce them to a wider audience. But since sipping spirits neat isn't everyone's cup of tea, I decided to smooth that introduction to mezcal neophytes by way of a cocktail, a margarita, if you will. Except that mezcal doesn't always play well with others, certainly not with just lime and Triple Sec. It needs the richness of a little brandy to balance its smokiness and the complexity of the bitters to smooth out its southern Mexican accent. Peychaud bitters have a more harmonious flavor than Angostura, I feel, and their rosy color makes the drink glow.

1. *Make the margarita mixture.* In a large pitcher, stir together the lime juice, sugar and ¾ cup water until the sugar has dissolved. Add the mezcal, brandy and bitters. Cover and refrigerate until chilled, about 1 hour.

2. *Shake and serve.* Moisten the rims of three 6-ounce martini glasses with the cut side of the lime half. Spread coarse salt on a small plate, then upend the glasses into the salt to crust the rims. Fill a cocktail shaker about ¾ full of ice and measure in ¾ cup of the margarita mixture for three drinks. Cover and shake for about 15 seconds to thoroughly chill the mixture—that's how long it takes for the perfect amount of ice to melt into the drink. Strain into the prepared glasses and you're ready to offer a unique experience. Finish the remaining margaritas in the same way.

Mexican Mojito
Mojito Mexicano
MAKES EIGHT 12-OUNCE DRINKS

8   large sprigs of fresh mint

1½ cups Simple Syrup (page 53)

Ice cubes (you'll need about 2 quarts)

2   cups 100% silver tequila (a favorite of mine in mojitos is El Teroso)

1½ cups fresh lime juice

Sparkling water or club soda

Why, you might ask, a Mexican mojito? They're Cuban—well, at least Caribbean—but not Mexican, right? But I ask you to stop for a moment and consider the perfect mojito's ingredients: fresh lime juice, the brightness of an unaged spirit, a splash of sweetness, an aromatic fresh herb. That could describe a lot of stuff that comes out of Mexico, so why not just replace a mojito's rum with blanco tequila and enjoy the geographic shift into Mexico? I love the subtle complexity that tequila contributes. Rather than stirring, some prefer to upend a cocktail shaker over the glass, shake a couple of times to mix the ingredients thoroughly, then remove the glass and add a splash of soda.

Set out eight tall 12-ounce glasses. Put the leaves stripped off a single sprig of mint into each glass—you'll need about 10 leaves for each drink. Divide the Simple Syrup among the glasses (3 tablespoons/1½ ounces per glass). Use a muddler (or the handle of a wooden spoon or a long-handle ice tea spoon—though neither is anywhere near as effective) to crush the mint, releasing its flavor into the syrup—the more muddling, the fuller the mint flavor. Fill each glass with ice. Measure in the tequila (¼ cup/2 ounces per glass) and the lime juice (3 tablespoons/1½ ounces per glass). Use a long-handle, ice tea spoon to mix everything together. Top off each glass with a little sparkling water or soda and enjoy the refreshment.

Sizzling Mojito
Mojito Picantísimo
MAKES EIGHT 12-OUNCE DRINKS

For those of you who like tingly, spicy drinks, this is your libation. The fresh ginger bounces playfully off the habanero-infused sweetness and the rustic, herby aromas of the blanco tequila. The drink's sparkling splash amps up the volume, so you can be sure that Sizzling Mojitos will animate a group when nothing else will. Remember: the Sizzling Simple Syrup recipe makes more than you need; use only 1½ cups.

8   large sprigs of fresh mint

16   quarter-size slices of peeled fresh ginger

1½ cups Sizzling Simple Syrup (below)

Ice cubes (you'll need about 2 quarts)

2   cups silver tequila (a favorite of mine in this mojito is the aromatic El Teroso)

1½ cups lime juice

Sparkling water or club soda

Set out eight tall 12-ounce glasses. Put the leaves stripped off a single sprig of mint into each glass—you'll need about 10 leaves for each drink—and top with two ginger slices. Divide the Sizzling Simple Syrup among the glasses (3 tablespoons/1½ ounces per glass). Use a muddler (or the handle of a wooden spoon or a long-handle ice tea spoon—though neither is anywhere near as effective) to crush the mint and ginger, releasing their flavor into the syrup—the more muddling, the fuller the flavors. Fill each glass with ice. Measure in the tequila (¼ cup/2 ounces per glass) and the lime juice (3 tablespoons/1½ ounces per glass). Use a long-handle ice tea spoon to mix everything together. Top off each glass with a little sparkling water or soda and pass around the spicy refreshment.

Simple Syrup
MAKES 2 CUPS

1½ cups granulated sugar (the syrup tastes best made with organic evaporated cane juice)

1½ cups water

1   tablespoon fresh lime juice

In a small saucepan, combine the sugar, water and lime juice. Set over medium-high heat and bring to a simmer, stirring constantly to dissolve the sugar granules. Remove from the heat, cool and store in a closed container, preferably in the refrigerator for optimal freshness.

To make Sizzling Simple Syrup for a Sizzling Mojito: Add 1 tablespoon chopped fresh ginger and ½ habanero chile (not chopped) to the syrup as it is coming to a simmer. Once the mixture has completely cooled, strain out the ginger and habanero.

Watermelon Mojito
Mojito de Sandía
MAKES EIGHT 12-OUNCE DRINKS

8   large sprigs of fresh mint

4   cups cubed seedless watermelon—¾-inch cubes are perfect here

½   cup Simple Syrup (see page 53)

Ice cubes (you'll need about 2 quarts)

2   cups white rum (I like D'Aristi rum from Yucatan)

½   cup fresh lime juice

Sparkling water or club soda

If a standard-issue mojito weren't refreshing enough, one with muddled watermelon in the minty mix shoots it right off the charts. Hot summer weekend, sun beginning to set, backyard, friends. You get the picture. You need about 3 pounds of watermelon to yield the 4 cups of fruit you need for these drinks.

Set out eight tall 12-ounce glasses. Put the leaves stripped off a single sprig of mint into each glass—you'll need about 10 leaves for each drink—and top with ½ cup watermelon cubes. Divide the Simple Syrup among the glasses (1 tablespoon/½ ounce per glass). Use a muddler (or the handle of a wooden spoon or a long-handle ice tea spoon—though neither is anywhere near as effective) to crush the mint and watermelon, releasing their flavor into the syrup—the more muddling, the fuller the flavors. Fill each glass with ice. Measure in the rum (¼ cup/2 ounces per glass) and the lime juice (1 tablespoon/½ ounce per glass). Use a long-handle ice tea spoon to mix everything together. Top off each glass with a little sparkling water or soda and you're ready to serve.

Tecate Mojito
Mojito al Tecate

MAKES EIGHT 12-OUNCE DRINKS

8	large sprigs of fresh mint
1	cup Simple Syrup (page 53)
	Ice cubes (you'll need about 8 cups)
½	cup white rum (D'Aristi from Yucatan is good)
½	cup lime juice
4	12-ounce cans of Tecate beer (or other light, citrusy-tasting beer)

Think "mojito meets michelada" and you're on the right track here. Refreshing, distinctive, thoroughly entertaining and addictively delicious. I've chosen Tecate as the beer because it offers the kind of simple brightness this drink is looking for.

Set out eight tall 12-ounce glasses. Put the leaves stripped off a single sprig of mint into each glass—you'll need about 10 leaves for each drink. Divide the Simple Syrup among the glasses (2 tablespoons/1 ounce per glass). Use a muddler (or the handle of a wooden spoon or a long-handle ice tea spoon—though neither is anywhere near as effective) to crush the mint, releasing its flavor into the syrup—the more muddling, the fuller the mint flavor. Fill each glass with ice. Measure in the rum (1 tablespoon/½ ounce per glass) and the lime juice (1 tablespoon/½ ounce per glass), then fill each glass with beer—it'll take about ½ can for each. Use a long-handle ice tea spoon to mix everything together. Serve your beautiful refreshment.

Limey (+/- Spicy) Beer on the Rocks
Michelada

MAKES ONE 12-OUNCE DRINK

A lime half for moistening the glass rim

Coarse salt

Ice cubes (you'll need a generous cup)

¼ cup fresh lime juice

1 12-ounce beer (such as Bohemia for lighter beer lovers, Dos Equis or Negra Modelo for darker beer lovers)

TO YOUR OWN LIKING, ADD ONE OR MORE OF THE FOLLOWING

Hot sauce (usually about ½ teaspoon) such as Tabasco, Tamazula or Valentina

Worcestershire sauce (usually about ½ teaspoon)

Jugo Maggi (usually about ⅛ teaspoon)

I know it's anathema to beer connoisseurs to "season" their golden, effervescent elixir, but this drink—when made with the right beer—is incredibly good, incredibly refreshing. You simply can't think of it as you do Beer with a capital B—I mean that beautifully handcrafted, coddled creation that you sip slowly, savoring every nuance. This is a beer "cocktail," if you will, that adds zing to easier-drinking brews by having some lime (and, potentially, hot sauce, Worcestershire, even Jugo Maggi) stirred in and being served over ice in a salt-rimmed glass. I've written this recipe for a single serving—using a 12-ounce beer—because that's how you'll make them, customizing them to your guests' tastes.

Moisten the rim of a pint beer glass (or mug) with the cut side of the lime half. Spread coarse salt on a small plate, then upend the glass into the salt to crust the rim. Fill half full of ice and pour in the lime juice, followed by the beer. If you (or your guests) want, add hot sauce, Worcestershire and/or Jugo Maggi; stir just enough to combine everything. It's time to enjoy what a *michelada* is all about.

How to Have a Tequila Tasting

It always strikes me a little odd when people snicker at the thought of a tequila tasting. They rarely snicker when invited to a tasting of cognac or Scotch or single-still bourbon. But tequila—sadly, unfortunately—still has too much "spring break" baggage, too many memories of knocking back shot after shot, while simultaneously trying to keep them down. If that's the memory, the snickers are justified: no one would argue that spring break tequila is worthy of serious tasting.

But all of the 100% agave tequilas are. So those—and *only* those, not the "golds" and the *mixtos*—will be our focus here.

SETTING: Setting a few bottles of tequila on a table won't really convey the handcrafted beauty of what you'll be tasting, so I suggest you set up a separate table for tasting, or at least designate a special table by laying down a tablecloth. And set out some pens and paper, so that your friends can write down the names of what they like.

GLASSWARE: Like many Mexican and American tequila aficionados, I don't like tasting tequila from the old-fashioned skinny Mexican shot glasses called *caballitos*. Number one, I can't enjoy the tequila's come-hither aroma from a thumb-print-wide, filled-to-the-brim shot glass. Number two, facing that little *caballito*, I have a near-involuntary impulse to knock back the whole thing, which, of course, isn't the way to savor anything. Especially when it's accompanied by a grimace, a lick of salt and a suck of lime. No, if you want to taste—*really* taste—all the deliciousness that the tequila has to offer, do it in a snifter (small ones—about 6 ounces—are ideal). Snifters always lull people into a slow, complete appreciation of what's in front

(continued on next page)

of them. Ideas for where to find inexpensive snifters to make your tequila tasting perfect? Look at a restaurant supply house (online at Restaurant Depot—therdstore.com) or a big box supplier, where you can find small snifters for very little. My second choice: white or all-purpose wine glasses.

AGES: Tequila comes in three ages: fresh (called silver or *blanco*, from just born—right out of the still—to two months old), youthful (called *reposado*, the word for "rested," two to twelve months spent in oak), and mature (called *añejo*, the word for "old," over twelve months spent in oak barrels that don't exceed 600 liters each). Unlike brandy, which is basically "white lightning" when it comes from the still, tequila has all the complexity that comes from the eight to twelve years of the agave plants' growth to maturity. Which means there's something important and delicious there, even if it is a little brash. So don't look down your nose at *blancos*: they have the most alluring, unadulterated agave flavor you'll find. Most of the time, *blancos* are my favorite.

Unless, of course, I'm wanting to sip a spirit that's got the edge taken off. Smoothed out pure agave flavor usually comes labeled *reposado*, especially if it's aged in large, "neutral" (aka "old") oak barrels—the wood flavor doesn't mask the plant's beauty.

But then again, after dinner, I often think of enjoying that agave loveliness when it's wearing the cloak of oak aging, redolent of the caramel-y vanilla scent that wood gives. If the oak is new—and/or the aging is very long—you may find the oak aging overpowering. The tequila may start tasting like an odd brandy or bourbon or whiskey. Which is definitely not the point with tequila, even though we've been taught that good booze is old booze. With tequila, you have to think outside that box: sometimes it's at its peak when absolutely fresh (think fresh-tasting gin); sometimes it's good with some age, but never to the point that the agave flavor has gone into hiding.

PROVENANCE: Agave, like wine grapes, tastes of where and how it's grown, making what's in a bottle of handcrafted 100% agave tequila one of the few ways you can actually, vividly "taste" a place without really going there. Jalisco—the Mexican state that produces more tequila than anywhere else in the country (in fact, the lowlands town of Tequila gives its name to this intriguing distillate)—has two distinct regions: the highlands and the lowlands. Highland agaves mature more slowly in the cooler temperatures and red, iron-rich, sandy soil, producing tequilas that tend to be aromatically complex, but still quite delicate. Lowland agaves mature more quickly in the warmer temperatures and dark earth, producing tequilas that tend to be more simply focused in their flavor—rustic and earthy with clear hints of minerality. Those are just generalizations, of course; there are exceptions and amplifications all over the place. And tequilas that come from the periphery of the state, or from other (mostly bordering) states that by law can label their agave distillate "tequila" add even more layers of nuance. Which is why I never tire of tasting the artisanal tequilas: I can taste one tequila after another, and find myself surprised and happy with all the delicious diversity. I'll bet you will, too.

SUGGESTIONS FOR A TASTING: My allegiances change pretty regularly when it comes to tequila—meaning, I believe, that practically every handcrafted 100% agave tequila has something to recommend it. Nonetheless, I offer you the following jump-off point for planning a tasting of tequilas, each with its own clear point of view. Encourage those who want to taste to sip from the freshest (*blanco*) to the most aged (*añejo*), making notes of the aromas and flavors they pick up and, most important, which ones they really like. You may want to engage a tequila-loving friend to taste through the tequilas ahead of time so he or she can help other guests make their ways through their evaluations.

FOR AN "EXPERIENCE OF THE HIGHLANDS" TEQUILA TASTING

El Tesoro *Blanco*—This is a crisp *blanco* that has a long finish—beautifully "clean" with hints of agave, green herbs and cinnamon.

Don Julio *Reposado*—This *reposado* tequila features an enticing, sweet nose (you'll likely pick up the aroma of banana, ripe guava, sweet spices) that carries straight through to what you taste. Some people pick up a little passion fruit flavor as well.

Corazon *Añejo*—Here's an *añejo* tequila with all the aromatic allure of fresh-roasted agave hearts (sweet, roasty, a little woodsy), but one that stays bright and true to its agave roots . . . in spite of the smoothness that comes from long oak aging.

FOR AN "EXPERIENCE OF THE LOWLANDS" TEQUILA TASTING

Herradura *Blanco*—This classic *blanco* is refreshingly light compared to other lowlands offerings, while delivering on straightforward minerality (think rainwater when you smell it) and the aroma of robust herbs like thyme and mint.

Cielo *Reposado*—A honey-colored *reposado* tequila, Cielo greets you with an attractive sweet nose (I always detect a touch of buttery sweet corn) that resolves beautifully into a rich taste on your tongue. I always think the last, lingering flavor reminds me of cinnamon oil.

Chinaco *Añejo*—An *añejo* with a nose of dry wood and butterscotch, Chinaco's palate has hints of *cajeta* balanced by oak and takes you into a long finish.

Crimson *Jamaica* "Flower" Cooler
Agua de Jamaica

MAKES ABOUT 2 QUARTS, GIVING YOU EIGHT 12-OUNCE GLASSES WITH ICE

2   cups (2 ounces) dried *jamaica* "flowers"

1¼ cups sugar

Ice cubes (you'll need about 2 quarts)

If the sweet-cinnamony-milky agua de horchata *is as common as Coke in Mexican street stalls,* jamaica *gives Pepsi a run for its money. It's a tangy, cranberry-red cold tea made from the "flowers" of a plain-Jane plant that's a distant cousin to the showy tropical hibiscus (the one with the huge red flowers). And, if I'm striving for complete accuracy, I'll have to tell you that* jamaica *isn't really made from the flowers of that plant at all, but rather the flowers' calyces (the coverings of the flower buds). All of which I bring up only because lots of writers, waiters, tea connoisseurs and Mexican food enthusiasts describe* agua de jamaica *as "hibiscus flower tea," rather than "hibiscus cousin calyx tea." Which, of course, sounds neither comprehensible nor delicious.*

Yet, everyone "gets" jamaica *the second they have their first delicious taste of it. A little like cranberry juice, you might say, because of the drink's tang, but it's more complex, with hints of cherry and farmers' market grapes. Maybe you'll notice a little herbiness, too, as if someone crushed in a leaf or two of chocolate mint. Anyway, it's just plain tasty.*

Working Ahead: Agua de jamaica *can be made several days in advance and refrigerated, tightly covered, in a stainless steel, glass or hard plastic container (it will stain soft plastic).*

In a medium (3-quart) stainless or enameled saucepan, bring 1½ quarts of water to a boil. Add the "flowers" and sugar. Stir for a minute or so, while the liquid returns to a boil and the sugar dissolves. Cover and let steep for at least an hour, but no more than 2 hours. Pour the mixture through a colander or strainer into a large bowl, pressing on the "flowers" to extract as much liquid as possible. Stir in 3 cups water. This recipe makes a tart version of *agua de jamaica*; feel free to stir in more sugar, if that appeals to you. Serve over ice.

Mexican Cosmo
Cóctel Cosmopolitano estilo Mexicano
MAKES TEN 6-OUNCE DRINKS

2   cups 100% agave silver tequila (a really bright one like Cazadores is good)

1   cup Cointreau

¾   cup fresh lime juice

1   cup *Jamaica* "Flower" Cooler (page 60)

½   cup plus 1 tablespoon superfine sugar

    Ice cubes (you'll need 6 or 7 cups—small ones are best)

This is a drink that I can say really satisfies Cosmo lovers, but it does take the Cointreau to balance everything just right. For an over-the-top touch, pulverize dried jamaica "flowers" in a clean coffee/spice mill, stir into some granulated sugar and use the rosy mixture to crust the rims of your glasses, margarita style.

1. *Make the Cosmo mixture.* In a large pitcher combine the tequila, Cointreau, lime juice, *jamaica* and sugar. Stir until the sugar is dissolved. Cover and refrigerate until chilled, about 1 hour.

2. *Shake and serve.* Fill a cocktail shaker about ¾ full of ice and measure in 1½ cups of the Cosmo mixture for three drinks. Cover and shake for 10 to 15 seconds. Strain into 6-ounce martini glasses and pass around to your guests. When you're ready, finish the remaining Cosmos in the same way.

Jamaica Sangria with Cointreau
Sangría al Jamaica

MAKES TWELVE 6-OUNCE GLASSES

2   750 ml bottles young, fruity red
    wine

1½ cups *Jamaica* "Flower" Cooler
    (page 60)

¾   cup Cointreau or Triple Sec

    Ice cubes, for serving

Certain agua de jamaica *flavors (and certainly the color) echo what I love about young red wine. Add a little orange liqueur—even some chopped fruit if that appeals—and you've got a pretty cool twist on sangria.*

Working Ahead: Your Jamaica Sangria can be mixed together, covered and set in a cool place for several hours before serving.

In a very large pitcher (or two smaller ones), combine the wine, *jamaica* and Cointreau. Cover and refrigerate until chilled, at least 1½ hours. When you're ready to serve, pour into wine glasses over ice.

Tangy Tamarind Cooler
Agua de Tamarindo
MAKES ABOUT 2 QUARTS, GIVING YOU EIGHT 12-OUNCE GLASSES WITH ICE

1   pound (about 16 large) fresh tamarind pods—flexible ones with shells that flake off easily

OR 1 14-ounce bag frozen tamarind pulp (available at Mexican groceries)

About 1 cup sugar

Ice cubes (you'll need about 2 quarts—small ones are best)

The third in the Mexican agua fresca triumvirate, together with jamaica and horchata, is tamarindo, the tangy brown pulp of a barky, seedy pod that's extracted, sweetened and diluted. The pods are harvested from a huge tree that migrated from Southeast Asia, and you can find them in pretty much every Mexican grocery and many well-stocked supermarkets. Though the pods provide you with the most wonderful flavor (think richly aromatic, molasses-y brown sugar and tangy citrus), they're a lot of work. You may want to wander over to the frozen food cases in a Mexican grocery and look for tamarind pulp—no need to peel, devein, soak and seed.

More than Mexico's other two iconic aguas frescas, tamarindo tends to separate as it stands. Though a simple stir will bring it together, you may want to blend everything just before serving: typically an amusing (and remarkably stable) foam is created when tamarind meets blender.

1. *Prepare the tamarind base.* To turn tamarind pods into the base for cocktails or other drinks, first clean them all: hold a pod in one hand, loosen the stem with the other, then firmly pull out the stem and all the runners that trail down between the shell and pulp; peel off the shell. In a large (3-quart), non-aluminum saucepan, bring 1 quart water to a boil. Add the tamarind, remove from the heat and let stand until completely soft—1 to 2 hours, depending on the freshness of the pods. Using your hand or the back of a large spoon, thoroughly dislodge the softened brown tamarind pulp from the fibrous material and seeds. Strain into a large pitcher, discarding the solids. You should have 1 quart of tamarind pulp; if you don't, add water to reach that quantity.

If using frozen pulp, simply blend the defrosted pulp with 2 generous cups of water to bring the quantity of the pulp up to 1 quart. Pour into a large pitcher.

NOTE: This concentrated tamarind base is used in the specialty tamarind drinks, pages 64 and 65.

2. *Dilute the tamarind base, sweeten and serve.* Add *1 quart* water to the tamarind base. Stir in enough sugar to sweeten the drink to your taste. Cover and refrigerate until you're ready to serve. Pour over ice in tall glasses, stirring before pouring.

Variation: Tamarind-Apple Cooler. Follow the above recipe, substituting apple cider (preferably fresh-squeezed and unpasteurized) for the water in Step 2 and reducing the sugar to ⅔ cup.

Mexican Snakebite
"La Culebra"
MAKES EIGHT 12-OUNCE DRINKS

2 cups tamarind base (to prepare the base, see page 63, Step 1)

3½ cups ice-cold apple cider, preferably fresh-squeezed and unpasteurized

4 12-ounce, ice-cold, full-flavored Mexican beers (my preference is for Bohemia or Dos Equis lager)

The cocktail traditionally known as a "snakebite" is equal parts beer and cider (typically sparkling hard cider with full-flavored, often dark beers in Europe). Looking at the cocktail through Mexican eyes brought tamarind into the mix. In fact, I welcomed it into the mix because of the rich, tangy complexity it adds to Mexico's often rather light-tasting beers. To make a less beery-tasting cocktail, add ½ cup sugar to the 2 cups tamarind base. Very interesting flavors emerge.

In a blender, combine the tamarind base and *half* (1¾ cups) of the cider. Blend to thoroughly combine. Pour into a pitcher and stir in the remaining cider. Cover and refrigerate until you're ready to serve.

When that moment comes, measure ⅔ cup of the tamarind–apple cider mixture into each of eight tall glasses, then slowly top off each one with *half* a cold beer. Serve right away.

Spicy Tamarind Margarita
Margarita Picosa de Tamarindo

MAKES EIGHT 6-OUNCE DRINKS

1½ cups tamarind base (to prepare the pulp, see page 63, Step 1)

½ to 1 canned chipotle chile *en adobo*, seeds scraped out

¾   cup sugar

1½ cups *reposado* or *añejo* tequila (Cazadores *añejo* is a choice I like)

1   cup fresh lime juice

A lime half for moistening the glass rims

Coarse (kosher) salt

Ice cubes (you'll need a generous quart—small ones are best)

1. *Flavor and cook the tamarind base.* In a blender or food processor, combine the tamarind base, chipotle and sugar. Process until smooth. Scrape into a small (2-quart) saucepan, set over medium heat and simmer briskly, stirring regularly, until shiny and reduced to a generous cup, about 15 minutes. Cool.

2. *Make the margarita mixture.* In a large pitcher, stir together the tamarind base, tequila and lime juice. Cover and refrigerate until chilled, about 1 hour.

3. *Shake and serve.* Moisten the rims of three 6-ounce martini glasses with the cut side of the lime half. Spread coarse salt on a small plate, then upend the glasses into the salt to crust the rims. Fill a cocktail shaker about ¾ full of ice and measure in 1½ cups of the margarita mixture for three drinks. Cover and shake for 10 to 15 seconds to thoroughly chill the mixture. Strain into the prepared glasses and hand to your guests. When you're ready, finish the remaining margaritas in the same way.

Creamy Almond-Rice Cooler
Horchata de Almendra
MAKES ABOUT 1½ QUARTS, GIVING YOU SIX OR SEVEN 12-OUNCE GLASSES WITH ICE

6   tablespoons raw white rice

6   ounces (about 1¼ cups) blanched
    almonds

    A 2-inch cinnamon stick, prefer-
    ably Mexican *canela*

1   cup milk or canned evaporated
    milk

⅔ to ¾ cup sugar

    Ice cubes (you'll need about 2
    quarts—smaller ones are best)

Agua de horchata is the Coke of Mexican street stalls. Except that it has a milky texture, cinnamon-y taste and no fizzy sensation. So it's really only Coke-like in terms of popularity.

Now, the most economical version of agua de horchata *is made with rice, sugar, cinnamon and water. But my favorite is a little creamier on the tongue, throwing a few almonds into the mix and stirring in a little milk at the end. I have two pieces of advice: if you're going to make* horchata, *canned evaporated—not sweetened condensed—milk gives the best flavor and is the most traditional in Mexico, and toasting half the almonds creates a more complex flavor that's closer to Spain's original* horchata de chufa. *Or follow the Yucatecan cooks' lead and use coconut milk instead of almonds; I've spelled out the details in the variation recipe that follows.*

Working Ahead: The agua de horchata *can be made several days ahead, tightly covered and refrigerated.*

1. *Soak the rice and almonds.* In a medium-size bowl, combine the rice, almonds and cinnamon stick. Stir in 2½ cups water, cover and let stand at least 8 hours or, preferably, overnight.

2. *Blend and strain.* Scrape the mixture into a blender jar and blend for several minutes, until a drop rubbed between your fingers no longer feels very gritty. (If you have access to a high-speed Vitamix blender, you'll get the smoothest results.) Add 2 cups of water, then blend for another minute. Set a medium mesh strainer or large colander over a mixing bowl and line it with two layers of dampened cheesecloth. A cup or so at a time, pour in the almond-rice mixture, gently stirring to help the liquid pass through. (Or, easier, pour it all into the strainer and let gravity pull it through, about 20 minutes.) When the liquid has passed through, gather up the corners of the cheesecloth and twist them together to trap the dregs inside. Squeeze the package firmly to extract any remaining liquid.

3. *Finish the* horchata. Add 1½ cups of water and the milk. Stir in enough sugar to sweeten the drink to your taste. If the consistency seems thicker than whole milk, stir in additional water. Cover and refrigerate until you're ready to serve. Pour over ice in tall glasses, stirring before pouring.

Variation: Coconut *Horchata.* Omit the almonds and increase the rice to 1¼ cups. In step 3, reduce the 1½ cups of water to ½ cup and replace the milk with a 14-ounce can of coconut milk; use the full ¾ cup sugar. If you wish, replace the cinnamon stick with a few pieces of lime zest (colored rind only).

Coconut *Horchata* "Colada"
Horchata de Coco "Colada"

MAKES EIGHT 8-OUNCE DRINKS

2 cups ice cubes

2 cups cubed, peeled-and-cored
   fresh pineapple

2 cups white rum

3 cups Coconut *Horchata*
   (page 66)

When the words "piña colada" stop conjuring up positive memories, put together a batch of these: an icy blend of creamy coconut horchata, rum and fresh pineapple. It'll set a new standard.

In a blender, combine *half* of all the ingredients. Blend until creamy smooth. Pour into four 8-ounce (highball) glasses. When you're ready, make another round in the same way.

Horchata-Banana Daiquiri
Daiquirí de Horchata
MAKES EIGHT 8-OUNCE DRINKS

2   cups ice cubes

2   bananas

¼   cup fresh lime juice

¼   cup sugar

2   cups white rum

3   cups Almond-Rice Cooler
(page 66)

This is pretty much the classic old blended banana daiquiri that the folks at Acapulco's old famous Villa Vera Hotel say they invented back in the glamorous '50s days of Elizabeth Taylor and Eddie Fisher. Classic, but with an horchata twist.

In a blender, combine, *half* of all the ingredients. Blend until smooth, then pour into four 8-ounce (highball) glasses. When you're ready, make another round in the same way.

Fresh Fruit Cooler
Agua Fresca de Frutas
MAKES ABOUT 4 QUARTS, GIVING YOU SIXTEEN 12-OUNCE DRINKS WITH ICE

8   cups prepared fresh fruit, peeled, pitted, seeded, hulled and/or cored, cubed—as appropriate for your fruit (ballpark grocery-store quantities are listed below)

⅓ to ½ cup fresh lime juice

¾ to 1½ cups sugar, depending on the type and sweetness of the fruit

Ice cubes (you'll need about 3 quarts)

A perfect agua fresca *is the intersection of practically any honestly ripe-ripe fruit (can you ever achieve it except at the height of a fruit's season?) and the well-considered additions of water, sugar and lime juice. A perfect agua fresca is never thick or cloying or filling, like some smoothies, and, in fact, captures the pure essence of the fruit in a diluted way. Ripe fruit provides the brilliance you're transforming, while sugar carries the fruitiness throughout the drink, lime heightens and focuses the flavor and water turns it from fruit to thirst-quenching beverage. Clearly, we're talking more art than science— but within some guidelines. As you make your way through this rather loose recipe, trust your taste buds, fiddle with the ingredients a little, and you'll figure out how to best showcase what the fruit has to offer. Because I'm focused here on the use of non-citrus fruits (which you approach slightly differently), there's nothing about Mexico's wonderful limeades, orangeades, grapefruit-ades, tangerine-ades, which in restaurants I always order made with sparkling water for added dazzle.*

Scoop the fruit into a blender and add 2 cups water (if your blender is small, do the fruit in two batches). Process to a smooth puree. Pour into a very large (1 gallon) pitcher or glass Mexican *agua fresca* barrel. Add 4 cups water and the minimum amount of sugar and lime juice, stirring until the sugar has dissolved. Taste and start fiddling with additional water (most fruits will take 2 cups more), plus additional sugar and lime, until you've determined that you have the perfect balance. Serve in tall glasses over ice.

Rough Grocery-Store Quantities for Fruit
7 to 8 pounds of cantaloupe, honeydew, watermelon, papaya and pineapple
3½ to 4 pounds peaches, nectarines and mangos
About 3 pints strawberries and raspberries

Rick's Favorite Summer Soft Drink
Agua Fresca Veraniega

MAKES 3 QUARTS, GIVING YOU TWELVE 12-OUNCE GLASSES WITH ICE

6   (about 1¼ pounds total) mini seedless or Persian cucumbers, peeled and roughly chopped (you should have about 4 cups)

1   (about 3½ pounds) medium pine-apple, peeled, cored and cubed (you should have a generous 4 cups)

½   cup (loosely packed) roughly chopped fresh flat-leaf parsley

½   cup (loosely packed) roughly chopped fresh cilantro leaves

⅓   cup fresh lime juice, plus a little more if needed

¼   cup sugar, plus a little more if needed

Ice cubes (you'll need about 2 quarts—small ones are best)

My favorite aguas frescas aren't always the single-fruit kind. In fact, the most appealing to me occasionally weave in ingredients that aren't fruit at all, ingredients that take the idea of "soft drink" to a whole new level of refreshment. Which is what you'll experience when you make this one: it offers a hint of melon-iness (without having any melon) from the cucumber and backyard freshness of the herbs, and the deep tropical sweetness of the pineapple. Of course, lime is the seasoning that brings it all together. A simpler alternative—inspired by our Summer Margarita on page 50—simply blends cucumber with lime, sugar and mint. If mini cucumbers are not available, use 4 cups of any peeled, roughly chopped cucumber.

In a blender, combine all of the ingredients with 1½ cups water. Blend until completely smooth. (If your blender isn't large enough to hold everything, blend in batches.) Pour into a large pitcher, then stir in 6 more cups of water. Taste and add more lime or sugar if you think the drink needs it. Serve in tall glasses over ice.

Luxury Guacamole Bar
Cocktail Party for 12

Luxury Guacamole Bar Cocktail Party for 12

Most people I know get the idea instantly: you're standing in front of a bowl of creamy guacamole—aromatic with roasted garlic and cilantro—nestled next to a basket of chips, perhaps another of toasty grilled baguette slices. There's a bowl of salad-y-looking roasted poblanos, too, and another of crab with diced jícama. And there are salsas, some crumbled cheese, maybe some bacon and toasted pumpkin seeds. And before you know it, you're spooning guac onto chips or toasts, topping each with a little crab or poblano or just a little bacon and cheese. Essentially, you're customizing each guacamole bite, which can lead to a delicious experience. At least you hope so. But even if it doesn't, you've only committed to a bite. And experimentation is half the fun.

Think of this guacamole recipe as a guideline. It starts with a very simple guacamole, but a delicious one—roasted garlic, cilantro and lime bring avocado alive. Plus, it provides a platform to spoon that guacamole onto: chips are an obvious choice, but I've noticed that chips alone lull people quickly into *dipping*, when *layering* is more the message here. So I suggest adding grill-toasted baguette slices or even pita chips or some of those handmade crackers that are so popular these days.

What you put on top can be simple or complex: it is up to you, so I've offered a number of options. There are two salad-y *salpicónes*: one with crab and jícama, the other with roasted poblanos and either salmon or mushrooms; choose either, both or neither. There are two salsa recipes as well: a classic chopped tomato salsa and one with roasted tomatillo, orange and smoky chipotle; both will add luxury to your guacamole bar, but so can a good-quality store-bought salsa.

The garnishes are easy, so go overboard. You can buy toasted pumpkin seeds, crumbled fresh cheese, sliced pickled jalapeños, even crisp bacon crumbles. The point is to provide your guests with what they need to create a memorable experience for themselves.

Because guacamole needs to be kept cold (it thins out and discolors quickly when it warms up), you may want to create a crushed ice holder for your bowl (I've described how to do that for ceviche on page 115). Easier, however, is to buy a terracotta pot that fits your guacamole bowl, soak it for a few minutes in water, then refrigerate it for an hour or so to chill. It's a simple, old-fashioned, low-tech way to keep something cool for an hour or two. You can keep the motif (and cooling) going by having damp, cool terracotta pots to hold the bowls of salad-y *salpicónes* and salsas.

Fiesta Game Plan

Special Equipment
● This is a great party for everyone, because there is no special equipment needed.

Timeline
● (follow whatever corresponds to the menu you've chosen)

Up to a week ahead:
● Make a shopping list and buy all the basics from your regular grocery store. (Truth is, everything for this party can be purchased from practically any well-stocked grocery store. You may, however, want to search out better quality or value. Read on.)

● Buy firm avocados and let them ripen at room temperature, or order ripe avocados to be picked up later in the week from a reliable market. If you're headed to a Mexican market for other ingredients, you'll typically find *ripe*, inexpensive avocados there. So ripe, you'll likely want to buy them closer to party time, maybe even refrigerate them to stop further ripening—in the *warmest* part of you refrigerator to avoid discoloration.

● Locate red-ripe tomatoes for the salsa.

● I think it's worth the effort to locate a Mexican market for chiles (poblano chiles, canned chipotle chiles), Mexican *queso fresco* or *añejo* and crispy pork rind (*chicharrón*), if using. If visiting a Mexican market, you may also want to purchase a lot of your vegetables—fresh habanero, poblano and serrano chiles, jícama, tomatillos, limes—since they will usually be much cheaper. Also, in a Mexican market there will be more variety of interesting chips to choose from (the thicker ones are much better for this situation).

The day before:
● Make the Garlicky Habanero Macadamia Nuts, page 38.

Early on party day:
● Prepare the *salpicónes*, salsas and garnishes for the guacamole bar, scoop them into serving dishes and refrigerate. Pumpkin seeds, pickled jalapeños and *chicharrón* (or bacon) should be left at room temperature.

About three hours before the guests arrive:

● Mix the margarita mixture for the Champagne Margaritas and refrigerate.

● Make the guacamole, leave half of it in the mixing bowl and scoop the other half into a serving bowl. Cover both bowls with plastic wrap directly on the surface of the guacamole and refrigerate.

● Procure ice and store it in ice chests.

● Ice (or refrigerate) all other beverages you've chosen (beer, wine, sparkling water, soft drinks).

About one hour before serving time:

● Set out the macadamia nuts in a serving bowl.

● Set up the ice bucket for the Champagne, margarita mixture and other beverages.

● Set out the chips, tostadas and toasted/grilled bread in baskets.

Serving Strategy

● When the first guests arrive, offer them a Champagne Margarita or other beverage and have the macadamia nuts set out.

● When about half the guests have gathered, set out the guacamole, toppings and garnishes, and help the guests understand how to create their different guacamole tastes, recommending your favorite combination of flavors (I especially like the crab *salpicón* topped with bacon). Because guacamole doesn't like to stand too long at room temperature, after about an hour or so I switch out the guacamole with the half that has been kept refrigerated.

Embellishments

● **Guacamole Bar:** A really dramatic way to set up the guacamole bar is to use terracotta pots. You'll need bowls, preferably stainless steel, that nestle snugly into the pots (the largest one for the guacamole, medium-size ones for the salsas and salad-y *salpicónes*, small ones for the "sprinkling" toppings). Soak the pots in cold water several hours before serving and refrigerate if possible; even if you simply put the damp pots in a cool place, they'll keep the guacamole and toppings cool for an hour or two. For even greater assurance that you'll have a cool guacamole bar, you can fill small zippered plastic bags with ice cubes and nestle them in the bottom of each pot before fitting the bowls in place.

● **Serving the beverages:** The Champagne and the margarita mixture need to be kept cold throughout the party. One of the easiest ways to create an ice bucket at an outside party is in really big terracotta pots. Upend one, setting it on a level surface where water draining from melting ice will be no problem. Set a second pot on top of the first, fill it with everything that needs to be kept cold, then top with ice.

Roasted Garlic Guacamole with Help-Yourself Garnishes

Guacamole de Ajo Asado con Sabores a Escoger

MAKES 4 CUPS, SERVING 12 AS PART OF A PARTY

FOR THE GUACAMOLE

6   garlic cloves, unpeeled

6   medium-large (2½ pounds) ripe avocados

½ cup (loosely packed) coarsely chopped fresh cilantro (thick bottom stems cut off)

2   tablespoons fresh lime juice, plus a little more if necessary

    Salt

FOR THE GARNISHES, CHIPS AND BREAD

¾ cup (about 3 ounces) Mexican *queso fresco* or *queso añejo* or other garnishing cheese like salted pressed farmer's cheese, firm goat cheese or Romano, finely crumbled or grated

¾ cup (about 3 ounces) toasted pumpkin seeds

¾ cup sliced "nacho ring" pickled jalapeños (you'll need half of an 11-ounce can)

¾ cup (about 2 ounces) coarsely crumbled *chicharrón* (Mexican crisp-fried pork rind)

    OR ½ cup crumbled, crisp-fried bacon (you'll need to start with 2 to 3 medium-thick bacon slices)

1½ to 2 pounds large, sturdy chips (preferably homemade or from a local tortilla factory) or small (2- to 3-inch) tostadas.

    OR 2 baguettes (1 pound each), diagonally sliced ¼-inch thick, brushed with olive oil and toasted on a grill or under a broiler

1. *Make the Roasted Garlic Guacamole.* In a small dry skillet over medium heat, roast the unpeeled garlic until it is soft and blackened in spots, 10 to 15 minutes. Cool, then slip off the papery skins and finely chop. Cut around each avocado from stem to blossom end and back up again, then twist the halves apart. Dislodge the pit and scoop the avocado flesh into a large bowl. Add the garlic, cilantro and lime. Coarsely mash everything together. Taste and season with salt, usually about 1 teaspoon. Scoop into its serving bowl and cover with plastic wrap directly on the surface of the guacamole. Refrigerate until you are ready to serve.

2. *Serving the Luxury Guacamole Bar.* Scoop the garnishes into small serving bowls and the chips and bread into a large basket or bowl. Set out everything—put spoons in all the preparations and garnishes—for your guests to enjoy, encouraging them to spoon a little guacamole on a toast or chip, then top with a garnish that appeals.

Chopped Fresh Tomato Salsa
Salsa Mexicana (aka Pico de Gallo)

MAKES 1½ CUPS, SERVING 12 AS PART OF A PARTY

½ medium white onion, chopped into ¼-inch pieces

Hot green chile(s) to taste (usually 1 to 2 serranos or 1 small jalapeño), stemmed, seeded (if you wish) and finely chopped

12 ounces (about 2 medium-small round or 4 to 5 plum) red-ripe tomatoes, chopped into ¼-inch pieces

2 to 3 tablespoons (loosely packed) chopped fresh cilantro (thick bottom stems cut off)

About 2 tablespoons fresh lime juice

Salt

Scoop the onion into a strainer, rinse under cold tap water, shake off the excess and transfer to a medium bowl. Add the green chile(s), tomatoes, cilantro and lime. Stir well, taste and season with salt, usually about ½ teaspoon. Cover and refrigerate until you are ready to serve.

Orange-Tomatillo Salsa
Salsa Verde con Naranja
MAKES 1½ CUPS, SERVING 12 AS A PART OF A PARTY

8   ounces (about 4 medium) tomati-
    llos, husked and rinsed

½   small red onion, chopped into
    ¼-inch pieces

1 or 2 canned chipotle chile(s) *en
    adobo*, removed from the canning
    sauce, seeded and finely chopped

2   small seedless oranges

Set a medium (8-inch) nonstick (or foil-lined) skillet over medium-high heat. Lay in the tomatillos cut side down. When they are browned, 3 or 4 minutes, flip and brown the other side. Remove from the pan and cool. Scoop half of the tomatillos into a food processor and process to a coarse puree. Scrape into a medium bowl. Chop the remaining tomatillos into small pieces and add to the bowl. Scoop the onion into a strainer, rinse under cold tap water, shake off the excess and add to the bowl along with the chipotle(s). Using a small knife, cut the peel from the oranges. Cut sections (supremes) from the oranges by cutting between the white membranes to release segments with no white pith or membrane. Cut each segment into 3 or 4 pieces and stir them into the tomatillo mixture. Taste and season with salt, usually ½ teaspoon. Cover and refrigerate.

Crab-Jícama *Salpicón*
Salpicón de Jaiba

MAKES 2 CUPS, SERVING 12 AS PART OF A PARTY

8 ounces crabmeat, picked over for stray bits of shell

⅓ of a small jícama, peeled and cut into ¼-inch pieces (you'll have a generous ½ cup)

3 green onions, roots and wilted outer leaves removed, cut cross-wise into ¼-inch pieces (you'll have about ⅓ cup)

⅓ cup (loosely packed) chopped fresh cilantro (thick bottom stems cut off)

2 tablespoons fresh lime juice

Salt

In a medium bowl, combine the crab, jícama, green onion, cilantro and lime juice. Taste and season with salt, usually about a generous ½ teaspoon. Cover and refrigerate.

Roasted Poblano *Salpicón*
(with smoked salmon or mushrooms)
Salpicón de Chile Poblano (con salmón ahumado o hongos)

MAKES 1½ CUPS, SERVING 12 AS PART OF A PARTY

8   ounces (3 medium) fresh poblano
    chiles

½   medium red onion, chopped into
    ¼-inch pieces

4   ounces smoked salmon (the
    fully-cooked hot-smoked salmon
    available widely is good, as is
    traditional smoked salmon), skin
    removed, flesh broken into ¼-inch
    pieces

    OR 6 ounces fresh mushrooms
    (oyster mushrooms would be my
    first choice here), tough stems
    cut off, caps cut into ¼-inch-wide
    strips about 1 inch long

½   teaspoon dried oregano, prefer-
    ably Mexican

2   tablespoons fresh lime juice (you
    may want a little less if using
    smoked salmon)

    Salt (if using mushrooms)

Over an open flame or 4 inches below a preheated broiler, roast the poblanos, turning them regularly until evenly blistered and blackened all over, about 5 minutes for an open flame, about 10 minutes for the broiler. Place in a bowl, cover with a kitchen towel and let cool until handleable. Rub off the blackened skin, then pull out the stem and seed pod; briefly rinse to remove any bits of skin and stray seeds. Chop into ¼-inch pieces and scoop into a medium bowl. Scoop the onion into a strainer, rinse under cold water, shake off the excess and transfer to the bowl along with the mushrooms (or smoked salmon), oregano and lime juice. Taste and season with salt if using mushrooms, usually about ½ teaspoon. (If using smoked salmon you won't need salt.) Cover and refrigerate.

ROASTED POBLANO *SALPICÓN*

Beverages

Although the making of Champagne Margaritas will usually draw guests like a magnet, you'll probably want to have some wine and beer on hand for those who prefer that.

Wine: One or two bottles of white wine (I would enjoy a refreshing, not-too-oaky Chardonnay or dry Chenin Blanc with the guacamole) is what I'd buy.

Beer: One or two six-packs of medium-bodied beer (like Dos Equis lager, Montejo or Pacifico) should be enough, depending on how many of your guests you think will opt for the cocktail.

Water: Having a couple of bottles of sparkling water on hand (my favorite being San Pellegrino) for a really nice cocktail party like this is important, I feel.

CHAMPAGNE MARGARITA (PAGE 85)

Champagne Margarita
Margarita de Champaña
MAKES TWENTY-FOUR 6-OUNCE DRINKS

The finely grated zest (colored rind only) from 3 limes

3 cups fresh lime juice

3 cups Cointreau

3 cups 100% agave silver tequila (some of our favorites right now are Oro Azul *blanco*, Milagro silver and El Tesoro platinum)

Superfine sugar, if needed for added sweetness

Several lime halves for moistening the glass rims

Coarse (kosher) salt

3 bottles chilled brut Champagne or other sparkling white wine

The cocktail should be the star of your Luxury Guacamole Bar Cocktail Party. The quantities I've listed below (triple the recipe on page 46) will be enough for two drinks per person.

1. *Make the margarita mixture.* In a large pitcher, combine the lime zest, lime juice, Cointreau and tequila. Taste the mixture: If you like the bracing flavor (it will be quite tart), leave the mixture as is; if it's too tart for you, stir in a little superfine sugar. Cover and refrigerate until chilled, about 1 hour.

2. *Serve.* Strain the mixture to remove the zest. Moisten the rims of twelve 6-ounce Champagne glasses with the cut side of the lime half. Spread coarse salt on a small plate, then upend the glasses into the salt to crust the rims. Fill each glass halfway with the margarita (it'll take a generous ⅓ cup). Slowly fill the rest of the way with Champagne or sparkling wine, and hand to one of your lucky guests.

An All-Purpose Playlist

When a group gathers at my house, they've come to celebrate something—an occasion, a season, a special dish. They've never come for a "theme" party where everything has been cooked and served to recreate another style or place or time. That approach never feels very genuine to me. Instead, when folks are coming to my house, I want the freedom to cook what I'm excited about, what I want to eat, what I think will make a perfect meal for that moment. Same goes for the music I play as we're eating. And this playlist reflects my rather eclectic approach. I created it one Sunday morning when some friends were coming for brunch—kind of mellow, with an unexpected mix of old and new songs that I can guarantee only the greatest aficionados will have heard before. There are old classics from Daniel Santos, Agustín Lara, Tony Camargo, even a romantic old *bolero* from Los Tres Aces. There's a little traditional Mexican danzón played on marimba. Lila Downs sings the Oaxacan standard "Naila." Julio Iglesias and Astor Piazolla do modern tango. Even Maná's here, singing one of Mexico's most enduring pop hits.

Song Title, Artist, Album

1. "No Me Llores Más," Omara Portuondo, *Buena Vista Social Club Presents Omara Portuondo*

2. "Esperanza Inútil," Daniel Santos, *15 Exitos Originales*

3. "Sabor a Mi," Los Tres Aces, *Boleros*

4. "Mambo en Sax," Pérez Prado, *15 Exitos*

5. "Mi Novia," Agustín Lara Las, *15 Inolvidables de Agustín Lara*

6. "Biyuna," Astor Piazzolla, *Astor Piazzolla Plays*

7. "Vivir Sin Aire," Maná, *Unplugged*

8. "Dos Gardenias," Buena Vista Social Club, *Buena Vista Social Club*

9. "Bodas de Oro," Ry Cooder & Manuel Galban, *Mambo Sinuendo*

10. "So Danço Samba," Luiz Bonfá, *The Very Best of Latin Jazz* (Disc 2)

11. "Para Machuchar Meu Coração," Stan Getz and João Gilberto, *Getz/Gilberto*

12. "Naila," Lila Downs, *La Sandunga*

13. "A Media Luz," Julio Iglesias, *Tango*

14. "Esta Noche Corazon," Tony Camargo, *El Año Viejo*

15. "Se Fue," Armando Garzón, *Danzón*

16. "Chan Chan (Son)," Las Perlas del Son, *Si, Señor*

17. "Zacatlan," *Danzónes con Marimba*

Ceviches, Seafood Cocktails and Oysters

Getting the Right Fish for Ceviche

First, let's tackle the sourcing and safety of seafood you want to serve raw, in ceviche or otherwise. You need the absolute freshest, most wholesome fish or other seafood, which you probably won't find at your run-of-the-mill chain grocery store. Those working behind your chosen fish counter should be able to tell you which top-of-the-line purveyors they use, be able to attest to the freshness and provenance of their product, and show they maintain the highest sanitary standards. It's been my experience that many of the independent fish stores (and fish counters in high-end grocery stores) meet those standards.

Another approach is to ask a sushi restaurant if they'll sell you fish, because your fish needs to be "sashimi fresh." Through there are no FDA regulations for "sashimi fresh" or "sashimi grade," most of the really good seafood distributors designate a "number one" quality that meets the demands of the best sushi restaurants. And many retailers who purchase that "number one" fish sell it as "sashimi grade" in their fresh or frozen fish counters. Otherwise you'll have to use your nose (fresh fish smells clean, almost sweet,

never the slightest bit fishy), your eyes (fresh fish looks luminescent, never dull) and your fingers (fresh fish is firm, resilient).

Fresh or *frozen* fish counters? Shouldn't *fresh* be the only option when you're talking about "sashimi quality?" Actually, frozen is frequently your best option, because fish caught, processed and blast-frozen right on the boat may taste fresher than "fresh" fish that has taken days to make its way to your city. You simply have to know which seafood freezes most successfully (large-flake, steak-y fish and all crustaceans) and how to defrost it without affecting the texture (in my opinion, only one option: overnight in the refrigerator).

Freezing ensures wholesomeness, too. Many would-be ceviche makers worry they'll be unknowingly offering parasites with their ceviche. Deep-freezing fish (-30°F for 15 hours, or −4°F for seven days) kills any concerns. Bacteria—the other half of wholesomeness concern here—is addressed by the liberal use of lime, chile and cilantro, all effective antibacterials.

Lastly: what fish to choose. Hands down, my favorite fish for ceviche

is bright-white, wild-harvested Alaskan halibut, but it's pricey. Practically any snapper and bass are delicious. Mahi mahi and tuna also make a tasty ceviche, but one with a grayish color. (In fact, if there is a dark strip of flesh on any fish—what's typically called the "blood line"—I always trim it off because of its stronger flavor and murkier-looking texture.) I'm crazy about wild-caught salmon ceviche (I give it only a half hour lime bath), but it doesn't taste like anything I've had in Mexico. No, there the favorites are Spanish mackerel and its relatives, but unless those oily fish are right off the boat, they can be strong tasting.

Most researchers do not recommend using wild-caught freshwater fish for health reasons, and most of the farm-raised freshwater fish are too fine-textured to make good ceviche.

Still not convinced you can lay your hands on the right fish? Simply replace the fish in any ceviche recipe with small cooked shrimp or cooked bay scallops; you'll need only about half the lime juice.

YUCATECAN CEVICHE WITH SHRIMP,
SQUID AND HABANERO (PAGE 96)

Yucatecan Ceviche with Shrimp, Squid and Habanero
Ceviche Yucateco de Camarónes, Calamares y Habanero

MAKES 8 CUPS, SERVING ABOUT 12 AS A STARTER

1½ cups fresh orange juice

1½ cups fresh lime juice

1   fresh habanero chile, stemmed

1½ tablespoons sugar

    Salt

12 ounces cleaned squid (including the tentacles if you're so inclined)

2   oranges

12 ounces small to medium cooked shrimp (you can either cook these in the shell—see page 104—and peel and devein them, or buy them already prepared)

2   (7 ounces total) small "pickle" or Persian (baby) cucumbers, cut into matchsticks

1   small (about 12 ounces) jícama, peeled and cut into matchsticks

1   small red onion, thinly sliced

    About ⅓ cup (loosely packed) chopped fresh cilantro (thick bottom stems cut off)

This is a juicy, cooked-seafood ceviche with crunchy fresh vegetables and the inimitable flavors of Yucatan: the tanginess of sour orange (here I recommend a mixture of orange and lime to replace the more-difficult-to-find sour oranges); the aromatic, laser-point spiciness of habanero chile; and the bold herbiness of cilantro. Ceviche Yucateco has become a staple on our restaurant's ceviche bar menu because of the sunny, smile-provoking way the flavors and textures bounce around. I love the flavor-absorbing tenderness of simmered squid. If you don't, replace it with more shrimp.

Working Ahead: You can do all the basic preparations early in the day you're serving: juice the citrus and marinate it with the habanero, cook the squid, segment the oranges and, if you need to, cook the shrimp. Cover and refrigerate everything separately. The ceviche can be completely finished and kept in the refrigerator a couple of hours before serving.

1. *Season the juice.* In a large bowl, combine the orange and lime juices. Cut the chile in half; scrape out and discard the seeds (you may want to wear disposable gloves—the chile is extremely spicy). Add the chile to the juice, along with the sugar and 1 teaspoon salt. Stir to dissolve the sugar and salt, then cover and refrigerate for 30 minutes. (That'll give you medium-spicy juice; you may want to let the mixture steep less or more time to achieve your perfect level of spiciness.) Remove the chile and discard.

2. *Cook the squid.* Meanwhile, half fill a large (4-quart) saucepan with water, heavily salt it and bring to a boil. Add the squid. When the water comes to a simmer, reduce the heat to keep it gently bubbling away. Cook until the squid is fully tender, about 30 minutes, then remove from the heat and let cool to lukewarm in the broth. Remove the squid and slice into ¼-inch rings (cut the tentacles in half).

3. *Make orange segments.* Cut sections (supremes) from the oranges: Cut the stem and blossom ends off the oranges, then stand the oranges on a cutting board. Working close to the flesh, cut away the rind and all the white pith. With a sharp, thin knife, cut the orange segments from between the white membranes that divide them.

4. *Finish the ceviche.* Add the orange segments to the spicy juice, along with the squid, shrimp, cucumber, jícama and red onion. Cover, pressing all the solids snugly into the juice, and refrigerate for a half hour or so, to blend all the flavors. Taste and season with salt if needed, then stir in the cilantro and spoon your ceviche into decorative glasses for all your guests to enjoy.

Tropical Beach Ceviche
Ceviche Playero

MAKES ABOUT 3½ CUPS, SERVING 6 GENEROUSLY AS A STARTER

8 ounces sea scallops, cut cross-wise into thin slices (you can use small bay scallops, too, and simply cut them in half)

1 cup fresh grapefruit juice

1 large dried Oaxacan pasilla chile, stemmed

  OR 1 to 2 canned chipotle chile(s) *en adobo*

4 garlic cloves, unpeeled

2 tablespoons chopped *piloncillo* or dark brown sugar

  Salt

2 cups diced fresh tropical fruit (I like a mixture of mango, the large Mexican papaya and pineapple—but you can vary it depending on what's available)

½ small red onion, thinly sliced

  About 1 cup peeled, diced jícama

Though I'd never claim that this is a traditional ceviche (in spite of the fact that it's inspired by flavors from an exploration of the Oaxaca coast, near Huatulco), the sweet-smoky-tangy combination of tropical fruit, Oaxacan pasilla (or chipotle) chiles and grapefruit is just plain delicious. Mix in the soft texture of scallops and the crunch of jícama and red onion and you've got a total crowd pleaser. If you've got a Mexican papaya, peel it with a knife, cut it in half and scrape out the seeds, then dice the fruit. For mango, simply peel it with a knife, cut the flesh from the pit (mango is a "cling-pit" fruit) and cut it into small pieces.

  Working Ahead: Early in the day you're serving, you can marinate the scallops, drain them, prepare the flavoring and chop the fruit. Store each preparation separately, tightly covered in the refrigerator. The ceviche can be finished, covered and refrigerated an hour or two before serving.

1. *Marinate the scallops.* In a small nonreactive bowl (glass or stainless steel are best), combine the sliced (or cut) scallops and the grapefruit juice. Cover and refrigerate for about 45 minutes to an hour while you're putting together the remaining ingredients.

2. *Prepare the flavoring.* If using the Oaxacan pasilla chile, toast it in a small ungreased skillet over medium heat, turning it every few seconds for about a minute, until the kitchen fills with its smoky aroma. Cover with hot tap water and allow to rehydrate for about 30 minutes. If using canned chipotle chile(s), simply remove them from their canning sauce and place in a blender.

  In a small skillet over medium heat, roast the garlic, turning regularly, until soft and blotchy black in spots, 10 to 15 minutes. Cool and peel.

  Drain the scallops, measuring ⅔ cup of the juice and discarding the rest.

  If using the Oaxacan pasilla chile, remove it from the water and place in the blender. Add the garlic, *piloncillo* (or brown sugar), reserved grapefruit juice marinade and 1 teaspoon salt. Blend until smooth. Pour in a bowl.

3. *Finishing the ceviche.* To the flavoring mixture, add the fruit, onion and jícama. Stir in the scallops. Taste and season with salt, usually about ½ teaspoon. You can refrigerate your ceviche for an hour or so before serving, or scoop it into small dishes or glasses and enjoy right away.

Herb Green Ceviche with cucumber
Ceviche Verde con pepino

MAKES ABOUT 4½ CUPS, SERVING 8 TO 10 AS A STARTER

FOR A SCANT 1 CUP OF HERB SEASONING

½ head garlic, cloves broken apart, unpeeled

2 to 3 fresh serrano chiles

1 medium bunch cilantro (thick bottom stems cut off)

1 small bunch flat-leaf parsley (thick bottom stems cut off)

½ cup olive oil

Salt

FOR FINISHING THE CEVICHE

¼ cup fresh lime juice

1½ pounds "sashimi-quality" skin-less, boneless fish fillets—my favorites are Alaskan halibut, ahi tuna and aqua-cultured Kona Kampachi (a type of yellowtail)—cut into ½-inch cubes

2 (7 ounces total) small "pickle" cucumbers (the kind you get in the farmers' market) or Persian (baby) cucumbers, cut into ½-inch cubes

2 ripe large avocados, pitted, flesh scooped from skin and then cut into cubes

Lettuce leaves (butter lettuce works great here), for garnish

This is one of my favorite dishes of all times: that seductive texture of fresh fish with a citric sparkle, the savor of roasted garlic and green chile, and the oh-so-attractive vividness of fresh cilantro and parsley. Add a little farmers' market cucumber and buttery avocado, and you've made a dish no one will forget. My inspiration was an all-green ceviche I ate in Mexico, prepared by my Veracruzana friend Carmen Ramírez Degollado, and the chimichurri they serve on steak in Argentina.

I don't usually follow regular ceviche procedure here, thoroughly "cooking" the fish in lime juice for several hours before serving. Instead, I toss the raw fish with lime and flavorings, scoop it into something pretty and carry it to the table—that's the essence of freshness. But if that doesn't sound good to you, stir a couple of cups fresh lime juice into the raw fish, refrigerate it for a couple of hours until the fish has a cooked texture, drain it and add the herb mixture and vegetables. Or just use cooked shrimp instead of raw fish, which I did last week for dinner and loved the outcome.

One thing to keep in mind: you'll have more than you need of the herb mixture (we call it Mexican chimichurri in our kitchen). You'll thank me for that. Store it in a covered container in the refrigerator (pour a film of oil over the top). It'll keep for a month or more. I smear it on chicken before grilling or roasting it. I stir it into scrambled eggs. I add it to salad dressing and cream sauces. It'll make your everyday cooking taste special-occasion.

Working Ahead: As I said, the herb seasoning can be stored in the refrigerator for a month or more. All the basic prep work can be done early in the day you're serving; store everything separately, covered, in the refrigerator. Mix and season the ceviche shortly before serving—no more than an hour—waiting to add the avocado until the guests have assembled.

1. Make the herb seasoning. Set a dry skillet over medium heat. Lay in the unpeeled garlic cloves and chiles. Roast, turning frequently, until soft and blotchy brown in spots, about 10 minutes for the chiles and 15 minutes for the garlic. Cool until handleable, then slip the skins off the garlic, pull the stems off the chiles and roughly chop (no need to remove the seeds). Place in a food processor along with the cilantro (about 1 cup if packed), parsley (about 1 cup if packed), oil and 2 generous teaspoons salt. Process until nearly smooth (it will be pasty). Scrape into a storage container and refrigerate until serving time.

2. *Finish the ceviche.* In a large bowl, whisk together the lime juice and ½ cup of the herb seasoning. (Cover and refrigerate the remainder for another preparation.) Add the fish and cucumber, and stir to combine. To blend the flavors, cover and refrigerate for a half hour (for best results no more than an hour). Taste and season with a little more lime juice or salt if you think necessary, gently stir in the avocado (save out a little for garnish if you want), then serve on lettuce leaf–lined plates or in martini glasses.

HERB GREEN CEVICHE WITH CUCUMBER

SEE "SHUCKING OYSTERS" ON PAGE 117

100   Fiesta at Rick's

Fruity "Gazpacho Moreliano" with Crab or Cured Fish
Gazpacho Moreliano de Jaiba o Pescado Curtido

SERVES 6 TO 8 AS A STARTER

1 large ripe mango, peeled, flesh cut from the pit and cut into ¼-inch pieces

OR ¼ of a ripe Mexican papaya, peeled, seeded, flesh cut into ¼-inch pieces (about 1½ cups of mango or papaya)

¼ of a ripe pineapple, peeled, cored, and cut into ¼-inch pieces (about 1½ cups)

½ medium jícama, peeled and cut into ¼-inch pieces (about 1½ cups)

⅔ cup fresh orange juice

⅓ cup fresh lime juice

Salt

6 to 8 ounces fresh crabmeat, picked over for any stray bits of shell

OR 8 ounces Ancho-Cured Salmon or Halibut (page 102), either works well—even a lightly smoked salmon can be good here, cut into ¼-inch pieces

About 3 to 4 teaspoons powdered ancho (or pasilla negro) chile

3 ounces Mexican fresh cheese like *queso fresco* or *panela*, crumbled (about ¾ cup)

OR 4 ounces fresh goat cheese or dryish (true Italian-style) ricotta— you'll need a cheese you can coarsely crumble

There are a few little stalls in downtown Morelia in west central Mexico— wedged into the beautiful, World Heritage colonial storefronts, between the ubiquitous shoe stores and bridal shops—that make pretty much just one thing. Gazpacho Moreliano. Which has nothing to do with gazpacho from Spain—no tomatoes or cucumbers or onion—except that everything is finely chopped and served cold in a cup or a bowl. Truth is, that's what the word gazpacho originally meant: cold, finely chopped soupy mixture. And in Morelia, that translates as a mixture of ripe tropical fruit with crunchy jícama, tangy lime, powdered ancho chile and fresh cheese. Think fruity and savory and spicy—it gets nearly all the taste buds going. And the combo looks beautiful with crab or cured fish, especially as a first course or a dish you serve (in a bowl, not cups) with drinks, tapas style.

Though it's available widely these days, you might choose to make your own ancho powder: Heat the oven to 300 degrees. Stem dried ancho chiles, rip them open and remove the seeds. Tear them into flat pieces and spread into a single layer on a baking sheet. Bake until nearly crisp, 10 to 15 minutes. Let cool (the pieces will crisp completely as they cool). In an electric spice/ coffee mill, pulverize the chiles in small batches. (If you want very fine powder, pass it through a fine-mesh strainer.) Store in a tightly closed container, preferably in the freezer or a cool, dry, dark place.

Working Ahead: The fruit mixture (Step 1) can be made, covered and refrigerated for a couple of hours before serving. The final assembly should be done just before serving.

1. *Make the Gazpacho Moreliano.* Combine the mango or papaya with the pineapple, jícama, orange and lime juices and 1 teaspoon salt. Taste and add a little more salt if necessary to give the mixture a nicely sweet-savory balance. Let stand for 10 or 15 minutes.

2. *Layering and serving the dish.* Divide half the mixture between six and eight glasses—small highball glasses or martini glasses are perfect here. Divide the crab (or cured fish) among the glasses, then top each with a scant ¼ teaspoon of the ground chile and some of the crumbled cheese (½ tablespoon of *queso fresco*, 1 tablespoon of goat cheese). Top each glass with a portion of the remaining fruit mixture and another portion of the chile and cheese. Serve right away.

Ancho-Cured Salmon or Halibut

MAKES ABOUT 14 OUNCES CURED FISH

½ cup powdered ancho chile (or guajillo chile or a mixture of paprika and a little cayenne)

½ cup kosher salt

1¼ cups sugar

1 pound skinless salmon or halibut fillet in a single piece—an inch-thick piece is best here

If you're interested in health and ecology, as I am, you'll likely choose wild-caught salmon because it's more health promoting than most farm raised, plus it's very, very tasty; and that wild-caught salmon will likely be from Alaskan waters, Alaska's fisheries being among the most well regulated in the world. Since this salmon isn't ever cooked, most experts recommend that you freeze it, then defrost it overnight in the refrigerator before curing it. The freezer comes in handy when slicing cured fish, too: 20 or 30 minutes in a freezer firms it for easy slicing. Cured fish will keep for about a week in the refrigerator; wrap it tightly.

In a bowl combine the powdered chile, salt and sugar; mix well. Spread *half* of the mixture into a 13 x 9-inch glass baking dish (or something similar—no aluminum or plastic). Lay the fish on top, then sprinkle with the remaining chile mixture. Cover and refrigerate for about 24 hours (timing is important in curing fish, though a couple of hours either way isn't going to hurt the fish). Scrape off the curing mixture. (I like to hold the fish up and "squeegee" the curing mixture off with my fingers.) Slice thinly or cube—whatever is appropriate for your preparation or presentation. (Use a very sharp thin-blade slicing knife, wetting it with cold water between slices, and cutting the fish on the bias, about a 45° angle to the countertop, will give the prettiest results.)

Mexican-Style Shrimp Cocktail
Cóctel de Camarón
MAKES 4 CUPS, SERVING 6 TO 8 AS A STARTER

1   pound (71 to 90 pieces per pound) peeled, cooked small shrimp

¾   cup ketchup

¼   cup Mexican hot sauce (such as Valentina or Tamazula)

½   cup (loosely packed) chopped fresh cilantro (thick bottom stems cut off)

2 to 3 tablespoons fresh lime juice

1   small white onion, cut into ¼-inch pieces

¾   cup clam juice, shellfish stock or water

    Salt

1   ripe avocado, pitted, flesh scooped from the skin and sliced crosswise

2 to 3 dozen crackers (standard-issue saltines, artisanal crackers or the homemade Red Chile Crackers on page 41)

    OR 8 to 12 ounces of tortilla chips

2   limes, cut into wedges

Unexpected as it may be for many Americans, market stalls and street stalls all over Mexico put together shrimp cocktails for hungry crowds every day and serve them up with packets of soda crackers. And not just on the beaches. Honestly, one of my favorite street-stall shrimp cocktails is at Mexico City's El Caguamo, which follows the pretty traditional pattern of making "cocktail" sauce from ketchup, Mexican hot sauce and fresh-squeezed lime, then mixing in shrimp, avocado, cilantro and onion. Elemental satisfaction.

Working Ahead: The sauce can be made, covered and refrigerated for several days before serving. Finish the cocktail within an hour or so of serving.

In a large bowl, combine the shrimp, ketchup, hot sauce, cilantro, lime juice and onion. Stir in the clam juice, stock or water. Taste and season with salt if you think it needs it. Refrigerate until you're ready to serve.

Serve the cocktail in small bowls topped with slices of avocado, accompanied by saltine crackers (for a very authentic touch) or tortilla chips and lime wedges for your guests to squeeze on.

Roasted Tomato Shrimp-and-Octopus Cocktail
Cóctel de Camarón y Pulpo con Jitomates Asados

MAKES 4½ CUPS, SERVING 8 AS A STARTER

1½ pounds octopus, cleaned (I love the small ones—about ½ pound each)

1 small red onion, sliced about ¼ inch thick

2 bay leaves

Salt

12 ounces small to medium (40 to 60 pieces) shrimp

1 pound (2 medium-large round or 6 medium plum) ripe tomatoes

OR 1½ cups canned tomatoes in juice (preferably fire roasted), drained (you will need about ¾ of a 28-ounce can)

3 garlic cloves, peeled and halved

1 tablespoon olive or vegetable oil

2 tablespoons balsamic or sweet sherry vinegar

2 tablespoons brown sugar

¼ cup Tamazula hot sauce (or whichever is your favorite Mexican offering)

1 small ripe avocado, pitted, flesh scooped from the skin and cut into ½-inch cubes

3 tablespoons chopped cilantro (thick bottom stems cut off)

2 to 3 dozen crackers (standard-issue soda crackers, artisanal crackers or the homemade Red Chile Crackers on page 41)

This preparation takes the basic Mexican street-style shrimp cocktail to the next level, mixing in tender pieces of octopus with the shrimp, and dressing them with this complex, richly textured roasted tomato cocktail sauce. Inspiration for the octopus addition comes from a stall at Chicago's (now very Mexican) Sunday morning Maxwell Street Market, where one of my favorite vendors offers two options for his tender shrimp and octopus: stir in cocktail sauce and avocado or pour on steaming tomato-laced broth spiked with green chile. This version of cocktail sauce is developed from my long-standing love affair with the smoky, sweet flavor of roasted tomatoes, onions and garlic.

Working Ahead: *The sauce can be made, covered and refrigerated for several days before serving. Finish the cocktail within an hour or so of serving.*

1. *Cook the octopus.* If you bought cleaned octopus, the eyes should have been removed; if not, cut them off. (Not a great way to start a recipe for most Americans, but something you need to know.) Cut open the head cavity and wash it out, making sure the ink sac has been removed. Check to make sure the beak (the hard mouth area where all the tentacles come together) has been cut out; if not, use a small knife to cut it away. Cut off the straggly last inch or so of each tentacle.

In a large (4-quart) saucepan, combine the octopus, ⅓ of the onion, the bay and 1 teaspoon salt with 2½ quarts water. Bring slowly to a simmer over medium heat, reduce the heat to maintain a gentle simmer, and cook until very tender when pierced with a thin-blade knife, about 1¼ hours. (Weight with a heat-proof plate to keep submerged.) Remove the cooked octopus to cool on a plate and raise the heat to high under the pan of cooking liquid.

2. *Cook the shrimp.* When the liquid comes to a boil, add the shrimp, cover and time 1 minute. Remove from the heat, set the lid askew and pour off all the delicious liquid—but no shrimp—into a heat-proof bowl to save for making seafood soup. Re-cover the pan and let the shrimp steam for 5 minutes, then fill the pan with cold water to stop the cooking. Let stand a minute or so. Drain thoroughly. Peel the shrimp.

3. *Make the sauce.* If using fresh tomatoes, roast them on a rimmed baking sheet about 4 inches below a very hot broiler until splotchy black and thoroughly soft, 5 or 6 minutes per side. Remove and cool. While the tomatoes are cooling, reduce the oven temperature to 425 degrees or heat to 425 degrees if using canned tomatoes. Spread the *remaining* onion and the garlic on a baking sheet and drizzle with the oil. Toss to combine. Roast, stirring a few times, until richly browned, about 15 minutes.

If you have roasted fresh tomatoes, pull off their blackened skins. Scoop the tomatoes (fresh roasted or canned roasted) into a food processor and pulse several times to chop them into small pieces. Scrape into a large bowl. Without washing the food processor, scoop in the onion and garlic, then pulse until chopped into pieces about ⅛ inch. Scrape in with the tomato and stir in the vinegar, brown sugar and hot sauce. Taste and season highly with salt, usually about 1½ teaspoons.

4. *Finish the cocktail.* If you're a person who likes shrimp cocktail really cold, refrigerate the sauce until chilled. Add the octopus, shrimp, avocado and cilantro to the sauce and stir to combine. *Cóctel de Camarón* looks beautiful presented in martini glasses or little glass bowls (especially if they are nestled into a larger bowl filled with crushed ice). Serve with crackers on the side.

ROASTED TOMATO SHRIMP-AND-OCTOPUS COCKTAIL

Scallops (or Shrimp) with Spicy Green Chile–Lime Marinade
Callos de Hacha (o Camarónes) en Aguachile

SERVES 6

1¼ cups fresh lime juice

1 to 2 fresh serrano chiles, stemmed

Salt

1 pound super-fresh sea scallops, tough little "foot" pulled off (if it's still there)

OR 1 pound large fresh shrimp, peeled and deveined

About 1 cup (loosely packed) cilantro leaves, for garnish

This ultra-simple raw-seafood "ceviche" is only as good as the freshness of the ingredients you use to make it. That's why you typically find it only on the coasts, primarily in Mexico's upper west coast shrimping communities where it's a regional specialty. (Nowadays, though, many of Mexico's top-notch seafood restaurants in big cities are starting to feature it.) If you're a sushi fan, you'll love this dazzlingly flavored dish: raw scallops (or, in Mexico, the more popular shrimp) are sliced and doused with just-squeezed lime juice, chopped serrano chiles and cilantro. Simple, bright, spicy. To make slicing easier, you may want to firm the scallops or shrimp in the freezer for 10 minutes. My preference is to let the shellfish soak up the spicy lime for about 10 minutes before serving, but that sacrifices a little of its melting texture.

Working Ahead: A couple of hours before serving, you can juice the lime and slice the shellfish. Keep everything tightly covered in the refrigerator.

1. *Prepare the marinade.* In a blender, combine the lime juice, chiles and a generous ½ teaspoon salt. Blend until smooth. Taste (it'll be spicy).

2. *Finish the dish.* Slice the scallops across the grain (meaning that you'll turn each scallop on its side for slicing) into ⅛-inch-thick disks. (If using shrimp, cut each in half lengthwise, creating two crescents.) Divide the slices among six dinner plates, laying them out in a single layer. Sprinkle lightly with salt. (*You may cover each plate with plastic wrap and refrigerate it for a couple of hours or so before serving.*) Douse each serving with about 3 tablespoons of the spicy lime mixture (scallops or shrimp should be about half submerged). Sprinkle each plate liberally with cilantro leaves and serve right away.

Red Chile–Tuna Tartar
Tártara de Atún y Chile Guajillo

MAKES 2½ CUPS, ENOUGH FOR 6 TO 8 AS A STARTER

1 pound "sashimi-quality" fresh tuna fillet—best if it is 1-inch-thick pieces

6 garlic cloves, unpeeled

6 (about 1½ ounces) dried guajillo chiles, stemmed, seeded and torn into flat pieces

½ cup fresh lime juice

Salt

½ small red onion, cut into ¼-inch pieces

⅓ cup (loosely packed) chopped fresh cilantro (thick bottom stems cut off), plus leaves for garnishing

When I want to start off a party with a dish that's both up-to-the-minute and very traditionally Mexican tasting, I gravitate to this rustic red chile–infused tuna tartar. Many supermarkets carry frozen "sashimi-quality" tuna, which I defrost in the refrigerator overnight to retain its tender, meaty texture. Dressing that essence of freshness with a lime-brightened blend of red guajillo chile and roasted garlic offers yin-yang in every bite. Your tartar can be piled on tortilla chips or small tortillas (or on grilled bread, bruschetta style). Or it can be served in glass bowls or martini glasses—I usually add some chopped, peeled jícama to round it out. For a restaurant-style presentation, form little "cakes" of tartar on plates (a biscuit cutter makes a good mold) and serve with baby greens and grilled bread or warm tortillas.

Working Ahead: The red chile seasoning can be made a day or two ahead, covered and refrigerated. Early in the day you're serving, the tuna can be diced, tightly covered and refrigerated. Combine the tuna, seasoning, cilantro and freshly chopped onion just before serving.

1. *Deep-chill the fish.* Wrap the tuna in plastic wrap and place in the freezer for an hour or so to firm for easier cutting.

2. *Toast the garlic and chiles.* Place a large skillet over medium heat and scatter the garlic on one side. When the pan is hot, toast the chile pieces one by one: use a metal spatula to press the pieces flat against the hot surface until they blister and release their aroma, about 10 seconds per side. (When properly toasted, the inside of each chile piece will have lightened in color, but not developed any dark spots.) Transfer to a bowl, cover with hot tap water and weight with a plate to keep submerged. Meanwhile, turn the garlic occasionally until it is completely softened (it will blacken in spots)—it will take 10 to 15 minutes. Cool until handleable, then peel.

3. *Prepare the red chile seasoning.* When the chiles have soaked 30 minutes, drain and place in a blender jar with the garlic and lime juice. Blend to a smooth puree, adding a little water if necessary to keep everything moving through the blades. Press through a medium-mesh strainer into a bowl. Season with salt, about 1 teaspoon. Refrigerate until ready to serve.

4. *Finish the tartar.* With a sharp knife, cut the tuna into small dice—I like ¼-inch cubes—and scoop into a bowl. When you're ready to serve, scoop the onion into a strainer, rinse under cold water, shake off the excess and add to the tuna. Mix in the red-chile seasoning and chopped cilantro. Serve—whether on a crispy base like a chip, molded on a plate or in a small bowl or glass—decorated with cilantro leaves.

Summertime Seafood Cocktail Party for 12

Summertime Seafood Cocktail Party for 12

Ceviche sums up summer, or it rekindles memories of warm beachside afternoons in Tulum, Puerto Vallarta, maybe Cabo San Lucas . . . or it stops us dead in our tracks.

Ceviche captures all of the sunny brightness fresh lime, cilantro and green chile can summon . . . but, of course, it's typically made from raw fish, which brings out major insecurities in many home cooks, especially concerning its sourcing and safety.

So why even attempt ceviche at home, let alone a ceviche party? Especially a ceviche party with *raw oysters*? I'm offering it because (1) insecurities spring from lack of knowledge or experience, and I plan to provide the former so that you can gain the latter; (2) ceviches don't always have to be made with that potentially anxiety-provoking raw fish; and (3) if done with an eye to accessibility and balance, a ceviche party will impress the socks off your friends.

Getting the Right Fish for Ceviche

Please read the information on page 94 about procuring fish for raw-fish ceviche. It will give you confidence. Only one last hurdle.

Tackling Oysters

As the summer wanes, I'm ready to go back to oysters. Not that we can't get good oysters during those months that don't end in an "r," an old adage many still adhere to—lightning-speed communication and transportation mean we can lay our hands on great oysters from cold waters year-round. Still, during the summer many of our continent's oyster beds reach water temperatures that are warm enough to encourage spawning . . . leading to less-than-optimal oyster taste and texture, occasionally without warning. Simply put, I'm personally not as excited about a plate of raw oysters at the height of summer.

And then, by September, I'm back to being gung ho about serving and eating oysters. So gung ho, in fact, that I usually want to throw an oyster-eating party, to savor with abandon that unique texture and steely taste that makes so many of us crazy for that gourmet delicacy. But I've discovered that not every oyster aficionado is as comfortable as I am with serving oysters on the half shell for a party at home. Probably because they don't know just how easy it can be—and how dramatic the outcome. As with ceviche, insecurities typically spring from a lack of knowledge and experience, especially experience in the simple technique of oyster shucking. I can teach you that in a matter of minutes (see page 117).

Good oysters can be easier to procure with confidence than sashimi-fresh fish for ceviche. Virtually all are farm raised in meticulously monitored beds and come with inspection tags that track them back to a specific stretch of coastline. To determine freshness, all you need to know is when they were plucked from the water, which an inspection tag will indicate.

And where do you buy these fresh oysters? As with sashimi-fresh fish,

SHUCKING OYSTERS

- Marinate and drain the scallops for ceviche, prepare the flavoring, and cut up the fruit and vegetables; refrigerate separately.

- Cook the shrimp if you didn't purchase cooked shrimp.

- If serving oysters, make the Orange-Habanero *Miñoneta*.

- Make the base for the Summer Margarita; refrigerate.

About three hours before the guests arrive:

- Make Rick's Favorite Summer Soft Drink; refrigerate.

- Set out baskets of chips, tostadas and crackers to accompany the guacamole, ceviches and shrimp cocktail.

- Ice (or refrigerate) beer and wine.

About one hour before serving time:

- Make guacamole, scoop into a serving bowl, cover with plastic wrap directly on the surface and refrigerate.

- Mix up and season the ceviches and the shrimp cocktail, scoop into serving bowls, cover and refrigerate.

- Set up your bar area with the soft drink, beer, wine, everything for the Summer Margarita and the ice.

Shortly before serving:

- If oysters are on the menu, line a large deep platter with crushed ice and pile on the bivalves. Set out the *Salsa Negra* and *Miñoneta*.

Serving Strategy

- When the first guests arrive, welcome them with Rick's Favorite Summer Soft Drink, a Summer Margarita, wine or beer. Set out the guacamole.

- When you're ready for the main attraction, set out the ceviches and shrimp cocktail. If you're serving oysters, station one person close by to shuck them as the guests are ready.

Embellishments

- **Serving guacamole, ceviches and seafood cocktails:** The guacamole, ceviches and seafood cocktails need to be kept cool to stay appetizing. For casual parties, a low-tech way to conserve coolness is to nestle bowls (stainless is efficient) into cold, damp, clean terracotta flower pots: First, make sure your serving bowls fit snugly into the pots. Then, run the pots under water, shake off the excess and refrigerate for several hours. When ready to serve, fit the bowls into the pots and fill with guacamole, ceviches and seafood cocktail. A beautiful way to serve the chips and crackers is to pile them onto a large terracotta saucer (a 15-inch one) around the base of the cold terracotta flower pots that contain the guacamole and so forth.

● **Homemade ice bowls are a really impressive way to serve guacamole, ceviches and seafood cocktails:** To make an ice bowl, fill a large metal bowl with crushed ice. Make a well in the center and press in a smaller metal bowl. Fill the smaller bowl with rocks to weigh it down. Around the rock-filled bowl, pour water over the crushed ice to cover. Freeze for several hours, until firm. Remove the small bowl (if it doesn't pop right out, pour warm water in it to loosen) and wrap a warm towel around the outside of the large bowl. Flip out your ice bowl, line it with a couple of rectangles cut from banana leaves and fill with the guacamole, ceviche or shrimp cocktail. Set the ice bowl in a large terracotta saucer to catch the water from the bowl.

● **A dramatic way to serve shucked oysters:** A large terracotta saucer (a 15-inch one) also works well for serving oysters. Cover the bottom of the saucer with plastic so that as the ice melts, the water doesn't run out of the drainage hole. Fill the saucer with crushed ice. In the center nestle two small bowls—one for the *Salsa Negra* and one for the *Miñoneta*. Shuck oysters, nestling them into the ice around the salsas.

● **Serving the beverages:** The *agua fresca* can be left in a pitcher at room temperature for a couple of hours. I put ice in the glasses rather than the pitcher to avoid diluting the beverage over time. If you entertain a lot, I recommend getting the now-common pitchers with the freezable ice core or chamber. They allow you to keep beverages at room temperature for longer periods of time without risking spoilage.

The margarita base can be left at the room temperature for longer than an *agua fresca* (tequila is a preservative), but the warmer the base, the more it will be diluted by ice in the shaker. Though it's a commitment, hand-shaking the margaritas is far superior to any other option.

Serving beer can be as simple as opening up an ice chest or as inventive as the huge terracotta pots I've recommended for other parties. Or, for outdoor parties, renting delivery bikes with ice-able containers. Or renting ice-pop carts (aka *paleta* carts) for stocking with (dry) ice and bottles.

Oysters on the Half Shell with *Salsa Negra* and Orange-Habanero *Miñoneta*
Ostiones Frescos y Sus Salsas

SERVES 12 AS PART OF A COCKTAIL PARTY

FOR ABOUT 1¼ CUPS SALSA NEGRA

1   whole can of chipotle chiles *en adobo*

1   tablespoon molasses

3   tablespoons balsamic or sweet sherry vinegar

2   tablespoons dark brown sugar

2   tablespoons soy sauce

    Salt

FOR 1¾ CUPS ORANGE-HABANERO MIÑONETA

1   small fresh habanero chile, stemmed

½   cup fresh orange juice

½   cup fresh lime juice

    Salt

2   medium tomatillos, husked, rinsed and finely chopped

½   small white onion, finely chopped

2   tablespoons (loosely packed) chopped fresh cilantro

FOR THE OYSTERS

2 or 3 limes, cut into wedges

    Mexican hot sauce like Tamazula or Valentina (optional)

6   dozen fresh oysters (or more if your crowd is oyster crazy)

1. *Make the* Salsa Negra. Combine the can of chipotles (including their canning sauce), molasses, vinegar and brown sugar in a blender or food processor, along with ¼ cup water. Process until smooth. Scrape into a small saucepan, set over medium-low heat and simmer until dark and reduced to the consistency of tomato paste, about 30 minutes. Remove from the heat and stir in the soy and enough water to give it the consistency of runny ketchup. (If the seeds bother you, press the sauce through a medium-mesh strainer.) Cool, taste and season with salt if you think the soy sauce doesn't add enough saltiness (the salsa should be heavily seasoned). Scrape into a serving bowl and refrigerate until ready to serve.

2. *Make the* Miñoneta. Cut the habanero in half and place one or both halves in a small bowl (depending on how spicy you want the *Miñoneta* to be). Add the juices, cover and refrigerate for an hour or two—the longer the chile stays in the juice, the spicier it will become. Fish out the chile pieces and discard. Season the juice highly with salt, usually about 1 teaspoon. Mix the chopped tomatillo, onion and cilantro in a small serving bowl, then pour on the juice.

3. *Serve.* Set out the *Salsa Negra* and *Miñoneta*, along with the lime wedges and hot sauce if you have it. Shuck the oysters, handing them directly to your guests or presenting them on crushed ice. Encourage your guests to experiment with the flavors of *ostiones a la mexicana.*

Shucking Oysters

Most people are intimidated at the thought of shucking oysters—sharp, craggy shells clamped so tightly shut that the seam between top and bottom is nearly invisible. If you've dreamed of serving up oysters on the half shell to friends and family, it's easier than you might think. The basics:

● Oysters have a top (flat) and bottom (cupped). To shuck an oyster, the bottom should be on the countertop or cutting board.

● Oysters have a front (rounded) and back (most pointed). Think of the back as the "hinge" that holds the two shells together, the point at which you want to pry the two shells apart. To shuck an oyster (if you are right-handed), steady the front of the oyster firmly against your work surface with your left hand, leaving your right hand free to pry the two shells apart.

● You can pry the top and bottom shells apart with the pointed end of a bottle/can opener (the kind commonly referred to as a "church key") or a small flat-head screwdriver, but the most efficient piece of oyster-opening equipment is a stubby, sturdy, short-bladed oyster knife with a guard. They are readily available online or from fishmongers, cookware shops, cutlery shops and restaurant supply companies.

● To protect the hand that's steadying the oyster—protect it from the shell or your prying device—use a folded kitchen towel or, better, one of those mesh gloves that most professional oyster shuckers wear. The protective gloves are usually available wherever they sell oyster knives.

TO SHUCK AN OYSTER: With the rounded "bottom" side of the oyster against your work surface, hold the front side of the oyster firmly with one (possibly gloved) hand. (Some shuckers fold a kitchen towel, lay the oyster on one end, then fold the towel up over the oyster, leaving the pointed, "hinge-end" of the oyster exposed; this allows for a firm, protected grasp of the oyster.) Use an oyster knife (or one of its stand-ins) to wedge between the top and bottom shells, inserting it at the pointy back end of the oyster. When you're about ¼ inch in, rotate the knife and feel the two shells release from each other. Run your knife along the inside of the top shell to release the oyster, then remove and discard the top shell. Slide your knife under the oyster to release it, flipping the oyster over as you go (this presents the oyster looking very plump and makes for easy eating).

Spicy Cilantro-Lime Shaved Ice for Oysters
Raspado Picante de Limón y Cilantro para Ostiones

MAKES A GENEROUS QUART, ENOUGH FOR 3 TO 6 DOZEN OYSTERS

3 to 4 fresh lemongrass stalks (4 or 5 ounces), roughly chopped (you need about 1½ to 2 cups of the chopped)

3   cups water

¼   cup sugar

1   small fresh serrano chile, stemmed and roughly chopped

A scant teaspoon salt

½   cup plus 1 tablespoon fresh lime juice

½   medium bunch of cilantro, thick bottom stems cut off

If serving fresh-shucked oysters with Orange-Habanero Miñoneta, Salsa Negra and lime isn't enough (or perhaps doesn't appeal), a spicy-herby-tangy shaved ice spooned onto an oyster might just be the ticket. It doesn't take much to imagine how this punchy raspado plays with those persuasive oyster flavors most of us hanker after. This ice has another use, too, as a dessert: simply raise the sugar to 1 cup and reduce the salt to ¼ teaspoon. You'll have a dessert folks will talk about for a long time.

If no 8 x 8-inch pan is available, a 13 x 9-inch pan will work. Just stir the ice more frequently in the freezer.

1. *Make the base.* In a small (2-quart) saucepan, combine the lemongrass, water, sugar, serrano and salt. Bring to a boil, remove from heat, cover and let steep 20 minutes. Uncover (the mixture should be close to room temperature) and strain into a blender jar, pressing firmly on the lemongrass to extract as much liquid as possible. Cover and refrigerate until chilled, about ½ hour. Add the lime juice and cilantro, and process until smooth.

2. *Freeze the raspado.* Pour the mixture into an 8 x 8-inch pan (a metal one works best) and set in the freezer. After 45 minutes, thoroughly stir the mixture, breaking up the large crystals that have formed. Return to the freezer for another 15 minutes, then stir it again. Repeat the freezing-stirring process every 15 minutes until you have a panful of large, fluffy crystals. (The whole process takes about 2 hours.) Scrape the finished *raspado* into a freezer container, cover and freeze until you are ready to serve.

Beverages

It's always difficult to predict how much of each beverage to have on hand unless you know the crowd really well. But as a caterer, it's often my job to guess. Here's what I'd do:

Summer Soft Drink: A single recipe (page 71) makes 3 quarts (12 large servings), which should be enough for your party.

Wine: White wine, not red, is what this food calls for, but neither ceviche because of liminess) nor oysters (because of brininess) is the easiest match. For ceviche, think a crisp Sauvignon Blanc, dry Riesling or—a personal favorite—Oregon Pinot Gris; oysters (which can be great with those same wines) are made for something sparkling. Two to three bottles will be enough.

Beer: Have at least 18 beers on hand. Choose half from the lighter Mexican beers like Pacifico or Tecate, half from the fuller-flavored beers like Bohemia or Tecate Lager.

Summer Margarita
Margarita Veraniega
MAKES TWENTY-SEVEN 6-OUNCE MARGARITAS

9 cups thin-sliced, peeled, seeded cucumber: you'll need 3 large 16-ounce (European) cucumbers or 6 standard 8-ounce (6-inch-long) cucumbers

4½ cups 100% agave silver tequila (we like El Milagro or Cazadores in this drink)

3 cups fresh lime juice

3 cups Simple Syrup (page 53)

A lime half for moistening the glass rim

Coarse (kosher) salt

Cucumber slices for garnish

Ice cubes (you'll need 18 or 20 cups—small ones are best)

I have chosen to triple the recipe on page 50 (making enough for 27 margaritas); if you think your guests are more a wine-beer-soft drink crowd, doubling the recipe may be enough.

1. *Make the margarita mixture.* In a blender, combine the cucumber, tequila, lime juice and simple syrup. Blend until the mixture is as smooth as you can get it. Strain into a pitcher, cover and refrigerate until chilled, about 1 hour.

2. *Shake and serve.* Moisten the rims of three 6-ounce martini glasses with the cut side of the lime half. Spread coarse salt on a small plate, then upend the glasses into the salt to crust the rims. Fill a cocktail shaker ¾ full with ice, then measure in 1½ cups of the margarita mixture. Cover and shake for 10 to 15 seconds. Strain into the prepared glasses. Garnish with cucumber slices (I usually cut a slit in each slice and impale one on the side of each glass). When you're ready, finish more rounds of margaritas in the same way.

Tropical Party Playlist

This long playlist—about two hours—from my iPod is one I rely on often when having friends over for a relaxed evening. It does everything I want music to do while I'm enjoying food and friends: it eases everyone into a fun groove, ready for something good, perhaps something unexpected. You'll notice there isn't anything stereotypical, no mariachis. Without calling too much attention to itself, as mariachis are wont to do, the music here swings in a nicely mellow way that reflects the Cuban roots of much that I've chosen. There's early work from Beny Moré and Ray Barretto and later (but still timeless) hits from Buena Vista Social Club, with stops at "tropical" classics from the likes of Tito Puente, Cachao and Cal Tjader. There's some Brazilian groove here, too—it always sets such a cool mood, I think—from early and recent Sergio Mendes and from Bebel Gilberto.

Song Title, Artist, Album

1. "Cumbanchero," Rafael Canchola Hernandez, *Introducing . . . Ruben Gonzalez*

2. "Cuál Es la Idea," Tito Punte and His Orchestra, *Cuban Carnival*

3. "Estoy Aquí," Shakira, *Pies Descalzos*

4. "Bananeira (Banana Tree)," Sergio Mendes, *Timeless*

5. "Bombón Chá," La Orquestra Aragón and Richard Egües, *Grandes Hits con la Orquesta Aragón*

6. "Bonito y Sabraso," Beny Moré and Orchestra Rafael de Paz, *Cuban Originals*

7. "Bruca Manigua," Ibrahim Ferrer, *Buena Vista Social Club Presents Ibrahim Ferrer*

8. "El Nuevo Barretto," Ray Barretto, *Salsa Explosion*

9. "Galletana," Orquesta America, *La Gloria del Cha Cha Cha*

10. "Garota de Ipanema," Baden Powell, *Personalidade—The Best of Brazil: Baden Powell*

Song Title, Artist, Album (*continued*)

11. "Guantanamera," Tito Puente, *Pottery Barn: Margarita Mix*

12. "Guateque Campesino," Ibrahim Ferrer, *Buena Vista Social Club Presents Ibrahim Ferrer*

13. "Herido de Sombras," Ibrahim Ferrer, *Buena Vista Social Club Presents Ibrahim Ferrer*

14. "Isora Club," Cachao, *Master Sessions, Vol. 1*

15. "Jovenes del Ritmo," Israel "Cachao" López, *Show*

16. "Mais Que Nada," Sergio Mendes, *The Very Best of Latin Jazz (Disc 1)*

17. "Malandro Quando Vaza," The Ipanemas, *Samba Is Our Gift*

18. "Oye Como Va," Tito Puente, *20th Century Masters: The Best of Tito Puente*

19. "Oye El Consejo," Ibrahim Ferrer, *Buenos Hermanos*

20. "Qué Bueno Baila Usted," Beny Moré, *¡Viva Margarita!*

21. "Quizás, Quizás," Ruben Gonzalez, *Chanchullo*

22. "Sabor a Mi," Pérez Prado, *Cuban Originals: Pérez Prado*

23. "Salsa y Dulzura," Ray Barretto, *El 'Ray' Criollo*

24. "Samba da Benção," Bebel Gilberto, *Tanto Tempo*

25. "The Soul Drummers," Ray Barretto, *Show 3 World*

27. "Soul Sauce (Fila Brazillia Remix)," Cal Tjader and Fila Brazillia, *Verve Remixed*

28. "Tanoca Vignette," Tania Maria, *The Best of Tania Maria*

29. "Tanto Tempo," Bebel Gilberto, *Tanto Tempo*

30. "Viva Cepeda," Cal Tjader, *Show 5 World*

Small Dishes for Party Snacking (Mexican Tapas)

One of my favorite places to eat in Mexico doesn't even have any tables. It's a sliver of a storefront eatery, tucked away in the shady, now-tony Condesa section of Mexico City, with just enough width for a serving counter down one side and space for a single-file of hungry patrons to stand, plates in hand, enjoying some of the most delicious *tacos de cazuela* anyone has ever tasted. El Güero, as people know the place, is just like the tiny tapas bars that dot much of Spain, each with just enough space to display earthenware dishes full of simmered or sauced or tangy-dressed local specialties to spoon onto plates for whoever's huddled around. Only this place has no dry sherry or bottles of beer to serve alongside. No, at El Güero, folks stop by on their way to work or for a quick, mid-morning *almuerzo* bite of herb-green chorizo with potatoes, pork and nopales, with red chile sauce or cactus paddle salad, served up with a glass of fresh-squeezed tangerine or grapefruit juice.

Which is not to say that Mexico's "tapas" can't play later in the day. They most certainly can. And should. So I offer you a chapter of Mexican "small plates," Mexican tapas, if you follow me.

Now, Mexico's tapas aren't typically served with slices of crusty bread as they would be in Spain. More often than not, they're served with warm corn tortillas, turning each spoonful into a soft taco. Stunningly delicious, in my opinion, but maybe a little too restrictive to be as versatile as these delicious preparations deserve to be in the American kitchen. Sometimes in Mexico, I've been served a typical "soft taco filling" as the topping on a crispy tostada. And I say: if tostadas work, why not crunchy toasts as a base, for a bruschetta-style presentation. Or perhaps just spoon these simple, delectable preparations onto plates and let folks choose whether they're in the mood for warm tortillas or tostadas or toasts. This food is too good to pigeonhole.

It might surprise you to know that El Güero makes twenty to twenty-five different preparations every day, all presented in traditional earthenware *cazuelas*. Some are warm—maybe saucy, maybe not. Others are cool, often salad-y, though none feature anything as fragile as lettuce. And this little eatery isn't all that exceptional—simply a very good example of what you can find in neighborhoods all through the country. It's just that the preparations change with regional tastes and with the circumstances in which they're served. Just a few miles away from El Güero, at the Sunday Lagunilla market, a family of cooks presents similar "fillings" in bright-colored plastic buckets and offers them folded into thick, just-made blue corn tortillas with a little cheese; they call them quesadillas. The same thing is going on up in Toluca, a couple of hours from Mexico City. But there they are making oval, corn-masa *tlacoyos*, breaking them open and stuffing them full of any number of regional flavors.

I could go on to the ladies in Oaxaca's Benito Juarez market, who specialize in *moles* and fava bean salads and the like. And on to the market

in Merida, Yucatan, and to the port town of Veracruz, where my favorite vendors offer a huge array of fish preparations served warm and cool, plus shredded meat *picadillos*. I'm embarrassed to continue the list, because the incredible regional variety of these "small dishes" is so great that they make my offerings in this chapter—though very tasty—seem small.

And to that array of soft taco fillings-*cum*-small dishes I'd be remiss not to add all the shared plates served as starters in restaurants. So please merely think of what I've sketched out in this chapter as a small sampling of what Mexico holds in store.

I start you off with a couple of restaurant-y *quesos fundidos* (adding beer-braised mushrooms to the melted cheese is a revelation), as well as one of my favorites: cubed fresh cheese in warm tomatillo sauce. There are some of those traditional soft taco fillings here, like the tuna in *escabeche*, the pickled pigs' feet and the two shredded beef salads. Believe it or not, but those Devilish Shrimp are a market taco filling in Acapulco, as are the plantain-stuffed chipotles in Veracruz (yes, they can be eaten as a taco filling, though most cooks choose to serve them solo). And the salads? They are a mix of traditional and contemporary. I find that folks always welcome them.

Tuna in Jalapeño *Escabeche*
Atún en Escabeche de Chile Jalapeño

MAKES 3 SCANT CUPS, SERVING 6 AS A SOFT TACO FILLING, BRUSCHETTA OR TOSTADA TOPPING, OR TAPA

1   12-ounce can pickled jalapeños

¼   cup good-quality olive oil

1   large white onion, cut into ¼-inch slices

2   6-ounce cans tuna (you can use tuna in a pouch here, if you like)

¼   cup (loosely packed) roughly chopped flat-leaf parsley (optional)

Though I'm not one of the world's greatest fans of canned tuna, I really like the way spicy-tangy pickled jalapeños—together with caramelized onions and fresh-tasting flat-leaf parsley—take that tuna in a deliciously Mexican direction. Not to mention that the ingredients are probably already in your pantry and that you can make it in about 10 minutes. The casual dish you turn out here is particularly good piled on tostadas (or chips) or on grilled or toasted bread, bruschetta style. It's great picnic food.

A brand of pickled jalapeños like Embasa typically includes a lot of vegetables—perfect for this recipe.

Working ahead: The dish can be made a day ahead, leaving out the parsley; cover and refrigerate. Bring to room temperature, stir in the parsley, and check seasonings shortly before serving.

Remove the jalapeños and vegetables (typically carrots and onions) that have been packed with them; reserve the liquid. Cut the stems off 2 to 3 of the jalapeños, cut them in half and scrape the seeds out. Thinly slice them (you need about ¼ cup), then thinly slice some of the vegetables (you need about ¼ cup of these also).

In a large skillet, heat the olive oil over medium. When hot, add the onion and cook until richly golden, about 10 minutes. Remove from the heat and stir in ¼ cup of the jalapeño pickling juice. Let cool. In a medium-size bowl, stir together the onions, tuna, sliced jalapeños and vegetables, and parsley (if you're using it). Cover and refrigerate if not using right away.

Wild Mushroom *Queso Fundido*
Queso Fundido con Hongos Silvestres

SERVES 4 AS A SOFT TACO FILLING

¾ ounce (about ½ cup) dried porcini (or other wild) mushrooms

2 tablespoons olive or vegetable oil

Hot green chile(s) to taste (roughly 1 large jalapeño or 2 serranos), stemmed, seeded (if you wish) and finely chopped

1 medium white onion, cut into ¼-inch pieces

1 large ripe tomato, cored, seeded (if you wish) and cut into ¼-inch pieces

3 tablespoons beer, preferably a full-flavored beer like Mexico's Bohemia

8 ounces Mexican melting cheese (such as Chihuahua, *quesadilla* or *asadero*) or Monterey Jack, mild cheddar or brick, shredded (you'll have about 2 cups)

If you love the flavor of wild mushrooms—I mean true wild mushrooms, not just "exotic" cultivated mushrooms like shiitakes or colorful oysters—this queso fundido is a wonderful way to experience it. A little dried mushroom, briefly rehydrated, infuses the whole dish with flavor, while the beer adds a lovely hint of malty sweetness and a creamy texture.

If making the dish with fresh mushrooms (wild or cultivated) appeals to you more, you'll need about 5 ounces. Trim the stems and chop them into small pieces (you'll have about 2 loosely packed cups), then cook them in 3 tablespoons of oil over medium-high for about 3 minutes with a sprinkling of salt. Add the other fresh vegetables and continue on with Step 2.

Right off the stove, while the cheese is at its gooeyest, a soft taco of Wild Mushroom Queso Fundido with a spoonful of roasted tomatillo salsa is the stuff of memories.

Working ahead: The dish can be prepared through Step 2; cover and refrigerate. Just before serving, heat the vegetables to sizzling and continue with Step 3.

1. *Rehydrate the mushrooms.* Scoop the mushrooms into a small bowl, cover with boiling water and let stand for 20 minutes, stirring for even rehydration. Drain off the liquid (it's great added to mushroom soups), pressing on the mushrooms to remove all the water. Chop into ¼-inch pieces.

2. *Prepare the flavorings.* Heat the oil in a large (10-inch) skillet over medium-high. Add the chile(s), onion, tomato and mushrooms and cook, stirring nearly constantly, until the onion begins to soften and brown, 7 or 8 minutes. Add the beer and stir until the liquid has evaporated and the mixture is once again dry looking.

3. *Finish the* **queso fundido.** With the skillet of beery vegetables over medium-low, sprinkle in the cheese. Stir slowly and constantly until just melted—too long over the heat and the cheese will become tough, oily and stringy. Immediately scoop into a warm serving dish (a small fondue dish with a tea light below is ideal) and serve with warm tortillas for making soft tacos or chips to dip.

WILD MUSHROOM *QUESO FUNDIDO*

TEQUILA-INFUSED *QUESO FUNDIDO* READY FOR SERVING

Tequila-Infused *Queso Fundido*
Queso Fundido al Tequila

SERVES 4 AS A SOFT TACO FILLING

1   tablespoon olive or vegetable oil

1   large ripe tomato, cored, seeded
    (if you wish) and cut into ¼-inch
    pieces

1   medium white onion, cut into
    ¼-inch pieces

    Hot green chile(s) to taste
    (roughly 1 large jalapeño or 2
    large serranos), stemmed, seeded
    (if you wish) and finely chopped

3   tablespoons tequila, preferably a
    silver tequila

8   ounces Mexican melting cheese
    (such as Chihuahua, *quesadilla* or
    asadero) or Monterey Jack, mild
    cheddar or brick, shredded (you'll
    have about 2 cups)

½   cup (loosely packed) chopped
    cilantro (thick bottom stems cut
    off)

I'm rarely wowed by tequila-infused dishes. Mostly I feel the tequila gets lost, meaning a waste of perfectly good tequila. In this queso fundido, *the tequila not only shines through with its agave brightness, but gives the melted cheese a luscious texture. Seared salsa ingredients (tomato, onion, chile, cilantro) mingle with unctuous cheese, the whole thing shot through with that unmistakable scent of silver tequila.*

Queso fundido *needs to be eaten as soon as it's made, either spooned into warm tortillas for soft tacos or scooped up with chips. (Remember: this is not a* Tex-Mex chile con queso *dip.) A small fondue pot set over a tea light can keep the cheese attractively fluid for a few minutes longer than a warm serving bowl. And no one would fault you for serving salsa with* queso fundido.

Working Ahead: *You really can't, except perhaps to chop the vegetables and shred the cheese.*

---

1. *Prepare the flavorings.* Heat the oil in a large (10-inch) skillet over medium-high. Add the tomato, onion and chile(s), and cook, stirring nearly constantly, until the onion begins to soften and brown, about 7 minutes. Add the tequila and cook, stirring, for a minute or so, until reduced to a glaze. (If you tip the pan toward an open gas flame, the tequila will ignite. If you choose this route, simply shake the pan back and forth until the flames subside and the tequila has reduced to a glaze.)

2. *Finish the* queso fundido. With the skillet of tequila-infused vegetables over medium-low, sprinkle in the cheese. Stir slowly and constantly until just melted—too long over the heat and the cheese will become tough, oily and stringy. Scoop into a warm dish, sprinkle with the cilantro and serve right away with tortillas for making soft tacos or chips to dip.

Creamy Chicken and Greens with Roasted Poblano and Caramelized Onion

Pollo a la Crema con Quelites, Chile Poblano Asado y Cebolla Caramelizado

MAKES 4 CUPS, SERVING 8 TO 10 AS A SOFT TACO FILLING OR TAPA

2 fresh poblano chiles

3 tablespoons olive or vegetable oil, plus a little more if needed

3 medium (about 1¼ pounds) boneless, skinless chicken breast halves

Salt

1 medium white onion, sliced ¼ inch thick

3 garlic cloves, peeled and finely chopped

5 cups (lightly packed) coarsely chopped, stemmed greens (about 1-inch pieces are good)—you'll need about 6 ounces spinach, 4½ ounces Swiss chard, 3 ounces wild lamb's quarters (quelites)

1 cup chicken broth

A little fresh thyme, if you have it

1 cup Mexican crema (page 200), crème fraîche or heavy (whipping) cream

When you're setting out some small dishes for friends to enjoy nibbling through, this is the creamy go-to dish to balance your tangy and less-saucy offerings. For me, this dish has the perfect balance: meaty from chicken, vegetable-y from greens and onions and roasted poblanos, creamy from crema. It's straightforward good cooking that practically everyone finds incredibly delicious.

A few notes about ingredients: (1) Though the chicken is delicious sautéed, as described here, in summer I grill it to add a little smokiness. (2) I've made this dish with all kinds of greens, and each adds something special. Spinach is sweet and velvety, chard is more toothsome and bold flavored, lamb's quarters are meaty and richly, sweetly green tasting (like French beans). (3) Many of the commercially made cremas available in Mexican grocery stores are more like mild sour cream (though they're a little less curdy) than Mexican crema, which is rich and velvety. For true Mexican taste and texture, make your own crema (page 200) or use store-bought crème fraîche.

Working Ahead: The poblano can be prepared and the chicken cooked a day or so ahead; store separately, well covered, in the refrigerator. Pick up the preparation at Step 3 shortly before serving.

1. Roast the chiles. Roast the poblanos directly over an open flame or 4 inches below a broiler, turning regularly until blistered and blackened all over, about 5 minutes for a flame, about 10 minutes for the broiler. Cover with a kitchen towel and cool until handleable. Rub off the blackened skin, then pull out the stem and seed pod. Briefly rinse to remove any stray seeds or bits of skin. Slice ¼ inch thick.

2. Brown the chicken. In a large skillet, heat the oil over medium-high. Generously sprinkle the chicken breasts with salt on both sides and lay them into the pan in a single layer. When browned underneath, about 4 minutes, flip them over and reduce the heat to medium. Cook on the other side until browned and medium-rare (a little slit in the thickest part will reveal a rosy interior), 5 or 6 minutes more. Transfer to a plate.

3. Finish the dish. To the skillet (still over medium heat), add the onion. If there isn't enough oil to lightly coat the onion, add a little more. Cook, stirring regularly, until richly browned and sweet, 8 or 9 minutes.

Meanwhile, cut the chicken into ½-inch cubes.

Add the garlic and chile slices to the skillet and cook 1 minute, then add the greens, broth and thyme (if you have it). Raise the temperature to medium-high. Cook until the liquid is nearly gone and the greens are almost tender, about 5 minutes. Add the *crema, crème fraîche* or cream and cook until it is noticeably thicker (it'll be a rich glaze) and the greens are fully tender, about 5 minutes more.

Taste and season the mixture in the skillet with salt, usually ¼ teaspoon. Stir in the chicken, let heat through for a minute or two, scoop into a serving bowl and enjoy without hesitation.

CREAMY CHICKEN AND GREENS WITH ROASTED POBLANO AND CARAMELIZED ONION

Devilish Shrimp
Camarónes a la Diabla

SERVES 6 AS A TAPA

FOR THE SAUCE

2   garlic cloves, unpeeled

8   medium-large (about 2 ounces) dried guajillo chiles, stemmed and seeded

¼   teaspoon dried oregano, preferably Mexican

¼   teaspoon black pepper, preferably freshly ground

    A big pinch of cumin, preferably freshly ground

1   cup fish broth, chicken broth or water, plus a little more if needed

2   tablespoons vegetable oil or olive oil

3 to 4 tablespoons red hot sauce (in Acapulco, many cooks choose Tamazula brand)

    Salt

    Sugar, about a scant teaspoon

FOR FINISHING THE DISH

2   tablespoons butter

1   small white onion, sliced ¼ inch thick

1   pound shrimp (see headnote)

I can't even think about these tangy, spicy shrimp, a beloved specialty of Acapulco and environs, without my mouth watering, without my head filling with heady memories of a racing heart and spice-induced runny nose. I love the full-flavored rush that comes with each bite of hot sauce–infused, slow-simmered red guajillo chile sauce mixed with butter-softened onions and sweet shrimp. These Devilish Shrimp aren't just spicy-hot. They're luxuriously rich and complex. And spicy-hot.

A note about shrimp: *In Acapulco, the shrimp for Camarónes a la Diabla are typically shell-on, meaning you can make quite a mess of yourself working through a plate of them. I prefer to peel the shrimp, leaving the tails on; I devein the shrimp, too, though it's not obligatory. Choose shrimp with a size to match your purpose: smaller ones (40 to 50 per pound) are perfect for serving tapa style.*

Working Ahead: *The sauce can be prepared several days ahead; cover and refrigerate. Complete Step 3 shortly before serving.*

---

1. *Make the sauce.* Roast the unpeeled garlic on an ungreased griddle or in a heavy skillet over medium heat, turning occasionally, until soft (they'll blacken in spots), about 15 minutes; cool and peel. While the garlic is roasting, toast the chiles on another side of the griddle or skillet a couple at a time; open them flat and press them against the hot surface with a metal spatula until they are very aromatic and have lightened in color underneath—about 10 seconds per side. In a small bowl, cover the chiles with hot water and let rehydrate 30 minutes, stirring frequently to ensure even soaking. Drain and discard the water.

Combine the oregano, black pepper and cumin in a food processor or blender. Add the drained chiles, garlic and ½ cup of the broth. Blend to a smooth puree, scraping and stirring every few seconds. (If the mixture just won't go through the blender blades, add a little more liquid.) Press through a medium-mesh strainer into a bowl.

Heat *1 tablespoon* of the oil in a heavy, medium-small (2- to 3-quart) pot (such as a Dutch oven or Mexican *cazuela*) over medium-high. When the oil is hot enough to make a drop of the puree sizzle sharply, add the puree and stir constantly until it reduces into a thick paste, 5 to 7 minutes. Stir in the remaining ½ cup broth or water, partially cover and simmer over medium-low, stirring occasionally, for 20 to 30 minutes as the flavors come together. Add the hot sauce and, if necessary, stir in a little more broth or water to bring the sauce to a medium, saucy consistency. Taste and season with a generous teaspoon salt and the sugar.

2. *Finish the dish.* In a large skillet, melt the butter with the remaining *tablespoon* of the oil over medium-high heat. Add the onion and cook, stirring, until slightly softened, 2 to 3 minutes. Add the shrimp, sprinkle with salt and cook, stirring, until the shrimp are done, about 3 minutes longer. Add the sauce and stir everything together for about 1 minute. Your Devilish Shrimp is ready to serve.

DEVILISH SHRIMP

Yucatecan Shredded Steak Salad with habanero and cilantro
Dzik de Res (aka Salpicón de Res a la Yucateca)

MAKES 3 CUPS, SERVING 6 TO 8 AS A SOFT TACO FILLING, BRUSCHETTA OR TOSTADA TOPPING, OR TAPA

1   pound well-trimmed skirt steak, trimmed of any surface fat and cut into 3-inch sections

2   garlic cloves, peeled and quartered

1   small red onion, thinly sliced

Salt

4   large radishes, cut into matchsticks or thinly sliced

1   fresh habanero chile, stemmed, seeded and finely chopped

2 to 3 tablespoons (loosely packed) chopped fresh cilantro

6   tablespoons sour orange or lime juice

1   romaine heart

1   ripe avocado, pitted, flesh scooped from the skin and cut into ¼-inch cubes

If you've had, say, a Thai beef salad, you'll know what to expect from this classic Yucatecan appetizer/cold taco filling: a tangy, crunchy, spicy, meaty salad that's playful on your palate. Dzik makes a bright, but substantial, dish to put out as part of a snacky grazing menu—or to offer guests as a casual appetizer. I love how the habanero lights everything up, while the avocado cools it down.

Here, I suggest you serve the dzik in a contemporary way, in romaine leaves that your guests can fold around the filling, creating a lettuce taco. If warm corn tortillas are more to your liking, serve the dzik on sliced lettuce with a basket of tortillas alongside, letting your guests make their own steak salad tacos. Dzik is delicious both ways.

Dzik makes a great tostada and bruschetta topping, too.

No time for simmering beef? A crab or shrimp version (salpicón de jaiba o camarón) is easy: replace the cooked shredded beef with 12 ounces of cooked crab or small cooked shrimp.

Working Ahead: The beef can be simmered and shredded a day or two ahead; cover and refrigerate. It can be combined with the vegetables and flavorings a couple of hours ahead; refrigerate, covered, until ready to serve.

---

1. *Cook the meat.* In a large (4-quart) saucepan, bring 6 cups water to a boil. Add the meat. When the water has returned to a brisk skimmer, skim off any grayish foam that rises to the top. Add the garlic, *half* of the onion and 1 teaspoon of salt. Simmer over medium to medium-low heat for an hour or so, until the meat is fall-apart tender. If there is time, let it cool in the broth. Drain and discard all but the meat. Shred into coarse strands.

2. *Finish the* dzik. In a medium bowl, combine the meat with the remaining *half* of the onion, the radishes, habanero, cilantro, sour orange or lime juice and a generous 1 teaspoon salt. Cover and refrigerate for 30 minutes or so for the flavors to blend.

For a beautiful presentation, choose 12 nice-looking romaine leaves and cut them about 5 inches long from the top. Cut the base section of those leaves (and any whole leaves you haven't used) crosswise into ¼-inch slices. Lay the 5-inch romaine leaves on a serving platter. Top each one with a little of the sliced romaine, then about ¼ cup of the *dzik* and a little scattering of diced avocado.

Crispy Flank Steak Shreds with Golden Onions and Red Chile Salsa
Mochomos con Cebolla Dorada y Salsa Roja

SERVES 8 AS A SOFT TACO FILLING OR TAPA

FOR THE MEAT

4   garlic cloves, peeled and roughly chopped

1   teaspoon dried oregano, preferably Mexican

2   bay leaves

    Salt

1   pound flank steak

FOR SERVING

    About 1 cup Red Chile Roasted Tomato Salsa (page 143)

2   ripe avocados, pitted and flesh scooped from skins

    About ½ cup (loosely packed) chopped cilantro (thick bottom stems cut off), plus a little extra for garnish

2   limes, each cut into 8 wedges, plus 1 tablespoon fresh lime juice

    Oil to a depth of approximately 2 inches for frying (peanut oil works best here, or canola or safflower oil that's specifically refined for frying—you'll need about 7 cups for a 4-quart saucepan)

⅓   cup flour

1   large white onion, thinly sliced (¼ inch thick or a little less)

    About 2 dozen warm corn tortillas for making soft tacos

This is hands-down one of my favorite dishes and one of the most popular appetizers we've ever served in Topolobampo. It's certainly more dramatic than most of the northern Mexican pan-crisped, shredded beef (or pork) machaca that was my inspiration. The reason? At the restaurant our mochomos are made from flank steak, with its clearly visible long grain, making it possible to turn out very thin strings that fry crunch-crisp and fluffy. Success rests in having the patience to shred the beef as fine as angel hair pasta. Serving can be simple and fun: pile the crispy, beefy strings on top of crispy onions (no need for either to be warm) and serve them with simple guacamole, red chile salsa, lime and warm corn tortillas for your guests to make super-delicious soft tacos: crunchy from the beef and onions, unctuous with guacamole, spicy with salsa, perfect with the earthy, corny, toasty tortilla. Or, dress up the mochomos with a restaurant-style individual serving. Guacamole gets spooned in the middle of a plate, surrounded by red chile salsa; over the guacamole goes a little pile of crispy onions, topped with crispy beef. Lime goes on the side.

Working Ahead: The salsa can be prepared and the meat simmered and shredded several days ahead; refrigerate them separately, covered. The guacamole can be prepared several hours ahead; cover with plastic wrap directly on the surface and refrigerate. Meat and onions can be fried several hours ahead (unless it's a very humid day); loosely cover and leave at room temperature.

1. *Simmer the meat.* In a large (4-quart) saucepan, measure 6 cups water. Add the garlic, oregano, bay and 2 teaspoons salt, set over high heat and bring to a boil. Add the flank steak, and, when the liquid returns to a simmer, reduce the temperature to between medium and medium-low (to maintain a very gentle simmer). Skim any grayish foam that rises during the first few minutes of simmering, then cover and cook until the meat is tender, about 1½ hours. If there is time, let the meat cool in the broth.

2. *Make the salsa, prepare the guacamole.* Make the salsa (page 143). In a medium bowl, coarsely mash the avocado with the cilantro and lime juice. Taste and season with salt, usually about ½ teaspoon.

3. *Shred and fry the meat, fry the onion, serve the dish.* Shred the meat into long, thin strands (this takes a while, but within reason, go for the thinnest possible—nothing larger than a strand of angel hair pasta).

Heat the oil to 375 degrees (a thermometer is pretty essential to keep the heat consistent and avoid greasy onions). Measure the flour into a large bowl. Add the onions, and toss to coat. In batches, shake off excess flour from handfuls of onions then carefully sprinkle them around the pot of oil. Stir gently until the onions are deep golden, about 30 seconds. Remove with a skimmer or slotted spoon to drain on paper towels. Sprinkle with salt.

Let the oil return to 375 degrees, then quickly drop the meat shreds into the oil one by one, making sure they don't clump together. Stir until completely crispy, about 30 seconds. Remove with a skimmer or slotted spoon to drain on paper towels. Sprinkle with salt.

For a family-style service, spread the crispy onions onto a serving platter, creating a bed onto which you can carefully pile the crispy beef. Sprinkle the whole thing with a little chopped cilantro. Scoop the salsa, guacamole and lime wedges into individual serving bowls to pass together with the onions and beef. You might want to show your guests how to create what I consider the perfect *mochomos* taco: a warm tortilla daubed with guacamole, drizzled with salsa, piled with crispy onions and beef, dribbled with a squeeze of lime.

CRISPY FLANK STEAK SHREDS WITH GOLDEN ONIONS
AND RED CHILE SALSA (PAGE 140)

Red Chile Roasted Tomato Salsa
Salsa Roja

MAKES A GENEROUS 1½ CUPS

1   large (12-ounce) red-ripe tomato

2   garlic cloves, unpeeled

8   (about 2 ounces) dried guajillo
    chiles, stemmed and seeded

1   canned chipotle chile *en adobo*,
    seeds scraped out

    Salt

1. *Roast and toast.* Place the tomato and garlic on a rimmed baking sheet and roast 4 inches below a very hot broiler until soft and blotchy black, 5 or 6 minutes per side. Cool, then pull off the peel from both the tomato and garlic.

In an ungreased skillet or on a griddle heated over medium, toast the guajillos, pressing them flat with a metal spatula until they are aromatic and have lightened in color underneath—about 10 seconds per side. (If the heat is right, you'll hear a slight crackle when you press down the chiles, but you shouldn't see more than the slightest wisp of smoke.) Collect in a small bowl, cover the chiles with hot water and let rehydrate, stirring occasionally, for about 30 minutes. Drain and discard the water.

2. *Finish the salsa.* Roughly chop the tomato. Scoop into a blender jar along with all its juices, the garlic, drained guajillos and chipotle. Blend until smooth. (If your blender won't fully puree the skins, press the salsa through a medium-mesh strainer to get rid of any bits of skin.) Stir in enough water to give the sauce an easily spoonable consistency, usually about ¾ cup. Taste and season with salt, usually about 1 teaspoon. Scrape into a serving bowl and the salsa is ready.

Fresh Cheese in Roasted Tomatillo Salsa
Panela en Salsa Verde

MAKES ABOUT 3 CUPS, SERVING 6 TO 8 AS A SOFT TACO FILLING OR TAPA

8   ounces (about 4 medium) tomatillos, husked, rinsed and cut in half

2   large garlic cloves, peeled

    Hot green chile to taste (roughly 1 serrano or 1 small jalapeño), stemmed and roughly chopped

    Salt

12 ounces Mexican *panela* cheese, cut into ¾-inch cubes—you'll have 3 loosely packed cups (see *Cheese Options* in headnote)

¼   cup finely chopped white onion

    About ¼ cup (loosely packed) chopped cilantro (thick bottom stems cut off)

Let's be honest: when most of us living in the United States hear the word "cheese" we rarely think of milky-sweet fresh cheese—maybe a little ricotta or goat cheese or cottage cheese now and then, but those hardly conjure melty images that our English word "cheese" stirs up. Mexico approaches cheese from the opposite direction: rather than imagining a pool of Monterey Jack, folks hearing "queso" commonly see a dusting of the crumbly fresh stuff that's sprinkled as an enlivening garnish on so many dishes.

Out of that Mexican tradition comes this regional dish of fresh cheese—a very fresh-tasting, not very crumbly, slightly spongy west central Mexican cheese called panela—that's warmed until it softens slightly (fresh cheese doesn't really melt) in a robust salsa of roasted tomatillos, garlic, green chiles and cilantro.

Now, before you turn the page, convinced that panela cheese is beyond your scope, consider one important point: you don't have to replicate Mexico's regional original to have a great dish. In fact, it'd be almost impossible to find the small-batch, artisan panela that makes this dish so special on its home turf.

Cheese Options: You can try the dish with American-made panela (it's widely available in most Mexican groceries) or queso fresco, but I love it with one of the fresh-made artisan mozzarellas or farmer's cheeses available these days. Or form goat cheese into a 1-inch-thick disk on an ovenproof serving platter, spoon the sauce over the top and warm the whole thing in the oven.

Serving Options: In Mexico, Panela en Salsa Verde is often served in a hot stone mortar—a Mexican lava rock molcajete is heated in a 400-degree oven or on a grill for about 45 minutes before the cheese-salsa mixture is spooned in. (In a molcajete everything stays warm for a long time.) Put out warm tortillas for making soft tacos or serve as a tapa along slices of grilled/toasted baguette.

Working Ahead: The sauce can be made several days ahead; cover and refrigerate. Complete Step 2 just before serving.

1. *Make the sauce.* In a small nonstick skillet over medium-high heat, roast the tomatillos (start them cut side down) and garlic until soft and browned, 3 or 4 minutes per side. (If a nonstick skillet is unavailable, line a regular skillet with aluminum foil.) Scoop the tomatillos and garlic into a blender or food processor, add the chile and ½ cup water and blend until smooth. Taste and season with salt, usually a generous ½ teaspoon.

2. *Finish the dish.* Pour the salsa into a medium (3-quart) saucepan and bring to a rolling boil over medium heat. Add the cheese. When the cheese is heated through, 2 to 3 minutes, pour the mixture into a warm serving dish. Scoop the chopped onion into a strainer and rinse under cold water. Sprinkle over the dish, along with the chopped cilantro.

Avocado-Dressed Shrimp *a la Mexicana*
Camarónes a la Mexicana con Aguacate

MAKES ABOUT 4 CUPS, SERVING 8 TO 10 AS A SOFT TACO FILLING, BRUSCHETTA OR TOSTADA TOPPING, OR TAPA

12 ounces (about 2½ cups) medium-small, peeled-and-deveined cooked shrimp

1 medium white onion, cut into ¼-inch pieces

1 large red-ripe tomato, cut into ¼-inch pieces (you should have a generous cup)

¼ to ⅓ cup fresh lime juice

Hot green chile(s) to taste (usually 3 serranos or 1 to 2 jalapeños), stemmed and roughly chopped

1 medium, ripe avocado, pitted, flesh scooped from the skin and roughly chopped

⅓ cup (loosely packed) roughly chopped cilantro (thick bottom stems cut off), plus sprigs for garnish

Salt

A simple creamy shrimp salad with fresh vegetables. Creamy from avocado, lively with green chile and cilantro, and toothsome with crunchy white onion and ripe tomato—that's why this very simple shrimp salad is a la mexicana.

Working ahead: This salad is best when eaten within an hour or two of being made. Keep it refrigerated until just before serving.

In a medium bowl, combine the shrimp, onion and tomato. Measure the lime juice into a food processor or blender. Cover and turn on. Drop in the chile(s) and, when finely chopped, turn off and scoop in the avocado and cilantro. Process until smooth. Thin to a "creamy dressing" consistency with water, usually 2 to 3 tablespoons. Taste and season with salt, usually about 1 teaspoon. (You will have about 1½ cups.) Mix the dressing into the shrimp mixture. Cover with plastic wrap directly on the surface of the shrimp *a la mexicana* and refrigerate. When you're ready to serve, scoop into a serving bowl, decorate with cilantro sprigs and it's ready.

THREE TOSTADAS (*CLOCKWISE FROM TOP LEFT*): BEEF AND POTATO SALAD WITH SMOKY CHIPOTLE (PAGE 148); PICKLED PIGS' FEET WITH JALAPEÑOS AND *CREMA* (PAGE 149); AVOCADO-DRESSED SHRIMP *A LA MEXICANA* (PAGE 146)

Beef and Potato Salad with Smoky Chipotle
Salpicón de Res al Chipotle

MAKES ABOUT 3½ CUPS, SERVING 8 AS A SOFT TACO FILLING, BRUSCHETTA OR TOSTADA TOPPING, OR TAPA

¾ pound stewing beef (preferably from the chuck), cut into 1-inch cubes

2 garlic cloves, peeled and chopped

Salt

3 medium (about ¾ pounds total) boiling potatoes, peeled and cut into roughly ½-inch pieces

3 tablespoons apple cider vinegar

2 to 3 canned chipotle chiles *en adobo*, stemmed, seeded and thinly sliced

1 small red onion, cut into ¼-inch pieces

3 tablespoons good-quality olive oil

1 medium, ripe avocado, pitted, flesh scooped from the skin and cut into ¼-inch pieces

In central Mexico, this salad is a standard—served as an appetizer, main dish or taco filling—most likely because it's straightforward both in preparation and flavors. Meaty (beef and potatoes), smoky (chipotle), crunchy (red onion) and creamy (avocado). Easy.

Working Ahead: The salad can be completed a day or two ahead, covered and refrigerated. Bring it out an hour before serving, mixing in the avocado at the last moment.

1. Cook the meat. In a medium (3-quart) saucepan, bring 1 quart water to a boil. Add the meat, garlic and 1 teaspoon salt. When the water returns to a boil, reduce the heat to medium-low. Skim off the grayish foam that rises during the first few minutes of simmering. Partially cover and simmer until the meat is fall-apart tender, about 1 hour. With a slotted spoon, remove the meat to a plate to cool.

2. Cook the potatoes. Scoop the potatoes into the meat broth (if there isn't enough to cover the potatoes, add water) and simmer over medium heat until tender, about 15 minutes. Use the slotted spoon to scoop the potatoes into a medium bowl. Sprinkle with the vinegar.

3. Finish the salad. Break up the meat into coarse shreds and stir it into the potatoes, along with the chipotles, onion and olive oil. Let cool completely, then taste and season with salt if you think necessary. Cover and refrigerate until about 1 hour before you're ready to serve. When it's time to set out the filling for your guests, mix in the avocado and scoop it into a serving bowl.

Pickled Pigs' Feet with Jalapeños and *Crema*
Manitas con Crema y Chile Jalapeño

MAKES ABOUT 3½ CUPS, SERVING 8 AS A SOFT TACO FILING, BRUSCHETTA OR TOSTADA TOPPING, OR TAPA

2½ cups cleaned, coarsely chopped pickled pigs' feet (see headnote for cleaning procedure)

1 medium white onion, cut into ¼-inch pieces

⅓ cup (loosely packed) chopped cilantro (thick bottom stems cut off)

¼ to ⅓ cup chopped pickled jalapeños (remove the stems and, if you wish, the seeds before chopping)

⅓ cup Mexican *crema* (page 200), *crème fraîche* or sour cream

Salt, if necessary

I'm talking to intrepid food lovers here. Those who know the wonderful play of textures in pigs' feet—that crunchy, meaty, fatty deliciousness that's commonly pickled the world around. Pickled and nothing more. But add a little thick cream and jalapeño to the tangy mixture and those in the know will discover a new level of luscious.

It's difficult to tell you just how many jars or pounds of pickled pigs' feet to buy, since some come cleaner (read: with less fat, cartilage and bone) than others. A dependable choice is Hormel's pickled pigs' feet (though they don't include the pickled chiles and vegetables in Mexican brands). Three 9-ounce jars will yield about 2½ cups of cleaned, chopped pigs' feet. To clean the pigs' feet, drain off the pickling liquid, then cut out or pull out any bones or hard pieces of cartilage and discard. Chop what remains into ½-inch bits.

Working ahead: Though the pigs' feet can be cleaned a couple of days ahead, you'll want to stir in the rest of the ingredients shortly before serving.

In a large bowl, mix together the pigs' feet, onion, cilantro, jalapeños and *crema* (or one of its stand-ins). Taste and season with salt if you think necessary. Cover and refrigerate until you're ready to serve.

Plantain-Stuffed Chipotle Chiles in *Escabeche*
Chiles Chipotles en Escabeche Rellenos de Plátano Macho

MAKES 24 STUFFED CHILES, SERVING 8 TO 12 AS A TAPA OR SNACK

2   tablespoons sugar

    Salt

24   large (3 ounces total) dried cranberry-red chipotle chiles (aka *chiles moritas*)—the softer the better

1   medium carrot, peeled and cut into ⅛-inch pieces

6   tablespoons olive oil

3   garlic cloves, peeled and finely chopped

½   teaspoon ground allspice, preferably coarsely ground

3   sprigs of fresh thyme (or ½ teaspoon dried)

3   sprigs of fresh marjoram (or ½ teaspoon dried)

2   bay leaves

½   cup apple cider vinegar

1   small (1 ounce) cone *piloncillo* (unrefined sugar)

    OR 2 tablespoons packed dark brown sugar

1   medium red onion, thinly sliced

2   large, black-ripe plantains, peeled and cut into ½-inch cubes

Spicy-sweet-savory-tangy—that's one of my favorite flavor combinations. And these little tiny stuffed smoky chipotle chiles deliver on all counts. They're spicy from the chiles, of course, chipotles being one of the spicier chiles you'll encounter. And sweet from the plantains, which have a much fuller flavor and meatier texture than standard-issue bananas. And savory from browned onions and garlic that are woven into the filling. And tangy from the vinegary, spice-infused red onion escabeche *that bathes the plantain-stuffed chiles. In a nutshell, this is the perfect appetizer for folks who love spicy, bold flavors.*

A couple of pointers: if you're worried about the chiles being too hot, blanch them twice in the sweet-salty water. Because plantains brown so well in a nonstick skillet, I use one in the preparation of this dish.

Working ahead: Chiles can be blanched, and escabeche *and filling made a couple of days ahead. Stuff and marinate the chiles early on the day you're serving; cover them and leave at room temperature.*

1. *The chiles.* Measure 4 cups water into a small (2-quart) saucepan, add the sugar and 1 tablespoon salt. Bring to a boil over high heat. Cut a slit down the side of each chile from stem to point. Add to the boiling water, reduce the heat to medium and simmer for 5 minutes. Let cool in the water while making the *escabeche* and filling.

2. *The* escabeche. Scoop the carrot into a large (10-inch) skillet, drizzle on *4 tablespoons* of the olive oil and set over medium heat. Stir occasionally as the carrot cooks until crisp-tender, about 5 minutes. Add the ⅔ of the garlic, the allspice, thyme, marjoram, bay, vinegar, *piloncillo* (or brown sugar) and ¾ cup water. Bring to a simmer, stirring to dissolve the *piloncillo*, remove from the heat and add ⅔ of the onion and ½ teaspoon salt. Scrape into a bowl and cool.

3. *The filling.* Rinse out the skillet and set over medium heat. Add the remaining *2 tablespoons* of the olive oil and ⅓ of the onion. Cook, stirring regularly, until the onion begins to brown, about 5 minutes. Add the remaining ⅓ of the garlic and cook 1 minute longer. Scoop in the cubed plantain and cook, stirring occasionally and mashing the mixture a little, for 15 to 20 minutes until thick and homogeneous; regularly scrape up the browned bits from the bottom of the skillet. Taste and season with salt, about 1 teaspoon.

4. *The stuffed chiles.* Remove the chiles from the water. With your fingers or a demitasse spoon, carefully scrape out all the seeds that are clinging to the seed pod and attached to the veins and discard. Stuff each chile with the plantain mixture, then arrange them, cut side down, on a platter. Spoon the *escabeche* over them and let marinate for at least an hour before serving.

STEMMING THE CHILES
SEEDING THE CHILES
STUFFING THE CHILES WITH PLANTAIN FILLING
CLOSING THE CHILES AROUND THE FILLING
SPOONING THE ESCABECHE OVER THE CHILES
THE FINISHED CHILES

PLANTAIN-STUFFED
CHIPOTLE CHILES
IN *ESCABECHE*
(RECIPE ON
PRECEDING PAGES)

Mushroom Ceviche
Ceviche de Hongos

MAKES 3 CUPS, SERVING 6 TO 8 AS A SOFT TACO FILLING, BRUSCHETTA OR TOSTADA TOPPING, OR TAPA

8 ounces mushrooms (I like a mixture of small cremini or white buttons, shiitakes, oysters and chanterelles or other wild mushrooms)

6 tablespoons fresh lime juice

1 medium-large (about 8 ounces) red-ripe tomato, cored, seeded (if you wish) and cut into ¼-inch pieces

½ small white onion, cut into ¼-inch pieces

¼ medium bunch cilantro, chopped

1 fresh serrano chile, stemmed, seeded (if you wish) and finely chopped

1 tablespoon olive oil

   Salt

If you've tasted Mexico's classic, lime-marinated fish ceviche, you'll be able to imagine where we're going here. This Mushroom Ceviche echoes those flavors, except that mushrooms stand in for the fish. And just as ceviche is best when made with fish of distinctive texture and rich flavor, mushroom ceviche is most impressive when it contains the flavors of and textures of various mushrooms.

These fresh, bright, mushroomy-earthy flavors pair beautifully with the toasty flavor of crisp-fried corn tortilla chips. Serve them alongside your Mushroom Ceviche and encourage everyone to use the chips to scoop up some of the deliciousness. Or pile a little of the ceviche on individual chips and pass them to your guests.

Working Ahead: You can marinate the mushrooms in lime several hours ahead. After 1 hour, tip off all the lime juice that hasn't been absorbed by the mushrooms; reserve the juice for finishing the dish. Shortly before serving, combine the marinated mushrooms with the remaining ingredients, using the reserved lime to add more tanginess if you think necessary.

---

1. *Marinate the mushrooms.* Collect the mushrooms in a colander. Quickly rinse under cold water, then cut them up: Cut the button mushrooms into quarters. Remove and discard the stems from the shiitakes and slice the tops ¼ inch thick. Trim the tough stem ends of the chanterelles and slice ¼ inch thick. Cut off and discard most of the oyster mushrooms' stems, then cut the larger pieces in half.

In a large, nonaluminum bowl, combine all the mushrooms (you will have about 8 loosely packed cups of cut mushrooms) with the lime juice. Allow the mushrooms to marinate in the juice for about 1 hour, stirring regularly.

2. *Finish the ceviche.* To the mushrooms, add the tomato, onion, cilantro, serrano and olive oil. Mix well, taste and season with salt, usually about ¾ teaspoon. Cover and refrigerate if not using right away (preferably not more than an hour).

Spicy Jícama, Cucumber and Fruit Skewers
Alambritos de Jícama, Pepino y Fruta con chile y limón

MAKES 8 SKEWERS, SERVING 8 AS A TAPA OR SNACK

1 small (about ¾ pound) jícama, peeled and cut into ¾-inch slices

1 English (long, thin-skin, hothouse) cucumber, cut into ¾-inch slices

½ small pineapple, peeled and cut into ¾-inch slices

2 large (about 2 pounds total) mangos, peeled, flesh cut from the pit in large slices

8 bamboo skewers

1 lime, cut into 8 wedges

2 tablespoons powdered guajillo chile

2 teaspoons fine-ground table salt

Here's a slightly dressy way to serve that beloved street food snack of fruit or jícama or cucumber (or, in this preparation, all of them) jazzed up with lime, chile and salt—the seasoning pillars of Mexican street food. While I always want to include the fresh crunch of jícama on these skewers, the other elements are easily substituted. Try cantaloupe (or other melon), orange segments, peaches, raw quince or apple or pear. And, while pure powdered guajillo chile gives a distinctively Mexican character with its wonderfully rich flavor and bright (but not overpowering) heat, there are other options: guajillo can be replaced by powdered ancho chile, New Mexico or California chile, or paprika with a little super-spicy cayenne, árbol or chipotle chile powder mixed in.

Cutting the fruits and vegetables in circles creates a very beautiful presentation—and a fair amount of waste. Feel free to choose any shape you like. But, make sure to peel the jícama with a knife, not a vegetable peeler, so that you can go deeply enough to remove all the fibrous exterior.

Working Ahead: The skewers can be put together a day ahead; cover and refrigerate. Sprinkle with the spicy salt when you're ready to serve.

Using a 1½ inch round cutter, cut circles out of the jícama, cucumber, pineapple and mango slices. Thread the circles on the skewers and arrange them on a serving platter. Surround the skewers with lime wedges. In a small shaker (a salt shaker works fine here), thoroughly mix together the powdered chile and salt. Secure the top and lightly sprinkle the skewers. Serve the remaining chile-salt mixture on the side, for guests to add *al gusto*.

SPICY JÍCAMA, CUCUMBER AND FRUIT SKEWERS

Roasted New Potato Salad with Poblano Mayo
Ensalada de Papas Cambray Rostizadas con Mayonesa al Poblano
MAKES 3 CUPS, SERVING 6 TO 8 AS A TAPA

1½ pounds small new potatoes

A little vegetable oil or olive oil for coating the vegetables

Salt and black pepper, preferably freshly ground

2 large poblano chiles

4 garlic cloves, peeled

4 green onions, roots and wilted outer leaves removed, cut cross-wise into ½-inch pieces

1 egg yolk

¼ cup light vinegar (I prefer rice vinegar or Spanish cava vinegar)

1 cup olive oil (one that's not too strong is good here)

About ¼ cup (loosely packed) chopped fresh cilantro (thick bottom stems cut off)

OR ¼ cup chopped fresh flat-leaf parsley

I know that potato salad sounds a little familiar and not at all Mexican, but this preparation proves both those assumptions wrong. Crusty roasted new potatoes, with their creamy centers, take "potato salad" to new heights when combined with garlicky homemade roasted poblano mayo, "wilted" green onions and fresh cilantro.

Add crumbled bacon, diced ham or flaked, hot-smoked salmon to the mix and you have a more substantial, party-ready small dish. As is, it can add the perfect balance to your small-dish party offerings; it's just right for picnics, too.

Working Ahead: Though you could roast the vegetables a day or two ahead, then cool, cover and refrigerate them, I wouldn't really recommend it. The texture of freshly roasted potatoes that have never been refrigerated is beyond compare. However, the roasted poblano mayo can be made several days ahead without suffering. Since your finished salad needs to be refrigerated if not served within two hours (it contains homemade mayonnaise)—and refrigeration will change the potatoes' texture—I recommend combining all the ingredients shortly before serving.

1. *Roast the vegetables.* Heat the oven to 375 degrees. If the potatoes are bite size, keep them whole; if not, cut into halves or quarters. Put them into a bowl, drizzle with a little oil, sprinkle with salt and pepper, and toss to coat. Scoop onto one side of a rimmed baking sheet. Roast 10 minutes. Put the poblanos and garlic in the bowl, toss with a little oil to coat and scoop onto the other side of the baking sheet. Toss the green onions with a little oil and scatter over the potatoes. Return to the oven and roast until the potatoes are tender, the poblanos are evenly blistered and the garlic is soft, about 20 minutes. Cool.

2. *Make the mayonnaise.* Peel the blistered skin off the poblano, pull out the stem and seed pod, then quickly rinse to remove any stray seeds. Chop into small pieces and scoop *half* into a blender jar, along with the roasted garlic. (Set the rest of the chile aside.) Add the egg yolk, vinegar and ½ teaspoon salt. Blend until smooth. With the blender running, pour in the olive oil in a thin stream, creating a luxurious mayonnaise.

3. *Finish the salad.* Scoop the roasted potatoes and green onion into a medium bowl, along with the reserved chile. Sprinkle on the cilantro or parsley. Add a generous ½ cup of the mayonnaise (cover and refrigerate the remainder for spreading on sandwiches or making incredible salmon salad) and stir to combine. Taste and season with more salt if you think necessary. Scoop into a serving bowl and the salad's ready. Cover and refrigerate if not serving right away.

Grilled Cactus and Onion Salad with Crab and Red Chile

Ensalada de Nopales Asados con Jaiba

MAKES 4 CUPS, SERVING 8 TO 10 AS A SOFT TACO FILLING, BRUSCHETTA OR TOSTADA TOPPING, OR TAPA

7	medium (about 14 ounces total) fresh cactus paddles (*nopales*)
1	large white onion, sliced ¼-inch thick
2	tablespoons fruity olive oil, plus extra for brushing the cactus and onion
4	ounces crabmeat (fresh lump crab will garner the most attention)
3	tablespoons Mexican hot sauce (Tamazula, Valentina or Búfalo are good choices)
2	tablespoons Mexican *crema* (page 200), heavy (whipping) cream or sour cream
	Salt
¼	cup (loosely packed) chopped fresh cilantro (thick bottom stems cut off)
	OR 2 tablespoons chopped fresh flat-leaf parsley

Here's one for the adventurers—or for those who've been to practically any Mexican taquería or market fonda. As exotic (or desperate) as eating cactus may sound to many folks north of the Río Bravo, it's commonplace in Mexico. There, the cactus is typically cooked by boiling, giving it a tender texture . . . but leaching out a mucilaginous substance (to put it delicately) that's hard to get rid of. Grilling cactus—a common cooking technique in many grilled-meat taquerías, street stalls and restaurantes campestres—produces a slightly chewier result, but one that's less sticky, shall we say. Plus, grilling adds a gentle smokiness I find enticing in this beautiful salad.

If it's easier for you, feel free to cook the cactus on a grill pan and to replace the Mexican hot sauce with a couple of finely chopped canned chipotle chiles en adobo. This salad works well as a do-it-yourself soft taco filling or bruschetta topping; another playful way to serve it is in small butter lettuce leaves, creating lettuce-wrapped "tacos."

Working Ahead: The cactus and onion can be grilled a day or two ahead; refrigerate, covered, without cutting. Finish the salad within a couple of hours of serving, keeping it refrigerated until the last moment.

---

1. *Clean the cactus.* Holding a cactus paddle gingerly between the nodes of the prickly spines, trim off the edge that outlines the paddle, including the blunt end where the paddle was severed from the plant. Slice or scrape off the spiny nodes from both sides.

2. *Grill the cactus and onion.* Light a charcoal fire and let the coals burn until they are covered with gray ash and medium hot; position the grill grate and let it heat for a couple of minutes. Brush oil on both sides of each cactus paddle and each onion slice, then lay them on the grill in a single layer. Grill until deeply golden and clearly softening, 4 to 5 minutes per side. Remove the cactus and onions to a baking sheet to cool, making sure the cactus stays in a single layer. When cooled, cut each onion round in half, freeing the strips, and each cactus paddle into ¼-inch strips.

3. *Finish the salad.* Scoop the cactus and onions into a medium bowl. Add the crab. In a small bowl, whisk together the hot sauce, *crema* (or heavy or sour cream) and *2 tablespoons* olive oil. Taste and season with salt, usually about ¼ teaspoon. Drizzle the hot sauce dressing over the salad, sprinkle with the cilantro, toss everything together and scoop into a serving bowl. Cover and refrigerate if not serving right away.

Roasted Beet Salad with Red Onion, Poblano and Lime

Ensalada de Betabel, Cebolla Morada, Poblano y Limón

MAKES ABOUT 3 CUPS, SERVING 6 TO 8 AS A TAPA

1½ pounds small beets (about 1½ inches in diameter), well scrubbed, stem and root ends trimmed, peeled (if you like) and quartered (you'll have about 4 loosely packed cups)

1 large red onion, sliced ¼-inch thick

2 fresh poblano chiles

⅓ cup olive oil

2 to 3 tablespoons Worcestershire sauce

1 teaspoon salt

¼ teaspoon black pepper, preferably freshly ground

2 tablespoons fresh lime juice

2 to 3 tablespoons chopped fresh cilantro

This roasted beet salad skates into new territory for most North American eaters. Rather than pairing the natural earthy sweetness of beets with sweet-tartness (balsamic vinegar), boldness (blue cheese) and nuttiness (walnuts)— you've probably had that now-classic modern American salad more than once—I've gone green and bright. I love roasted beets with poblano chiles, red onions, lime and cilantro, plus a little Worcestershire to add depth. When I'm in the mood for a touch of dairy, I'll add a little Mexican fresh cheese (queso fresco) or crumbled goat cheese or shards of Spanish manchego shaved with a vegetable peeler. And during the summer, I choose a variety of different beets from the farmers' market and grill-roast them, along with the onion and poblano, in a perforated grill pan over a charcoal fire.

Working Ahead: *The vegetables can be roasted several hours ahead (even the day before in a pinch); cover and refrigerate. Finish the salad within a couple of hours of serving, leaving it at room temperature.*

1. *Roast the vegetables.* Heat the oven to 425 degrees. In a large bowl, combine the beets, onion and poblanos. In a small bowl, whisk together the olive oil, Worcestershire sauce, salt and pepper. Drizzle over the mixture and toss (I like to use my hands here) to coat everything evenly and break the onion slices apart. Scoop the vegetables onto a rimmed baking sheet, slide in the oven and roast, stirring carefully every 10 minutes, until the poblano is blistered and soft, about 20 minutes. Remove the chiles, then continue roasting, stirring every 10 minutes, until the beets are tender, 20 to 30 minutes more. Cool.

When the chiles are cool enough to handle, peel off the blistered skin, pull out the stems and seed pods, then quickly rinse to remove any stray seeds and bits of skin. Cut into ¼-inch slices about 2 inches long.

2. *Finish the salad.* In a wide shallow serving bowl, combine the beets, onion and poblanos. Drizzle with the lime juice, sprinkle with the cilantro and toss to combine. Taste and season with more salt and pepper if you think necessary. Your Roasted Beet Salad is ready to serve.

A Casual Weekend *Pozole* Party

A Casual Weekend *Pozole* Party for 25 guests of all ages

Calling a *pozole* party a "soup party" would make most Mexicans laugh. "A soup party?" they'd ask with a hint of condescension. "*Just* a soup party?" Meaning, no doubt, the kind of party that kind of goes in and out of fashion on our side of the border every few years. You know: three or four kinds of soup, some salads, some bread and butter.

A *pozole* party is anything but that, though it does involve a soupy bowl of *pozole*, that garlic-redolent, slow-cooked pork and hominy soup/stew. You see, a *pozole* party is *the* most common, classic, comfortable party that's thrown when folks in Mexico are entertaining big groups. It's celebrated from one end of the Republic to the other for birthdays, anniversaries, national holidays, whatever seems worth gathering a group for. And *pozole* making elicits the kind of culinary fervor that typically accompanies the making of barbecue or chili in our country.

So, don't you think it's odd that most Americans know virtually nothing about this super-common Mexican party ritual? Odd, because a *pozole* party has nearly every element most of us think of making for a perfect party: (1) *pozole* offers the enticement of a big slow-simmering pot that fills the house with dreamy, meaty aromas (a pot that needs little tending—perfect for sharing a few beers, as you might around a pot of gurgling chili); (2) one great big pot of *pozole* feeds the whole crowd; (3) everyone gets to customize their bowl with a variety of toppings; (4) *pozole* can be really spicy . . . or not at all, depending on how you doctor it up; (5) *pozole* is so casual that you can eat it with a spoon while standing up; (6) *pozole* welcomes beer . . . and tequila. Throw in a simple, help-yourself appetizer and a pass-around dessert that doesn't need a plate, and you've got a terrific party.

One comment about that great big pot: If you've got a turkey fryer, you're covered. If you don't, think of your investment as you would a turkey-roasting pan: you're glad you have one, even though you only unearth it once a year. And, as with a turkey roasting pan, there are inexpensive options (always available at Mexican groceries) and expensive, last-a-lifetime investments.

I'd put out guacamole—I suggest Sun-Dried Tomato Guacamole, but any of the others would be welcome, too. However, with the hominy in the soup and the tostadas that are served alongside, I recommend replacing (or at least augmenting) the usual tortilla chips with slices of jícama and cucumbers and daikon radish for folks to dip into the guac. If you have a favorite simple nut mix, don't hesitate to add it to your guacamole offering.

Keep drinks and dessert simple: a fresh fruit soft drink (Mexican *agua fresca*), beer and wine, plus some make-ahead rich bites of gooey chocolate packed in bar shape (Frontera Grill's Chocolate Pecan Pie Bars). The salty pretzel crust will make them ooh and aah.

Streamlining the accompaniments keeps the focus on your glorious pot of *pozole*.

Fiesta Game Plan

Special Equipment

Pozole **Pot:** You need a very large pot to make *pozole* for a crowd—one that holds about 30 quarts. Which is the size of most turkey fryers. Bingo. You want *pozole* making to be easy? Use a turkey fryer: perfect size pan, perfect size burner. And since *pozole* is soupy, the pan doesn't have to be a really heavy-gauge metal.

Meat Pot: If you make *pozole* over two days, you can use your large *pozole* pot first for the meat, then for the corn. Otherwise, you'll need a second, smaller pot—a 12- or 15-quart pot is fine. Which is the size I recommend everyone have in their kitchen anyway, for making stocks and soups and boiling pasta.

Baking Pans for Pie Bars: To bake enough Chocolate Pecan Pie Bars for 25 people you need two 8 x 8-inch baking pans.

Bowls for serving the *pozole*: *Pozole* is the main attraction here, as it is anywhere it's served in Mexico, and there's nothing dainty about the portion. It's always served in bowls that range between 16 and 24 ounces. Remember: there are lots of garnishes to pile on, so the bowl needs to be bigger than you might think. If you have access to a Mexican grocery, you'll almost always find inexpensive *pozole* bowls for sale alongside the *pozole* simmering pots (usually made of speckled enamelware) and tamal steamers. The *pozole* bowls will usually be ceramic or earthenware.

Timeline
A week or so ahead:

● Make a shopping list and buy all the basics from your regular grocery store.

● Buy firm avocados and let them ripen at room temperature, or order ripe avocados to be picked up later in the week from a reliable market.

● Lacking a very well-stocked grocery, locate a Mexican market and buy (or order by mail): chipotle chiles *en adobo*, dried *pozole* corn or fresh or frozen *nixtamal* corn, coarsely ground dried red chile, Mexican oregano, tostadas, Mexican chocolate. Also, in the Mexican market, you may want to buy fruit for making the fresh fruit *agua*; fruit you'll find is often riper and less expensive than what's in other grocery stores.

● Order from the meat market in your grocery store or from a Mexican grocery store the pork shanks, trotters and bone-in pork shoulder for pickup two days before your party.

1 to 2 days ahead:

● Make the Chocolate Pecan Pie Bars, cool, cut and refrigerate, covered.

● To take the pressure off your party day, I suggest you cook, cool, coarsely shred and store the meat for the *pozole*. Degrease the broth. Cover and refrigerate meat and broth separately.

Early on party day:

● Begin simmering the dried *pozole* corn or *nixtamal*.

● If you haven't cooked the meat, do it now. Cool it, shred it, place it in a pan for reheating, cover and refrigerate until later in the day.

● Add the meat broth to the *pozole* and keep at a low simmer until you're ready to serve.

● Prepare the garnishes for the *pozole*, scoop them into serving dishes, cover and refrigerate (onions, limes, cabbage, radishes) or leave at room temperature (chile, oregano, tostadas).

● Set up the drink area with glassware. Set red wine in place.

About 3 hours before the guests arrive:

● Remove the Chocolate Pecan Pie Bars from the refrigerator and arrange on a serving platter. Cover and leave at room temperature.

● Slice the vegetables for serving with the guacamole and arrange on a serving platter, leaving space for your guacamole serving bowl. Cover and refrigerate.

● Make the *agua fresca*. Pour into pitchers and refrigerate.

● Get ice and keep in ice chests.

● Ice (or refrigerate) beer and white wine.

About 1 hour before serving time:

● Make guacamole, scoop into a serving bowl, cover with plastic wrap directly on the surface and refrigerate.

● Set out the *agua fresca*, beer, white wine and the ice in the drink area.

Serving Strategy

● When the first guests arrive, welcome them with *agua fresca*, beer or wine. Set out the guacamole with the platter of vegetables.

● When you're ready to serve the *pozole*, set out the condiments. Typically, I do this right on the kitchen counter, so that I can ladle *pozole* into bowls directly from the stove. (Keep in mind: a *pozole* party is a casual party.) If your guests aren't familiar with how *pozole* works, talk them through topping their bowls with each of the condiments. Since tostadas are always eaten alongside *pozole*, encourage your guests to pick one up after they've doctored their *pozole* bowl.

● After your guests have had their happy fill of *pozole*, dust the platter of Chocolate Pecan Pie Bars with powdered sugar and pass them around for each to enjoy a sweet finish to the party.

Embellishments

● **Serving Guacamole:** Guacamole needs to be kept cold to stay firm and appetizing. For casual parties, my go-to guacamole service is to nestle a bowl (stainless is most efficient) into a cold, damp, clean terracotta flower pot. Make sure the bowl fits snugly into the pot. Run the pot under water, shake off the excess, then refrigerate for several hours. Make the guacamole, scrape into the bowl and refrigerate. When ready to serve, fit the bowl into the pot. A beautiful way to serve the vegetables is on a large terracotta saucer (a 15-inch one is ideal). Moisten and refrigerate it, then, at serving time, set the guacamole "pot" in the middle and arrange the sliced vegetables (or chips) around it.

● **Serving *pozole*:** As with *mole*, it's fun (and appropriate) to serve it from the vessel it was cooked in—here, a huge pot. If you're using a turkey fryer, set up the pot and burner outside (obviously, away from anything that could catch on fire), with all the condiments on a nearby table. To make sure that the cabbage, onion, lime and radish don't wilt, I've filled a deep, watertight tray with crushed ice and nestled in bowls of these condiments; the chile and oregano take smaller bowls and, of course, don't need to be cool.

● **Serving the beverages:** Any *agua fresca* you make can be left in a pitcher at room temperature for a couple of hours. I usually put ice in the cups or glasses rather than the pitcher because ice in a pitcher dilutes the beverage over time. If you entertain a lot, I recommend getting the now-common pitchers with the freezable ice core or chamber. They keep your drinks cool on the countertop without diluting them.

For the Overachiever

In Mexico it's traditional to serve *pozole* with crisp-fried tortillas (tostadas) to munch alongside. Though I think you should always have a basket of them on the *pozole* condiment table, for those who can't imagine doing without, you may want to pull the tostadas forward as an additional appetizer, using them as edible plates on which party-goers can pile a variety of toppings. I'd make one recipe each of the Beef and Potato Salad with Smoky Chipotle (page 148), Avocado-Dressed Shrimp *a la Mexicana* (page 146) and Pickled Pigs' Feet with Jalapeños and *Crema* (page 149). The last one will give the adventurous ones something to remember, and everyone else something to talk about.

For something novel to drink (and appropriate for *pozole*), you might like to offer Tecate Mojitos (page 55). Or, since *pozole* is famous for coming from the tequila-producing region, you may want to set up for a Tequila Tasting (page 57). It'll be one of the most enjoyable "courses" any of your friends have ever taken.

Sun-Dried Tomato Guacamole
Guacamole de Jitomate Deshidratado

MAKES A GENEROUS 2 QUARTS, SERVING 25 TO 30 AS A NIBBLE

9 medium-large (about 3¾ pounds) ripe avocados

1½ medium white onions, chopped into ¼-inch pieces (about 1 cup)

Fresh hot green chiles to taste (usually 6 small serranos or 3 small jalapeños), stemmed, seeded (if you wish) and finely chopped

¾ cup soft sun-dried tomatoes, chopped into ¼-inch pieces (patted dry on paper towels if oil-packed)

¾ cup (loosely packed) chopped fresh cilantro (thick bottom stems cut off), plus a little extra for garnish

Salt

About ¼ cup fresh lime juice

A little Mexican *queso fresco* or other fresh garnishing cheese such as feta or salted farmer's cheese, for garnish (optional)

Below are the quantities I'd make into guacamole for 25 people—triple the recipe on page 34. I'd have ready about 50 slices each of jícama and cucumber. Buy 3 medium jícamas and 3 long hot-house/English cucumbers.

Cut around each avocado, from stem to blossom end and back again, then twist the two halves apart. Dislodge the pit and scoop the avocado flesh into a large bowl. Using an old-fashioned potato masher or a large fork or spoon, mash the avocados into a coarse puree. Scoop the onion into a small strainer and rinse under cold water. Shake off the excess water and mix into the avocado, along with the chiles, tomatoes and cilantro. Taste and season with salt and lime juice—the guacamole usually takes about 2 to 3 teaspoons of salt; lime juice is a matter of personal preference.

Cover with plastic wrap directly on the surface of the guacamole and refrigerate until you're ready to serve (for best results, this needs to be within a couple of hours). Scoop the guacamole into a serving dish, sprinkle with a little chopped cilantro and *queso fresco* (if you're using it) and you're ready to serve.

Classic White *Pozole* with all the trimmings
Pozole Blanco Clásico con sus guarniciones

MAKES ABOUT 18 QUARTS, SERVING 25 TO 30

3 pounds (about 7 cups) dried *pozole* corn, preferably red *pozole* corn

OR 4 pounds (about 10 cups) fresh or frozen *nixtamal* corn, well rinsed

2 heads garlic, cloves broken apart, peeled and halved

7 pounds (3 medium) pork shanks

3 pounds (4 medium) pork trotters

5 pounds bone-in pork shoulder, cut into 3 or 4 large pieces

Salt

4 large (2 pounds) white onions, cut into ¼-inch pieces

About 1 cup coarsely ground spicy dried red chile (árbol chile is pretty classic here)

6 limes, cut into wedges

3 quarts thinly sliced cabbage or head lettuce (though not traditional, I love Napa cabbage for *pozole*)

2 dozen radishes, thinly sliced

About ⅓ cup dried Mexican oregano, preferably whole-leaf oregano

About 4 dozen tostadas (crisp-fried corn tortillas), store-bought or homemade (page 201)

This is white pozole that's so beloved around Guadalajara, not the red chile–infused pozole rojo that I grew to love while living in Mexico City. Both rely on a garlicky, velvety rich broth, the result of slowly simmering parts of a pig you don't often find in everyday grocery stores. Pig head is a part prized by food lovers, but that freaks out even some of the most intrepid cooks I know. So I'm suggesting pork shanks and trotters (aka pigs' feet) to create that beautiful texture and robust flavor; the combination even fools some of my Mexican friends into thinking I've used head.

If you've decided to make an honest-to-Mexico pozole, you shouldn't even think about using canned hominy. It's disappointingly mushy by comparison to fresh or frozen nixtamal (available at Mexican grocery stores) or dried pozole corn (available online or from specialty food stores).

With the broth made, the corn simmered to tenderness, and the meat coarsely shredded, all that's left is a few simple garnishes.

Working ahead: The pozole can be made a couple of days ahead; store the meat separately from the corn and broth. Cut up the fresh garnishes shortly before serving.

---

1. *Cook the corn.* Measure 14 quarts of water into a huge (30-quart) pot and add the corn (either the rinsed *nixtamal* or the dried corn) and garlic. Bring to a boil, partially cover the pot and simmer gently over medium-low heat until the corn is thoroughly tender—at a minimum allow about 3 hours for *nixtamal*, about 5 hours for dried corn. Add water as necessary to keep the water level more or less constant. Slower, longer cooking only means better *pozole*, as evidenced by the fact that in many places in Mexico huge pots of the fragrant mixture simmer overnight over wood fires before a fiesta.

2. *Cook the meat.* While the corn is simmering, cook the meat. Place all the meats in another very large (at least 12-quart) pot, cover with 8 quarts of water, add ¼ cup salt and bring to a boil. Skim off the grayish foam that rises during the next few minutes, then add *half* of the chopped onions. (Scoop the remaining onion into a strainer, rinse under cold water, shake off the excess, then place in a serving bowl, cover and refrigerate for serving.) Partially cover the pot and simmer over medium-low heat until all the meat is thoroughly tender, about 3 hours. Remove the meat from the broth and let cool. Or, if time allows, cool the meat in the broth for the best flavor and texture, then remove it.

Skim the fat from the broth; you'll have about 4 quarts broth. Add it to the corn, along with 2 tablespoons salt, partially cover and continue simmering until you're ready to serve.

Pull off the meat from the pork shanks and shoulder, coarsely shredding it. Collect in a large roasting pan. Cut the bones and knuckles out of the trotters. Discard the bones and knuckles, then chop what remains into ½-inch pieces. Add to the shredded meat (there will be about 12 cups meat in all). Cover and refrigerate if not serving within an hour.

3. *Serve the* pozole. When you're ready to serve, heat the meat in a 350-degree oven until just warm through (no need for the meat to be really hot), about 20 minutes. Taste the *pozole* and season with additional salt if you think necessary. Set out bowls of the condiments: the reserved onion, the ground chile, lime wedges, sliced cabbage or lettuce, sliced radishes and oregano. Set out the tostadas in a basket for the guests to enjoy alongside their *pozole*.

Spoon portions of meat into large soup bowls, then ladle in the *pozole* corn and broth. Let your guests add the condiments to suit their own tastes. Before sprinkling it over the bowl, each guest should powder the whole-leaf oregano by rubbing it between his or her palms.

PORK AND GARNISHES FOR *POZOLE*

Frontera Grill's Chocolate Pecan Pie Bars

MAKES THIRTY-TWO 2-INCH BARS

9   ounces (about 2 cups) pecan halves

1   9-ounce bag pretzel rods

1   pound (4 sticks) unsalted butter, plus extra for buttering the pan

½   cup granulated sugar

8   ounces semisweet or bittersweet chocolate, chopped into pieces not larger than ¼ inch

¾   cup (about 4½ ounces) finely chopped Mexican chocolate (such as the widely available Ibarra brand)

This recipe is a bar version of the Chocolate Pecan Pie that's been the signature dessert at Frontera Grill for well over two decades. We've replaced the flaky crust with a sweet-salty-buttery pretzel crust that I think is perfect for these luscious bars. Come to think of it, with these bars being so gooey-rich, you may want to cut the squares crosswise into triangles, so people can enjoy just a biteful at a time.

1. *Toast the pecans and prepare the crumb crust.* In a 325-degree oven, toast the pecans on a rimmed baking sheet until noticeably darker and toasty smelling, about 10 minutes. Let the pecans cool to lukewarm (but keep the oven heated), then coarsely chop them by hand—¼- to ½-inch pieces make luxurious-looking bars. Scrape into a large bowl.

Use a food processor to chop the pretzels into fairly fine crumbs. (You should have 2 cups of crumbs.) In a small saucepan over medium heat or in a microwave at 50% power, melt *2 sticks* of the butter. Scrape into the processor, along with the ½ cup granulated sugar. Pulse until everything is combined.

3   tablespoons all-purpose flour

6   large eggs

1½ cups firmly packed dark brown
    sugar

1½ cups corn syrup, preferably dark
    (or use a mixture of corn syrup
    and molasses, sorghum, Steen's
    cane syrup or most any of the
    other rich-flavored syrups)

1   tablespoon pure vanilla extract,
    preferably Mexican vanilla

    Powdered sugar, for garnish

Butter the bottoms and sides of two 8 x 8-inch baking pans. Cut a piece of parchment to fit the bottom of each pan, then press firmly in place. Butter the parchment paper. Divide the crumb mixture between the two pans and pat into an even layer covering the bottom completely.

2. *Make the filling.* To the pecans, add the two chocolates and the flour. Stir to combine, then divide evenly between the two pans. In the small saucepan or microwave at 50% power, melt the remaining *2 sticks* of the butter. In the bowl of an electric mixer, combine the eggs, brown sugar, corn syrup or corn syrup mixture and vanilla, and beat at medium-low speed (if your mixer has a choice, use the flat beater). Slowly add the melted butter, mixing until the batter looks smooth. Divide the batter between the two pans, pouring it slowly and evenly over the surface to ensure even distribution of the chocolate and pecans through the batter.

3. *Bake, cool and serve the bars.* Slide the pans into the oven and bake for 45 to 55 minutes, until the center is *almost* firm. Let cool to room temperature. Cover and refrigerate until firm for easy cutting. Use a small knife to loosen the sides, then turn out. Cut into 2-inch squares. Keep your Chocolate Pecan Pie Bars stored in the refrigerator until just before serving. Transfer to a serving platter, dust with powdered sugar, carry to your guests and await the moans of pleasure.

Beverages

It's always difficult to predict how much of each beverage to have on hand unless you know the crowd really well. But as a caterer, it's often my job to guess. Here's what I'd do:

Agua Fresca: Double the recipe on page 69, choosing fresh fruit you think will appeal. You'll have about 1½ gallons. Triple the recipe if yours is a nondrinking crowd or heavy in kids.

Beer: Have at least 24 beers on hand (even double that, if you think beer will be the main draw). Choose half from the lighter Mexican beers such as Pacifico or Tecate, half from the fuller-flavored beers such as Bohemia or Dos Equis Lager.

Wine: Typically, 4 to 6 bottles of wine will be enough for a party like this, since *pozole* seems to beckon beer more than wine. For white, I'd choose a Chardonnay with a touch of oak; if red's your thing, I'm thinking of Pinot Noir.

WATERMELON *AGUA FRESCA*

Inspirations from Taquerías, Mexican Diners and Street Vendors

When you say "Mexican food" to most Americans, tacos come to mind before, say, classics like *mole, pozole, barbacoa,* even *queso fundido*. Not that I bristle at that thought, any more than I bristle when Europeans assume that hamburgers sum up the best of American food. Neither tacos nor hamburgers tell the whole story. But they do tell an essential part of it, and we all have to agree that well-made tacos—and hamburgers—are thrillingly delicious, relatively simple to make, and easy for folks from Argentina to Zimbabwe to appreciate on the stage of world cuisine. In other words, tacos offer an alluring portal into Mexican flavor.

I'm thinking of supple Mexican tacos, of course, not the Mexican-American U-bent crispy tostadas filled with bland ground beef. Pardon my saying it, but for me those have all the allure of cardboard-wrapped pet food, even though they're dolled up with sour cream and vinegary-sweet—*but not too hot!*—taco sauce. Unfortunately, that's the taco that some successful American chains have exported around the world, convincingly proclaiming its Mexican-ness to hundreds of millions.

Which may lead you to wonder: if a genuine Mexican taco is so good, why wasn't *it* chosen for international promotion? Three reasons: tortillas, tomatillos and our American preconception of Mexico's culinary potential—or lack thereof.

First the hard one, the tortillas. Outside Mexico, few understand that the classic little corn tortilla that wraps the classic Mexican taco—often employed in pairs due to its melt-in-your-mouth tenderness—goes dry and stale within hours, certainly a day, of its baking. And refrigeration and freezing don't really help slow the process much. So, unless you live near a tortilla factory or make tortillas yourself—an admirable skill that takes time to perfect—you may never have tasted a fresh corn tortilla. And know one thing for sure: the flavor and texture of a fresh-baked tortilla made from fresh-ground corn *masa* can be a life-changing experience. A mouthful of reheated frozen corn tortilla, not so much.

So most Americans have learned to say they prefer crispy tacos (once fried, the corn tortilla has absorbed enough oil to preserve and protect it from rapid staleness) or ones made with wheat flour tortillas. While wheat flour tortillas are made and enjoyed in Mexico, they account for a very small percentage of daily tortilla consumption, a percentage that increases the closer you get to the United States, to the land of wheat and plenty. We understand wheat flour here—certainly a lot more than corn *masa* flour. Plus we understand how delicious and protective a good dollop of fat and sprinkling of salt can make that wheat flour tortilla. For better (nutrition) or worse (shelf life), fat and salt play no part in corn tortillas. All of which leaves the genuine Mexican taco, wrapped in its fresh-baked corn tortilla, hard to find outside Mexico and other spots where the Mexican diaspora has landed. Or in the kitchens of those dedicated to full-throttle international culinary enjoyment.

Tomatillos rarely make it into discussions of globalized Mexican food, in spite of the fact that in Mexico, their vividly bright flavor plays a major role in the salsas that bring alive authentic flavor. Their cultivation just never took off like tomatoes, that other native Mexican fruit that's beloved the world over. Yet I know, having been asked to cook Mexican food on many continents, that without the distinctive tang of tomatillos it's hard to achieve authentic flavor—stuff tastes, well, more American. We just have to face it: salsas and sauces made with tomatoes aren't as bright, as richly complex, as compelling as those made with tomatillos.

But on that huge stage of world cuisine, most people don't seem to expect that much from Mexican food, do they? Mexico's a developing country and rustic, simple street fare made from inexpensive ingredients—their less-than-perfect quality masked with a good dose of chile—has become the stereotype. And though stereotypes usually blossom out of truths, this is one I chafe against. Because, when you stop to look—truly look—at even the simplest street foods, the ingredients they're created from can dazzle even jaded foodies, the techniques used to create them are anything but slapdash, and the flavors of a genuine Mexican taco are anything but simple. In fact, those flavors can be downright transcendent.

I'm just hesitant to promote tacos too much—even the genuine article— for fear that everything I say will be heard through the filter of long-held American stereotypes. Nevertheless, I love this food too much to ignore the lively role it plays in Mexico's cuisine. So here's a chapter chock-full of really delicious inspirations from taquerias, street stalls and those Mexican diners called cafeterías—plus about a dozen salsas and sauces that make them sing.

I start with Grilled Skirt Steak Tacos on page 182 (who doesn't like those?) and follow it with my version of Grilled Pork Tacos al Pastor (page 188). The texture you achieve with the vertical spit-roasting of true pork tacos al pastor is nearly impossible for home cooks to recreate, but the flavor of this grilled version rings true.

Rolled crisp-fried tacos are a staple of *cafeterías*, and the version I've included here (page 192) offers you the opportunity to experience a classic Mexican texture you may not know: sauce-doused crispiness softening slightly, tantalizingly, to a consistency we have no word for. *Cafeterías* are also the domain of sauced tortilla dishes—we call them all "enchiladas," though in Mexico the specific sauce dictates their exact name: "enchiladas" (page 199) for a sauce that focuses on chile, "*enfrijoladas*" (page 196) for one made from beans, just to name a couple.

Crisp-fried or -baked tortillas, typically called tostadas, come in a range of sizes and carry a wide variety of regional toppings: Oaxacan *tlayudas* (page 202) baked over the coals and drizzled with smoky, tangy flavors; Yucatecan black bean *panuchos* (page 204) with pickled chicken, red onions and habanero; Chiapas red chile-beef tartar on crisp tortilla triangles (page 210). And I've included sandal shaped *huaraches* (page 206), even though they're thicker and never get crisp; these black bean-filled corn *masa* cakes are a perfect vehicle for roasted tomatillo salsa and a dusting of Romano-like *queso añejo*.

Tamales are available everywhere in Mexico, from simple market stalls called *fondas* to *cafeterías*, restaurants, even the street vendors that often huddle in churchyards when mass lets out. And the diversity of wrappers, fillings and batters cooks use is astonishing. Here, I'm just scratching the surface with Black Bean Tamales with Fresh Goat Cheese (page 212), Yucatecan "Pudding" Tamales (page 216) steamed in banana leaves, Pork *Picadillo* Sweet Corn Tamales (page 220), Roasted Garlic Tamales with Ricotta and Swiss Chard (page 222), and Butternut Tamales with Chipotle Chicken (page 224).

No doubt, all this delicious variety will whet your appetite for the full range of the Mexican kitchen. Can we ask anything more of a great taco or enchilada or tostada or tamal?

Grilled Skirt Steak (or Chicken) Tacos with Knob Onions (and Cactus)

Tacos de Arrachera (o Pollo) al Carbón con Cebollitas Asadas (y Nopales)

MAKES 12 TACOS, SERVING 4 AS A LIGHT MEAL

FOR THE MARINADE

1   head garlic, broken into individual cloves, unpeeled—about 12 cloves

¼   cup vegetable or olive oil

6   tablespoons vinegar—apple cider vinegar works well here

    A generous ½ teaspoon EACH ground black pepper and cinnamon

1   big pinch of ground cloves

    A generous 1 teaspoon dried oregano, preferably Mexican

    Salt

FOR FINISHING THE DISH

1   pound skirt steak, trimmed of surface fat as well as the thin white membrane called "silver skin"

    OR 1 pound boneless, skinless chicken breast halves—about 3

3   medium (about 6 ounces total) cactus paddles (optional)

2   bunches (about 12 total) knob onions, each about 1 inch in diameter (available at Mexican groceries and farmers' markets)

    Vegetable or olive oil for brushing or spritzing the onions, cactus and meat

Steak tacos are on practically everyone's list of favorites. They're easy to prepare, nearly universal in appeal, simply traditional in their Mexican flavor. And they welcome—almost encourage—tweaking and momentary inspiration. We've had grilled skirt steak tacos on the Frontera Grill menu for decades now, and this recipe captures the heart of what we put on the plate: garlicky marinated skirt steak, grilled over a hardwood fire and served with those sweet-grilled bulbous knob onions that are so much a part of Mexico's taquería flavor. I love them with some fresh-made guacamole and a bowl of charro beans flavored with bacon and cilantro.

The same dish can be—in fact, is—made regularly with chicken, and with grilled cactus, alongside or instead of the knob onions. And with roasted poblano peppers mixed in with the sliced meat. You can even substitute a no-frills squeeze of lime for the more complex garlic marinade.

Some cooks don't even grill skirt-steak tacos: the meat is disarmingly delicious when simply seared until crusty on a hot griddle, which is considerably easier for many of us.

1. *Make the marinade and marinate the meat.* In a small skillet over medium heat, roast the unpeeled garlic, turning occasionally, until softened (it'll be blackened in spots), 10 to 15 minutes. Cool, then peel and place in a food processor or blender, along with the oil, vinegar, spices, herbs and ¾ teaspoon salt. Process to a smooth puree. Lay the skirt steak (or chicken) in a non-aluminum baking dish. Scrape *half* of the marinade over the steak, then use a spoon to smear it over both sides. (Refrigerate leftover marinade for seasoning another round of grilled skirt steak or fish.) Cover and refrigerate for 30 minutes or so (or as long as 6 hours).

2. *Clean the cactus, if using.* Holding the cactus with gloves or tongs, trim off ¼ inch all the way around each cactus paddle. Holding your knife blade perpendicular to the paddle, scrape off all the spiny nodes from both sides.

3. *Grill the onions and cactus.* Heat one side of a gas grill to medium-high or light a charcoal fire and let it burn until the coals are covered with gray ash and still very hot. To set up the grill for indirect cooking, either turn the burner(s) on the other side of the grill to medium-low or bank the coals to one side.

12 warm corn tortillas

A small bowlful of lime wedges for serving

About 1 cup Roasted Tomatillo Salsa (page 208) or another of your favorites

Brush or spray the knob onions and cactus, if using, with oil and sprinkle with salt. Lay the cactus on the hotter side of the grill, the onions on the cooler side, bulbous ends toward the heat. When the cactus browns a little, about 3 minutes, flip the paddles over and cook until they are limp and browned (they will have darkened to olive colored); move them to the coolest part of the grill. When the onions start to soften and turn golden, about 10 minutes, use a spatula to flip them and cook the other side.

4. *Grill the meat.* When the onions are about done, brush or spritz oil over both sides of the steak (or chicken). Lay it over the hottest part of the grill. Grill, turning once, until richly browned and done to your liking, about 2 minutes per side for medium (chicken will take slightly longer). Move to the coolest part of the grill and let rest for a couple of minutes—this allows the juices to reabsorb into the meat rather than run out onto the board when the steak is cut.

5. *Serve the tacos.* Cut the long piece of skirt steak into 3- to 4-inch sections, then cut each section into thin strips *across the grain*, that is, in line with the full length of the skirt steak. (Or slice the chicken breast widthwise.) Slice the cactus into ¼-inch strips. Sprinkle everything with salt, scoop into warm serving dishes and set on the table, along with the warm tortillas, knob onions, lime wedges and salsa. Your guests will love making their own soft tacos.

"Drunken" Salsa
Salsa Borracha

MAKES 1½ CUPS

6 garlic cloves, unpeeled

6 large (about 2 ounces total) dried pasilla chiles, stemmed and seeded

⅓ cup fresh orange juice

⅓ cup dark beer, preferably Negra Modelo

1 tablespoon tequila (a bright-flavored silver tequila is good here)

Salt

This is my Stateside version of the classic salsa that's served with pit-cooked lamb barbacoa in central Mexico: the darkest of the dried chiles (pasilla negro), richly roasted with garlic, then blended with beer and tequila (the borracha part), a dash of orange and a dose of salt. Only difference in Mexico: pulque (that sourish "beer" made from the fermented sap of huge agaves pulqueros) is the booze, not my more zingy beer-plus-tequila combo. I've never seen fresh pulque for sale here; only the canned stuff, which, in my opinion, isn't worth the little you pay for it.

Working Ahead: The salsa keeps well for several days in the refrigerator, covered. It may thicken a little, requiring a spoon or two of water before serving.

1. Roast the garlic, toast the chiles. In a large (10-inch) skillet over medium heat, roast the unpeeled garlic, turning occasionally, until soft and blackened in spots, 10 to 15 minutes; cool and peel. While the garlic is roasting, toast the chiles on another side of the skillet: one or two at a time, open them out flat and press down firmly on the hot surface with a spatula until they are aromatic and have lightened in color underneath—about 10 seconds per side. In a small bowl, cover the chiles with hot water and let rehydrate for 30 minutes, stirring regularly to ensure even soaking. Drain, *reserving ⅓ cup of the soaking water.*

2. Finish the salsa. In a food processor or blender, combine the chiles, the *⅓ cup soaking liquid,* the garlic, orange juice, beer and tequila. Process to a smooth puree. Pour into a salsa dish, then stir in a little water to give your *salsa borracha* an easily spoonable consistency (it typically takes about ¼ cup). Taste and season with salt, usually about 1 teaspoon—it'll have rich depth, pungency, tanginess and an edge of sweetness, but it's the salt that pulls it all together.

Creamy Roasted Jalapeño Salsa
Salsa Cremosa de Chile Jalapeño Asado

MAKES ABOUT 1¾ CUPS

6 ounces (about 5 medium to large) jalapeño chiles, stemmed

10 garlic cloves, peeled

¼ cup fresh lime juice

½ cup vegetable oil

Salt

Few know of this salsa, though some version of it shows up pretty regularly in taquerías in central and southern Mexico, almost convincing those who spoon it on tasty tacos that its charismatic creaminess has something to do with mayonnaise. But it doesn't. That creaminess is the alchemical reaction of roasted jalapeños and garlic (some cooks boil, rather than roast, them) blended with lime and oil—no egg yolks in sight.

Working Ahead: I don't typically keep this salsa for more than a day or so. Or if I must push that to 3 or 4 days, re-blending is typically needed to re-homogenize it. Always: refrigerate the salsa, covered.

In a large (10-inch) skillet over medium heat, roast the jalapeños and unpeeled garlic until soft and blotchy brown, 15 to 20 minutes (the garlic may be done before the chiles). Cool, then peel the garlic and roughly chop the jalapeños. Combine the garlic, chiles and lime juice in a blender. Pulse to finely chop. Turn on the blender and slowly dribble in the oil. Pour into a salsa dish and add enough water to give it an easily spoonable consistency (I often add 2 tablespoons). Taste and season with salt, usually a scant teaspoon.

So You Want to Have a Street Food Party?

First, a little-known truth: creating rustic, earthy, enthralling street food is harder than pulling off a five-course formal dinner party. Why? There are three reasons. First, for the formal dinner party, much of the work can be done ahead; try to make street food ahead and it lacks all the fresh, won't-hold-for-a-minute vitality we're attracted to. Second, once you've delivered a dinner-party course to all your guests, you can sit with them, enjoying what you've created; street food is all about the one-serving-at-a-time immediacy, so you have to enthusiastically embrace the role of cook-for-the-night . . . or you'll be miserable. And third, our homes are typically designed for sit-down dinners, kitchen and dining areas separate from one another; crowding all your guests in the kitchen, where you'll make dishes for them one serving at a time, isn't always feasible.

Now, all that said, I'll tell you I love to do street food parties (remember: one of my greatest joys is cooking for people, *in front* of people), but I am careful how much—and exactly what—I tackle. After all, at some point, I want people to be full so I can join the party.

Though I've done street food parties indoors, they're easier around a grill. You can use the grill for cooking and keeping things warm. The aromas will put everyone in the street food mood anyway. Here's a good, manageable menu, I think.

- A favorite guacamole with chips and/or sliced vegetables (pages 26 to 34)

- Skewers of jícama and fruit cubes drizzled with fresh lime, sprinkled with hot powdered chile (page 154)

- Any of your favorite tamales (pages 212 to 224)

- Three-Chile Salsa (page 192)

Up to this point, everything can be prepared at least a few hours ahead (sprinkle jícama with chile just before serving). I sometimes like to make crispy, tostada-like *tlayudas* (page 202) with their avocado-tomatillo salsa, cooked chorizo and crumbled fresh cheese topping, because nearly every-thing can be done ahead except for the final grilling of the tortilla. If you choose to do them, I'd rec-ommend preparing a double batch of the tomatillo-avocado salsa so you can serve some with what follows:

- Grilled Skirt Steak (or Chicken) Tacos with Knob Onions (and Cactus; page 182).

I set up a table next to the grill and cover it with a tablecloth. (I made leg extensions for my fold-ing table from 12-inch lengths of PVC pipe, bringing it to a more comfortable counter height.) On it goes the salsa, a bowl of lime wedges, a tortilla warmer, some plates, napkins and forks for my friends, and a cutting board, knife and tongs for me. In another area, along with the drinks, I set out the guac 'n' chips and the jícama skewers for everyone to nibble on, away from the grilling action.

If I've chosen to do the Tlayudas, those ingredients will be on my table, too, and I like to grill and serve them first, before moving on to tacos and tamales.

I reheat the tamales in their steamer and set the steamer on the back of the grill to keep them warm. Then I grill the onions and (optional) cactus, slice up the cactus and keep both warm in a pan next to the tamales.

When the guests are ready for more than the opening nibbles, I start grilling skirt steak and chicken breasts, slicing them up and making tacos from the meat, onions and cactus, letting them embellish what I've handed them with salsa, lime, even a dab of guacamole. If my tortillas are very fresh, I reheat them one at a time right on the grill; if not, I reheat them according to the directions on page 197. The tamales are right there to pluck from the steamer and slide onto the plate next to the taco.

For dessert, I don't recommend anything you actually have to serve: a plate of cookies or brownies, perhaps, or a more involved *chocoflan* (page 290) that you can slice up ahead of time and let guests serve them-selves. By dessert time, you deserve a rest. Though I know everyone thinks of margaritas (and we have a wonderful selec-tion on pages 44 to 51) for a party like this, there's a well-reasoned argument for a variety of (easy to serve) good beer, maybe a bottle or two of red wine.

Grilled Pork Tacos *al Pastor*
Tacos al Pastor

MAKES ENOUGH FOR 20 TACOS, SERVING 6 AS A LIGHT MEAL

A 3½-ounce package *achiote* marinade

3 canned chipotle chiles *en adobo*, plus 4 tablespoons of the canning sauce

¼ cup vegetable or olive oil, plus a little more for the onion and pineapple

1½ pounds thin-sliced pork shoulder (¼-inch-thick slices are ideal—the kind Mexican butchers sell for making *tacos al pastor*)

1 medium red onion, sliced ¼-inch thick

Salt

¼ of a medium pineapple, sliced into ¼-inch-thick rounds

FOR SERVING

20 warm corn tortillas

About 1½ cups salsa (my favorite here is Three-Chile Salsa, page 190)

Of course, this doesn't make true tacos al pastor, *because for that you'd have to start with a spit full of at least 20 pounds of the thin-sliced, marinated pork. Then you'd roast it vertically in front of a gas- or charcoal-fired contraption like the one used for Greek gyros, with a pineapple skewered on top, dripping down its sweet, tangy juices. And finally, you'd shave off slivers of the roasty meat and pineapple to wrap in soft corn tortillas and douse with salsa. All of which is pretty unlikely for most of us, though that's the seminal experience* tacos al pastor *aficionados would love to capture at home. Instead, we either choose to delay gratifying our* tacos al pastor *cravings until we can travel (often long distances) to find a good or authentic one, or we enjoy a deliciously-close-to-tacos-al-pastor experience—like the preparation I've outlined here—at our backyard grill. Those of us who opt for the second, more-frequently-available option are in good company: ready-to-cook "pastor-style" meat (thin-cut pork marinated like I've described in the recipe below) is finding its way into Mexican grocery stores on both sides of the border, as well as into the stalls of certain street vendors who simply sear it on a hot griddle, chop it up and serve it in tacos or gorditas or on huaraches. So riding the wave of that "pastor evolution," I offer my backyard-grill version of central Mexico's most iconic taco.*

According to most food historians, the name, which translates as "shepherd's style," came to Mexico after a great number of Middle Eastern immigrants brought vertical spit cooking.

Working Ahead: The longer you marinate the meat, the more its texture will resemble cured ham; marinate for an hour or so for fresh-pork texture, overnight for cured texture. The marinade itself will hold for a week or more, covered and refrigerated. Obviously, freshly grilled meat is the best.

1. *Marinate the meat.* In a blender, combine the *achiote*, chiles, canning sauce, oil and ¾ cup water. Blend until smooth. Use ⅓ of the marinade to smear over both sides of each slice of meat (refrigerate the rest of the marinade to use on other meat or fish). Cover and refrigerate for at least an hour.

2. *Grill and serve.* Heat one side of a gas grill to medium-high or light a charcoal fire and let it burn until the coals are covered with gray ash and still very hot. To set up the grill for indirect cooking, either turn the burner(s) on the other side of the grill to medium-low or bank the coals. Brush both sides of the onion slices with oil and sprinkle with salt. Lay in a single layer on the hot side of the grill. When richly browned, usually just about a minute, flip and brown the other side; move to the cool side of the grill to finish softening to grilled-onion sweetness. Oil and grill the pineapple in the same way. Finally, in batches, grill the meat: it'll take about a minute per side as well. As the meat is done, transfer it to a cutting board and chop it up (between ¼- and ½-inch pieces). Scoop into a skillet and set over the grill to keep the meat warm. Chop the onion and pineapple into small pieces as well, add them to the skillet and toss everything together. Taste and season with salt, usually about ½ teaspoon. Scoop the meat mixture into a warm serving dish, and serve with the tortillas and salsa for your guests to make soft tacos.

GRILLED PORK TACOS *AL PASTOR*

Three-Chile Salsa
Salsa de Tres Chiles

MAKES 2 CUPS SALSA

2 large (about 2-inch-long) dried red chipotle chiles (aka moritas), stemmed

4 dried round cascabel chiles, stemmed

1 large dried guajillo chile, stemmed, seeded and torn into flat pieces

6 garlic cloves, unpeeled

1 pound (6 to 8 medium) tomatillos, husked and rinsed

Salt

About ½ teaspoon sugar (optional)

This is the recipe for Frontera's now-classic "red table salsa," the one we've served for twenty-three years. And its inspiration came from a taquería I went to in . . . Pilsen. Those in Chicago know that Pilsen, an old German-turned-Mexican neighborhood southwest of the city's downtown, offers just about the closest thing to Mexico-away-from-Mexico you'll find in the United States. Which is to say that this salsa is pure-bred Mexican, even if I didn't eat it there, being a blend of roasted tomatillos and garlic with three different dried chiles: chipotle for smoky sweetness, the round cascabel for nuttiness and the guajillo for brightness. If finding dried chipotles is a challenge, replace them with the canned ones en adobo; no need to toast and soak.

Working Ahead: Feel free to make this salsa ahead. It keeps well for up to a week in the refrigerator if well covered.

1. *Toast and roast.* Heat a large (10-inch) ungreased skillet over medium, then toast the chiles: scoop in the chipotle and cascabel chiles and stir until very aromatic—toasty—smelling, about a minute. Scoop into a small bowl. Use a metal spatula to press the flat pieces of guajillo firmly against the hot surface for a few seconds to toast them; flip and toast the other side. Collect the guajillos with the other chiles, cover with hot tap water and soak for about 30 minutes, stirring from time to time to ensure even rehydration.

In the same skillet, roast the garlic, turning regularly, until soft and blotchy-black in places, 10 to 15 minutes. Cool and slip off the papery skins.

Meanwhile, roast the tomatillos on a rimmed baking sheet about 4 inches below a very hot broiler until soft and blackened in spots, about 5 minutes per side. Cool, then scrape into blender jar, along with all the juices.

2. *Finish the salsa.* Drain the chiles and add to the blender, along with the garlic and ½ cup water. Blend until nearly smooth, then scrape into a salsa dish. Stir in enough water to give the salsa an easily spoonable consistency (it typically needs about ¼ cup more). Taste and season with salt, usually about 1 teaspoon, and the sugar, if using.

CRISPY SHRIMP TACOS (PAGE 192)

Huitlacoche Filling with Caramelized Vegetables for Crispy Tacos

Relleno de Huitlacoche con Verduras Caramalizadas para Tacos Dorados

MAKES ENOUGH TO FILL 12 TACOS

2 tablespoons olive oil

½ medium onion, cut into ¼-inch pieces

1 heaping cup diced peeled root vegetables or squash (I like a combination of carrot, parsnip and butternut or pie pumpkin)—best if the pieces are small, about ¼ inch

2 garlic cloves, peeled and finely chopped

1 cup *huitlacoche* (see headnote)

Hot green chiles to taste (2 to 3 serranos, 1 to 2 jalapeños), stemmed, seeded (if you like) and finely chopped

12 ounces (2 medium-small round) red-ripe tomatoes, chopped into ¼-inch pieces

OR 1 15-ounce can diced tomatoes, drained

Leaves from a large branch of *epazote*, chopped (or a small handful of chopped cilantro)

Salt

A delicious, if exotic, substitute for the shrimp in Crispy Shrimp Tacos (page 192) is huitlacoche. You know: Mexico's highly sought-after, earthy-sweet huitlacoche, the exact same stuff as the dreaded, nearly eradicated blight called corn smut in North America. Same taste on both sides of the border, though I doubt many Iowa farmers could or would attest to that. What this bi-national culinary conflict means for Mexophile cooks like me is simple. It's hard to find huitlacoche for cooking here in the United States, except in a few farmers' markets where Mexican (or otherwise enlightened) vendors sell the fresh stuff or in some Mexican groceries where canned is an option (though the quality varies widely from brand to brand). When it's fresh, you're looking for huitlacoche that's slightly soft but not so soft that the grayish outer covering of the lobes has broken, revealing the blackish inside. Its flavor should have a mushroom-y earthiness with a gentle corn sweetness (it is, after all, a mushroom growing in an ear of corn); if it tastes "dirty" it's overripe. For canned huitlacoche, look for lobes that are intact rather than mushy.

Working Ahead: The good news is that this huitlacoche filling can be frozen for up to a couple of months, so make it when you find the huitlacoche and then start planning a dinner around it. Defrost the frozen huitlacoche filling in the refrigerator overnight.

In a very large (12-inch) skillet, heat the oil over medium. Add the onion and diced vegetables. Cook, stirring occasionally, until soft and richly browned, about 10 minutes. Add the garlic and stir for a minute, then add the *huitlacoche*, chiles, tomatoes and *epazote* (or cilantro). Raise the heat to medium-high and cook, stirring regularly, until nearly dry, about 4 minutes. Taste and season with salt, usually about ¾ teaspoon. Cool.

Savory Tomato Broth and Pickled Vegetables for Crispy Tacos
Caldo de Jitomate y Verduras Escabechadas para Tacos Dorados

ENOUGH FOR 12 TACOS, SERVING 6

I love to douse shrimp tacos (any crispy tacos, really) with this tomato broth and top them with a little of the pickled vegetables. It's all about texture: softening crispness (one of Mexico's favorite textures) juxtaposed with the meatiness of the filling and the crunchiness of the vegetables. If a creamy element appeals, top off the pickled vegetables with diced avocado.

FOR THE TOMATO BROTH

12 ounces (2 medium-small round) red-ripe tomatoes, roughly chopped

    OR 1 15-ounce can diced tomatoes, lightly drained

½ small white onion, roughly chopped

2 garlic cloves, peeled and roughly chopped

1 tablespoon olive oil

2 cups chicken, fish or shellfish broth

    Salt

FOR THE PICKLED VEGETABLES

⅔ cup light vinegar (I like rice or cava vinegar)

1 bay leaf

1 sprig of fresh thyme (or a big pinch of dried thyme)

1 teaspoon sugar

2 medium carrots, cut into matchsticks (or 4 ounces matchstick-cut carrots from the produce section of the grocery store)

½ small white onion, thinly sliced

4 cups (loosely packed) thinly sliced Napa cabbage (you'll need about ⅛ of a head)

1. *Make the tomato broth.* In a blender, puree the tomatoes, onion and garlic. Press through a medium-mesh strainer into a bowl. Heat the oil in a medium (3-quart) saucepan over medium-high. When hot enough to make a drop of the puree sizzle sharply, add it all at once. Stir until noticeably darker and thicker, about 5 minutes. Add the broth. When the mixture comes to a boil, partially cover and simmer for 30 minutes over medium-low. If necessary add more broth (or water) to give the mixture a soupy consistency. Taste and season with salt, usually about ½ teaspoon.

2. *Make the pickled vegetables.* In a medium (3-quart) saucepan, combine the vinegar, bay, thyme and sugar with 1 cup water and ½ teaspoon salt. Heat the mixture just to a simmer. Scoop the carrots into a heat-proof bowl and strain in the vinegar mixture. When cool, add the onion and cabbage.

Savory Bean-Sauced Tortillas with Fresh Cheese
Enfrijoladas
YIELD: 4 SERVINGS

¾ cup cooked black beans

The broth from cooking 1 pound of black beans—about 5 cups (for the most authentic flavor, cook them with a few toasted avocado leaves if they're available)

Salt

8 ounces (about 1 cup) fresh Mexican chorizo sausage, removed from its casing

8 corn tortillas

A little vegetable oil, for brushing or spraying the tortillas

About ½ cup Roasted Tomatillo Salsa (page 208)

About ½ cup crumbled Mexican *queso fresco* or other fresh cheese like salted pressed famer's cheese or goat cheese

A couple of thin white onion slices, broken into rings

A few tablespoons coarsely chopped flat-leaf parsley

The first time—this was sometime in the early '80s—I stood outside that exact number on that exact Oaxacan street, just as I'd been told, I had to decide whether or not to go in. There was no sign saying "Doña Elpidia" or "fonda" or "restaurante": only a small tacked-up slip of paper with the words "waitress wanted." The place had been a boarding house, I later learned, but still served mid-morning almuerzo and an afternoon comida—now only to outsiders, since the boarders were long gone. The old patrona still wandered the kitchen and bird-filled courtyard, cooking and greeting. She was from the old school, and so were her traditional Oaxacan dishes. Deann and I picked a boxy table on the patio and tasted the famous banana leaf–wrapped tamales and hot chocolate whipped with water (never milk) and served in a small, slope-sided bowl. But it's the enfrijoladas that are most vivid in my memory: made with those white Oaxacan tortillas, the little local black beans flavored with avocado leaf and dried chile, the typical local garnishes of onion, fresh cheese and flat-leaf parsley, and sweet-tasting Oaxacan chorizo.

The following recipe for this Oaxacan specialty, which starts with the broth from simmering black beans, is designed around the Doña Elpidia version; enfrijoladas are popular elsewhere in Mexico, but these are the best I know. While many cooks puree beans and broth to create the sauce, I rely almost exclusively on the velvety natural consistency and rich dark color of black bean–simmering broth, only a few beans added to give substance. To be successful, everything for making the dish (tortillas, chorizo, bean broth, plates) has to be hot. Plain and simple: this is one of my favorite light meals, served with a romaine and watercress salad. Sometimes made even better adding sautéed sweet (ripe) plantains to the chorizo and replacing the salsa with a drizzle of thick cream.

Working Ahead: Of course, the bean broth can be kept in the refrigerator for several days before serving. Everything else can be prepped several hours ahead, if that helps. But, of course, the dish has to be finished when you're ready to serve it.

1. *Preliminaries.* Puree the cooked beans in a food processor until smooth, adding some of the bean liquid if necessary. Scoop the puree, along with the broth, into a medium (3-quart) saucepan and bring to a boil over medium to medium-high heat. Boil, whisking regularly, until reduced to 2 cups, about 35 minutes. The consistency should be very saucy, like a very light bean soup; if necessary, stir in a little water. Taste and season with salt, usually a generous teaspoon. Cover and set over the lowest heat.

In a small skillet, fry the chorizo over medium-low heat (add a little oil if it doesn't begin to render fat right away) until done, about 10 minutes, breaking up any clumps as it cooks. Keep warm over low heat or in a low oven.

2. *Warm the tortillas.* Lightly brush or spray both sides of each tortilla with oil. Slide into a plastic bag and microwave on high (100%) for 1 minute to warm and soften.

3. *Finish the* enfrijoladas. One by one, dip the tortillas into the hot bean broth, fold into quarters and divide among four warm dinner plates, slightly overlapping each pair. Spoon a portion (about ¼ cup) of the remaining hot bean broth over each pair of quartered tortillas, splash with some of the Roasted Tomatillo Salsa, then sprinkle with chorizo, crumbled cheese, sliced onion and chopped parsley. Serve immediately.

Reheating Store-Bought Corn Tortillas

MICROWAVE VERSION (1 TO 3 DOZEN): Buy factory-made medium-thick corn tortillas (preferably from a local *tortillería* or grocery store that makes them on premise). Unwrap them from the package they came in, then re-wrap them *by dozens* in one square of damp paper towels (wet the paper towels, then roll up and gently squeeze out the excess water; unroll and use to wrap the tortillas). Slide into a plastic bag (big enough so the tortillas will lie flat), but don't seal. Microwave for 1 minute per dozen, up to 3 dozen. Carefully remove from the bag. Immediately remove from the paper towel and store in a Styrofoam tortilla warmer or

small thermal chest (like the ones that will hold a 6-pack of cans). Styrofoam tortilla warmers typically come in two sizes: a small size that fits 1 dozen, and a larger size for 3 dozen. To ensure that the tortillas stay for a long time, it's best to buy the 1-dozen size. Unopened, the tortillas typically stay piping hot for an hour.

OVEN VERSION (4 TO 8 DOZEN): Buy factory-made medium-thick corn tortillas (preferably from a local *tortillería* or grocery store that makes them on premise). Heat the oven to 300 degrees. Unwrap the tortillas from the package they came in. Place a rack (like the one you'd cool cookies on, one

with "feet" that support the rack about ½ inch above the counter) in a roasting pan. Pour in ¼ inch of water. Lay a clean kitchen towel on the rack, making sure it doesn't touch the water. Lay the tortillas in stacks of 1 to 2 dozen on the towel. Cover with a second towel, then cover the pan with a lid or piece of aluminum foil (crimp the edges to seal). Slide into the oven and heat for 45 minutes if the stacks are 1-dozen high, 1 hour if the stacks are 2-dozen high. Turn off the oven. The tortillas can be served immediately or can be kept warm for an hour or so if you keep the lid (or crimped foil) securely in place.

ROASTED VEGETABLE ENCHILADAS WITH CREAMY
TOMATILLO SAUCE AND MELTED CHEESE

Roasted Vegetable Enchiladas with Creamy Tomatillo Sauce and Melted Cheese

Enchiladas Suizas de Verduras Asadas

SERVES 4 TO 6

1 pound (6 to 8) tomatillos, husked and rinsed

1 medium white onion, sliced about ¼ inch thick

3 garlic cloves, peeled

Fresh hot green chiles to taste (2 or 3 serranos, 1 or 2 jalapeños), stemmed

1½ tablespoons vegetable oil, plus extra for roasting the vegetables and brushing or spraying the tortillas

2 cups vegetable or chicken broth, plus a little extra if needed

½ cup Mexican *crema* (page 200), *crème fraîche* or heavy (whipping) cream

8 cups cubed vegetables (about ½-inch cubes are good)—delicious choices are chayote, carrots, white or red onions, small turnips, kohlrabi, mushrooms and peeled butternut squash

Salt

12 corn tortillas

⅔ cup shredded Mexican melting cheese (like Chihuahua, *quesadilla,* or *asadero*) or Monterey Jack, brick or mild cheddar

A few sliced rounds of white onion, separated into rings, for garnish

Fresh cilantro sprigs, for garnish

Practically everyone who visits Mexico City sits at one time or another at the coffee shop counter toward the rear of the old Sanborns in downtown Mexico City, the place where creamy enchiladas suizas were invented. And the perceptive ones know that within the four walls of that blue-and-white-tiled sixteenth-century-palace-turned-twentieth-century-retailer a good number of important historical events have transpired over the last five centuries. But none outshines, in my opinion, the development of the enchiladas suizas, a dish I think straddles the transition between old-fashioned regional cooking and that of the modern world stage. The original sauce was made with tomatoes, but it's evolved into tomatillos in most cooks' versions, offering a tangy counterpoint to the richness. And here I'm nudging the dish into yet another stage of evolution: richly textured roasted vegetables replacing shredded chicken, rolled into warm corn tortillas, doused with that luscious tomatillo sauce, nestled under a little melted cheese. Clearly a dish that's ready for prime time.

A note about vegetables: feel free to use broccoli, asparagus, zucchini and other green vegetables, too. Just roast them on a separate baking sheet, since they'll be done 5 to 10 minutes quicker than those suggested in the recipe.

Working Ahead: The sauce can be made a day or two ahead; refrigerate covered. After the tortillas have been heated in the oven, you need to work quickly and steadily toward serving in order to preserve their beautiful texture. Once out of the oven, the finished dish softens to near mush over a period of 15 to 20 minutes.

---

1. *Make the sauce.* Roast the tomatillos, sliced onion, peeled garlic and chiles on a rimmed baking sheet 4 inches below a hot broiler until the tomatillos are soft and blotchy black on one side, 4 or 5 minutes. Turn everything over and roast the other side. Remove and reduce the oven temperature to 400 degrees.

Scrape the tomatillo mixture into a blender or food processor. Process to a smooth puree. Heat the 1½ *tablespoons* of oil in a medium-large (4- or 5-quart) pot over medium high. When the oil is hot enough to make a drop of the puree sizzle, add the puree all at once. Stir nearly constantly for several minutes until darker and thicker. Add the broth and the *crema,* reduce the heat to medium-low, partially cover and simmer for about 30 minutes.

2. *Roast the vegetables.* Spread the cubed vegetables on a rimmed baking sheet. Drizzle or spritz with oil, sprinkle with salt and stir to coat evenly. Roast, stirring regularly, until the carrots are crunchy-tender, about 25 minutes.

3. *Finish the sauce, heat the tortillas.* If the sauce has thickened beyond the consistency of a light cream soup, stir in a little more broth (or water). Taste and season with salt, usually about 1 teaspoon. Lightly brush or spray both sides of each tortilla with oil. Slide into a plastic bag and microwave on high (100%) for 1 minute to warm and soften.

4. *Finish the enchiladas.* Smear a few tablespoons of the sauce over the bottom of four to six 9-inch individual ovenproof baking/serving dishes or smear about 1 cup of the sauce over the bottom of a 13 x 9-inch baking dish. Working quickly so the tortillas stay hot and pliable, roll a portion of the roasted vegetables into each tortilla, then line them all up in the baking dish(es). Douse evenly with the remaining sauce, then sprinkle with the cheese. Bake until the enchiladas are heated through (the cheese will have begun to brown), about 10 minutes. Garnish with onion rings and cilantro sprigs. These are best served piping hot from the oven.

Mexican *Crema*

A tub of *crème fraîche* will provide you the closest thing to real Mexican *crema*, since, to my knowledge, there are no artisanal Mexican dairies producing high-quality traditional creams and cheeses in wide distribution in the United States. *Crème fraîche* and *crema* are essentially the same, meaning that they are both cultured creams and that there is a lot of variety from brand to brand, region to region, season to season.

You can culture your own *crema* using the long-standing recipe:

Add 1 tablespoon live-culture buttermilk to 1 cup heavy cream slightly warmed to 80 degrees. Let stand until thickened (usually 6 to 12 hours) at warm room temperature, refrigerate until very thick. It's complexly delicious and nutty-tangy and much less expensive than a tub of *crème fraîche*. But it will quickly melt into a puddle when you spoon it on anything warm.

To avoid the quick melt, you can make your *crème fraîche* with the sour cream alternative: Mix equal parts of very good quality sour cream and heavy cream, let stand at warm room temperature until noticeably thicker (about 6 hours), then refrigerate for several hours until very thick. This version isn't as nutty as *crème fraîche*, but it's rich, tangy and substantial enough to stand up to warm foods.

Tostadas

A tostada is a crisp-fried tortilla, and these days they come in a wide array of sizes and contours: tiny two-bite rounds, diamond and triangle shapes, squares from small to large, the standard 5-inch disk. And lately no-fry, baked tostadas are storming the market; just recently, in Uruapan, Michoacan, I tasted a baked tostada made with sesame paste that was way better than good. Usually, baked tostadas are made from specially formulated tortillas that have a little oil in the dough, helping them toast crisp and tender, rather than hard. Making beautifully crisp baked tostadas at home depends on your finding just the right tortilla; out of twelve we tried only one was passable. My suggestion: buy the oven-baked ones or fry your own.

"Almost Oaxacan" Grilled Tostadas with Chorizo, Tangy Guacamole and Fresh Cheese

Tlayudas "Casi Oaxaqueñas" con Chorizo, Guacamole y Queso Fresco

SERVES 6 TO 8 AS A LIGHT MEAL

About 2 dozen corn tortillas, preferably ones from a local *tortillería*

FOR THE TANGY AVOCADO SAUCE

8 ounces (3 to 4 medium) tomatillos, husked, rinsed and roughly chopped

1 garlic clove, peeled and roughly chopped

Hot green chiles to taste (roughly 2 or 3 serranos, or 1 or 2 jalapeños), stemmed and roughly chopped

About ¼ cup (loosely packed) roughly chopped cilantro, thick lower stems cut off

1 large, ripe avocado, pitted, flesh scooped from skin and roughly chopped

Salt

FOR FINISHING THE TLAYUDAS

About 1 pound fresh Mexican chorizo sausage, casing removed

About 6 ounces Mexican *queso fresco* or other fresh cheese like salted pressed farmer's cheese or goat cheese, crumbled

About ¼ cup fresh-rendered, room temperature pork lard (preferably the kind with bits of brown cracklings in it—what's called *asiento* in Oaxaca), rendered bacon or chorizo fat or vegetable oil

Every night of the week on Libres in downtown Oaxaca, cooks throw the 15-inch leathery tlayuda tortillas directly on the coals (yes, no grill between coals and food). They crisp, helped along by a brushing of dark, roasty-tasting lard, while being topped with a splash of smoky salsa, runny-tangy guacamole, salty chorizo sausage or half-dried beef tasajo. And then they're folded in half and eaten sitting on a curb or wooden bench, with the dusty aroma of the historical neighborhood in the air. That's an experience you have only in Oaxaca.

You see, in that town, the specially made, leathery, pizza-size tlayuda tortillas have a whole culture built around them. They don't go stale as quickly as the softer, moister tortillas they called blandas, which has made tlayudas the tortilla choice for outings and trips, perfect for toasting or grilling to a fresh-tasting crispy crunchiness. But unless you live in a largely Oaxacan neighborhood here in the States, you likely won't be able to lay your hands on real, imported tlayudas.

But you can mimic the tlayuda approach with our tortillas, creating a facsimile. This facsimile satisfies in a different way, starting out as it does with an everyday-size tortilla (a puffy one from local tortilla factory gives the most tender crunch) that's grilled, brushed and topped, making it a great pass-around appetizer for a backyard party that has the grill at center stage. Think "light, grill-tinged, flavor-packed tostada" and you'll know intuitively what to expect.

1. *The tortillas.* If the tortillas are just made and very moist feeling, lay them out in a single layer and cover with a dish towel or napkin—the goal is to let them dry to leathery, so that they'll crisp thoroughly on the grill.

2. *Make the Tangy Avocado Sauce.* In a blender or food processor, combine the tomatillos, garlic, green chile, cilantro and ½ cup water. Process to a coarse puree. Add the avocado and pulse until nearly smooth. Pour into a salsa dish. If necessary, thin to a drizzleable consistency with a little more water (I often add 1 to 2 tablespoons more). Taste and season with salt, usually about 1 teaspoon.

3. *The chorizo and fresh cheese.* In a large (10-inch) skillet, cook the chorizo over medium heat, breaking up any clumps, until well browned, about 12 minutes. Scrape out onto a plate lined with paper towels to absorb excess fat. Transfer to a serving dish. Scoop the crumbled cheese into a serving dish.

4. *Grill and serve the* tlayudas. Turn on a gas grill to medium or light a charcoal grill and let the coals burn until medium-hot and covered with gray ash. When you're ready to serve, lay several tortillas on the grill and turn every 20 seconds or so until nearly crisp—depending on the heat of your fire this should take a couple of minutes. Brush the top of each tortilla completely (and a little generously) with the lard or oil. (For a more tender-flaky—but perhaps less authentic—texture, brush both sides with lard or oil and turn for another minute on the grill.) Sprinkle each with a tablespoon of chorizo. When the tortillas are completely crisp (they'll be richly browned underneath) and the chorizo is hot, remove them to a serving platter. Drizzle with the avocado sauce and sprinkle with the cheese. Let your guests enjoy the first round while you're making the remainder.

Oaxacan Pasilla Salsa
Salsa de Chile Pasilla Oaxaqueña

MAKES ABOUT 1 CUP

2 large dried Oaxacan pasilla chiles

OR 2 to 3 canned chipotle chiles *en adobo* (plus 1 tablespoon of their canning sauce)

8 ounces (3 to 4) medium tomatillos, husked and rinsed

3 garlic cloves, peeled and halved

Salt

Toni Sobel, my friend in Oaxaca, makes this iconic, smoky-sweet-tangy regional salsa by simmering tomatillos and garlic, then blending them with the Oaxacan cousin (at least flavor-wise) of the smoke-dried chipotle chile. Simple and perfect—which often go hand-in-hand in my experience. Except that some of you might like it even better if you roast the tomatillos and garlic to add deep, sweet, toasty flavor notes, too.

Working Ahead: The salsa can be made several days ahead. Refrigerate, covered, until shortly before serving.

If using dried Oaxacan pasilla chiles, toast them in a dry skillet over medium, turning them every few seconds for about a minute, until aromatic. Break off the stems and scoop into a small saucepan along with the tomatillos and garlic. Cover with water and simmer over medium heat just until the tomatillos turn from bright to olive green, 4 to 5 minutes. Drain and cool, then scoop the mixture into a blender or food processor. (If using canned chipotle chiles, remove them from the can and add them and their canning liquid to the blender or processor along with the tomatillos and garlic.) Cover and process until *almost* smooth. Pour into small dish. If very thick, stir in some water (I typically add 3 to 4 tablespoons). Taste and season with salt—usually a generous ½ teaspoon.

Easy Yucatan-Style Tostadas with "Pickled" Chicken and Black Beans

Panuchos Fáciles Yucatecos con Pollo en Escabeche y Frijoles Negros

MAKES 12 *PANUCHOS*, SERVING 4 AS A LIGHT MEAL

FOR THE CHICKEN

6   garlic cloves, unpeeled

¼   cup olive or vegetable oil

¼   cup vinegar (apple cider vinegar is common in Mexico)

⅔   cup chicken broth

    A pinch EACH of ground cloves and sugar

¼   teaspoon EACH ground black pepper and cinnamon (preferably Mexican *canela*)

½   teaspoon dried oregano, preferably Mexican

    Salt

6   (about 1¼ pounds total) boneless, skinless chicken thighs

1   medium red onion, sliced ¼ inch thick

FOR THE PANUCHOS

12 tostadas (crisp-fried or baked corn tortillas)

    About 2 cups coarsely mashed, seasoned, cooked black beans

4   hardboiled eggs, each cut into 6 slices (optional)

    A few tablespoons of chopped cilantro, for garnish

There's a classic version of panuchos *that by today's standards seems pretty involved. You carefully slit the side of perfect tortillas—the ones that have puffed like pita during baking—so that you can spread a thin smear of beans between the top and bottom layers, then you lay in a couple of hardboiled egg slices. After pressing the two sides together, you shallow-fry the whole thing without flipping (ensuring that it's crisp on the bottom, soft on the top). Finally, you top it with shredded chicken in tangy, aromatic* escabeche. *And you know what? After hours of work, they rarely come out perfect to my taste.*

Personally, I like the simpler approach better: a crisp corn tortilla topped with beans, maybe a slice or two of hardboiled egg, a big spoonful of simple chicken in escabeche. *That gives me time for roasting* xcatic *(banana) chile to add to the chicken, or to make a Roasted Tomato–Habanero Salsa (page 218). If you're not practiced at hardboiling eggs, here's the lowdown: Start the eggs in cold water, bring to a bare simmer, time 11 minutes, pour off the hot water, set under cold running water for 3 minutes, let stand 10 minutes.*

1. *Make the* escabeche *seasoning.* Cut a slit in the side of each garlic clove. Place in a microwaveable bowl, cover with plastic and microwave on high (100%) for 30 seconds. Cool until handleable, then slip off the paper skins. (For a more robust flavor, dry-roast unpeeled garlic cloves in a skillet over medium heat until soft and blotchy-black in places, about 15 minutes; cool and peel.)

One by one, drop the garlic cloves into a running blender or food processor, letting each get thoroughly chopped before adding the next. Scrape down the sides, then add the oil, vinegar, broth, cloves and sugar, spices, oregano and ½ teaspoon salt. Re-cover and process until the mixture is as smooth as you can get it.

2. *Cook the chicken and onion.* Pour the mixture into a large (10-inch) skillet and bring to a simmer. Nestle in the chicken. Gently simmer over medium-low until the chicken is cooked, usually about 18 minutes. Scoop the sliced onion into a bowl, then pour the hot cooked chicken mixture over. Cool, then remove the chicken and coarsely shred it. Stir into the onion mixture. Taste and season with additional salt if you think necessary.

3. *Make the* panuchos. Heat the beans in a microwave or small saucepan over medium; stir in enough water to give the beans the consistency of hummus. Smear a portion of the beans onto each tortilla, leaving a ½ inch uncovered on the edge. Lay 2 slices of the hardboiled eggs (if using) on top of the beans, then spoon about ⅓ cup of the chicken *escabeche* (either room temperature or warmed) on top. I think a sprinkling of chopped cilantro is beautiful and tasty.

Habanero Hot Sauce (for bottling)
Salsa Habanera (para embotellar)
MAKES ABOUT 3 CUPS

5   garlic cloves, unpeeled

½   cup peeled, roughly chopped carrot (you'll need 1 medium carrot)

½   cup white onion, roughly chopped (you'll need about ½ of a medium onion)

5   ounces (12 to 15) fresh orange habanero chiles, stemmed

1   cup apple cider vinegar

About 2 teaspoons salt

¼   teaspoon sugar

If you've made it all the way through habanero's explosive heat to that incomparable fruity, tropical habanero flavor, you're probably a card-carrying member of the habanero fan club. Still, to get to that seductive flavor you have to deal with the heat. Though in this hot sauce the habanero heat is a little less hot, tempered by carrot, whose orange-habanero color tricks the eye and sweetens the palate. It's easy to make in big batches, making it the perfect gift for picante-loving friends.

Working Ahead: As with most vinegar-based hot sauces, this one can be stored for a month or more in the refrigerator.

Roast the garlic in a skillet over medium heat, turning regularly until soft and blackened in spots, 10 to 15 minutes. Cool and peel.

In a small saucepan, combine the carrot, onion, habaneros, vinegar and 1 cup water. Bring to a boil, partially cover and simmer over medium-low heat until the carrots are thoroughly tender, about 15 minutes. Pour into a blender jar, add the roasted garlic, salt and sugar. Let cool for a few minutes, then blend until smooth. Thin with a little additional water (I often use another ¼ cup) if you think your hot sauce is too thick. Taste (very gingerly) and season with additional salt if you think necessary. Pour into jars or bottles and store in the refrigerator until you're ready to add some dazzle to a dish.

Sandal-Shaped Corn *Masa* Cakes with Black Beans, Salsa and Aged Cheese
Huaraches

MAKES 8 *HUARACHES*, SERVING 4 AS A LIGHT MEAL

1 pound fresh corn *masa* for tortillas

OR 1¾ cups dried *masa harina* for tortillas (such as Maseca brand) reconstituted with 1 cup plus 2 tablespoons hot tap water

Salt

¾ cup seasoned cooked black beans (either canned or homemade), drained

About 1½ cups Roasted Tomatillo Salsa (page 208), Three-Chile Salsa (page 190) or practically any other salsa

About ⅔ cup grated Mexican *queso añejo* or other garnishing cheese like Romano or Parmesan

3 or 4 radishes, thinly sliced

About ½ cup vegetable oil

⅔ cup chopped white onion

½ cup (loosely packed) chopped cilantro (thick bottom stems cut off)

If you're thinking of Mexico City's giant edible huaraches—pressed out by street vendors to be nearly 18 inches long and a foot wide—you'll see as you read through this recipe that I don't encourage such feats at home. First, I don't have a huge Mexico City huarache press. And second, I'd rather eat a turnover-size snack than a Guinness World Records–inspired gut buster.

No matter what the dimensions, huaraches are all basically the same: a sandal-shaped fat corn tortilla filled with a thin-thin layer of bean paste and baked until crusty on a hot griddle. When your (or someone else's) mouth is watering for a gutsy, delicious bite, you reheat the huarache on an oily griddle, crisping it nicely, then topping it with salsa, a grating of sharp cheese, cilantro, crunchy white onion and radish. A little chorizo or slivers of grilled steak make a huarache more filling; thin-sliced iberico ham or chopped shrimp (or crab or lobster) make it stunning.

1. *Make the* **huaraches.** In a medium bowl, mix together the *masa* (fresh or reconstituted) and ¾ teaspoon salt. If necessary, knead a few drops of water into the *masa* to give it the consistency of soft cookie dough. Cover with plastic wrap. In a food processor, process the beans until completely smooth. Stir in a little water, if necessary, to give them the same consistency as the *masa*.

Heat a well-seasoned or nonstick griddle or heavy skillet over medium. Divide the *masa* into 8 portions; cover with plastic. One by one, form and bake the *huaraches*: Line a tortilla press with two pieces of plastic cut to fit the press. Roll a portion of *masa* into an egg shape, then press your thumb into the middle to make a long, deep, wide hole. Spoon in 2 teaspoons of the beans, then pinch the dough up around the beans to completely enclose it. Roll into a cigar shape about 5 inches long. Between the sheets of plastic, *gently* press out into a 6-inch oval. Peel off the top sheet of plastic. Flip—uncovered side down—onto the fingers of one hand and gently peel off the second piece of plastic. In one flowing movement, roll the *huarache* off your hand and onto the griddle or skillet. After about 1 minute (when the *huarache* releases itself from the hot surface), flip and bake for another 2 or 3 minutes until lightly browned. Remove to a plate and cover lightly with plastic.

2. *Finish the* **huaraches.** Set out the tomatillo (or other) salsa, grated cheese and radishes. Pour enough oil onto your griddle or skillet to create a generous coating. Set over medium to medium-high heat. When quite hot, lay on as many *huaraches* as will fit in a single layer. When crisp underneath—about 1 ½ minutes—flip over. Spread about 1½ tablespoons salsa over the surface of the *huarache*, then dust with cheese. Let crisp underneath for a minute or two, then slide onto a serving platter or individual plates and sprinkle with the onion, cilantro and radishes. (If working in batches, go ahead and serve the first finished huaraches while you finish the remainder.) Pass the extra salsa for your guests to add as they wish.

SANDAL-SHAPED CORN *MASA* CAKES WITH BLACK BEANS, SALSA AND AGED CHEESE

Roasted Tomatillo Salsa
Salsa Verde

MAKES ABOUT 2 CUPS

1 pound (6 to 8 medium) tomatillos, husked and rinsed

Fresh hot green chiles to taste (3 to 4 serranos, or 1 or 2 jalapeños), stemmed

15 to 20 sprigs of fresh cilantro (thick bottom stems cut off), roughly chopped

1 small white onion, finely chopped

Salt

Though most Mexican food lovers in the United States think "tomato" when salsa is mentioned, tomatillos tend to be the go-to ingredient in Mexico: their tanginess adds brightness to salsa. And, if those tomatillos (and the green chiles) are roasted, there's a deeper, sweeter complexity in each mouthful. Honestly, if I could only have one salsa in my life, this would be it.

Working Ahead: *Feel free to make the tomatillo–green chile base several days ahead and refrigerate it, covered. Just before serving, correct the consistency with water, stir in the onion and cilantro, and season with salt.*

Note: *For a super-bright-tasting, very quick salsa, coarsely puree quartered tomatillos with all the rest of the ingredients and a little water in a food processor. Use right away.*

Roast the tomatillos and chile(s) on a rimmed baking sheet 4 inches below a very hot broiler, until blotchy black and softening (they'll be turning from lime green to olive), about 5 minutes. Flip them over and roast the other side. Cool, then transfer everything to a blender, including all the delicious juice the tomatillos have exuded during roasting. Add the cilantro and ½ cup water, then blend to a coarse puree. Scoop into a serving dish. Rinse the onion under cold water, then shake to remove excess moisture. Stir into the salsa and season with salt, usually a teaspoon.

TINY TOSTADAS WITH CHIAPAS-STYLE STEAK TARTAR
(PAGE 210)

Tiny Tostadas with Chiapas-Style Steak Tartar
Tostaditas de Carne Tártara (aka Carne Apache)

MAKES ABOUT 50 SMALL (2½-INCH) TOSTADAS, SERVING 12 TO 15 AS A SNACK OR PASS-AROUND APPETIZER

3   tablespoons vegetable oil

4   (about 1 ounce total) dried guajillo chiles, stemmed, seeded and torn into flat pieces

4   garlic cloves, peeled

⅔   cup fresh lime juice

    Salt

1¼ pound steak (practically anything works here, from tenderloin to strip steak and sirloin), chopped into ⅛-inch pieces or coarsely ground

½   medium red onion, cut into ¼-inch pieces

1   medium-large red-ripe tomato, cut into ¼-inch pieces

½   cup (loosely packed) chopped cilantro (thick bottom stems cut off), plus a little extra for garnish

    About 60 small (about 2½-inch) tostadas (see headnote)

    About ½ cup grated Mexican *queso añejo* or other garnishing cheese like Romano or Parmesan

Odd as it may seem, this tartar is (or can be) street food in Mexico . . . even in Chicago, sold from coolers on the sidelines of Sunday morning soccer matches in some neighborhoods. It's basically just a beef ceviche, famous from the southern Mexican state of Chiapas, where it's called carne tártara, as well as in the west and north-central sections of Mexico, where it typically goes by carne apache, conjuring images of less-civilized, raw-meat-eating days. My version weaves in red chile for color (beef cured only in lime can look gray) and sweet-earthy flavor.

I think the best tartars are made from hand-chopped beef, but that requires a very sharp knife, a fair amount of practice and a plain-old determination. If you choose to grind your meat, use a meat grinder fitted with the coarse die (for health reasons, I'd stay away from pre-ground beef for serving raw) or a food processor, first cutting the meat into ¾-inch pieces, partially freezing, then chopping in the processor in small batches. Whether chopping by hand, grinder or processor, you'll get the nicest-looking tartar if you freeze the meat for about 45 minutes before chopping to firm it up.

Carne Tártara is delicious as a pass-around appetizer piled onto little tostadas or sturdy chips (homemade or perhaps from a local taquería or tortilla factory). The more rustic texture of two-bite, oven-baked tostadas is delicious; simply cut good-quality tortillas into small rounds or triangles, spray both sides with oil and bake at 325 degrees until completely crisp. Many Mexican groceries are now selling delicious oven-baked tostadas in several sizes, produced in Mexico.

---

1. *Make the red chile marinade.* Measure the oil into a medium skillet and set over medium heat. When hot, add the flat chile pieces a few at a time, turning them until they are aromatic and have changed slightly in color (they lighten in color on the inside), about 2 to 3 seconds per side. Remove to a blender jar. Add the garlic to the pan and cook, stirring and turning regularly, until soft and richly browned, about 2 minutes. Scrape in with the chiles and add the lime juice and 1 teaspoon salt. Blend until smooth, then press through a medium-mesh strainer into a large bowl. Cool.

2. *Finish the* carne tártara. Add the meat to the red chile marinade and stir to thoroughly combine. Scoop the onion into a strainer, run under cold water, shake off the excess, then add it to the meat mixture along with the tomatoes and cilantro. Stir everything together, then taste and season with additional salt if you think the tartar needs it.

3. *Serve.* Scoop a little *carne tártara* onto each tostada, sprinkle with *queso añejo* and cilantro, and carry to your guests.

Smooth Árbol-Tomato Salsa
Salsa de Chile de Árbol y Jitomate
MAKES ABOUT 2 CUPS

1   pound (2 medium-large round or 6 to 8 plum) ripe tomatoes, quartered

5 to 8 dried árbol chiles, stemmed

3   large garlic cloves, peeled and halved

¼   teaspoon black pepper, preferably freshly ground

A pinch of cloves, preferably freshly ground

½   teaspoon dried oregano, preferably Mexican

1   tablespoon cider vinegar

Salt

½   small white onion, finely chopped (optional)

The raucous-tasting árbol chile salsa made with roasted tomatillos and garlic is boldly, thrillingly perfect, but not the only thing that chile has to offer. Here we're talking the kinder, gentler árbol, mellowed by simmering with tomatoes and garlic, nudged and cajoled by a couple of spices. Not that the chiles lose that legendary spiciness that hovers over every-thing—it's just spiciness dressed differently.

   Working ahead: This salsa will last (even improve) in the refrigerator for several days—just make sure to keep it well covered.

Place the tomatoes, chiles and garlic in a medium (3-quart) saucepan and just barely cover with water. Bring to a boil, partially cover and simmer over medium-low heat until the tomatoes are very tender but not falling apart, about 10 minutes. With a slotted spoon transfer the tomatoes, chiles and garlic to a blender (save the cooking liquid) and add the black pepper, clove, oregano and vinegar. Pulse the machine until everything is reduced to a relatively smooth puree.

Pour the puree into a serving dish and let cool to room temperature. Stir in enough of the cooking liquid to give the salsa an easily spoonable consistency (typically about 2 tablespoons), since this biting salsa is usually made a little soupy. Taste and season with salt, usually about 1 teaspoon. Scoop the chopped onion into a strainer, if using, rinse under cold water, shake off the excess moisture, then stir into the salsa. Your salsa is ready to serve.

Black Bean Tamales with Fresh Goat Cheese
Tamal de Frijoles Negros con Queso de Cabra

MAKES ABOUT 15 TAMALES

1   8-ounce package dried corn husks

1   cup drained, cooked, seasoned black beans (homemade are best, but canned will work), cooking liquid reserved from homemade beans

5   ounces (a scant ⅔ cup) fresh, rich-tasting pork lard or vegetable shortening (we've had good luck using Spectrum Organic All Vegetable Shortening), soft but not runny

½   teaspoon baking powder

    Salt

1   pound (about 2 cups) fresh coarse-ground corn *masa* for tamales

    OR 1¾ cups dried *masa harina* for tamales reconstituted with 1 cup plus 2 tablespoons hot water

    About ⅔ cup cooking liquid from the beans, chicken broth or water for thinning the *masa* and the optional second beating

8   ounces fresh goat cheese

I know most of us in the United States don't think of tamales as having pureed black beans in the batter or goat cheese as the filling, but luckily Mexico's not bound by our (rather narrow) constraints. As long as corn masa's the main batter ingredient (and, for some, lard is the shortening), there's little that tamales don't welcome . . . from achiote to chocolate to zucchini. Black beans give a satisfying moistness and bean-y earthiness; goat cheese offers a bolder-flavored freshness than you'll typically get in Mexico's queso fresco or requesón, but it's in the same tasty ballpark. To sum it all up: these are really good tamales—real crowd pleasers—especially served with Three-Chile Salsa (page 190).

Working Ahead: These tamales can be made several days ahead. Cool, wrap tightly and refrigerate. They can be frozen for about a month. Defrost in the refrigerator overnight, then reheat in a steamer.

1. *Soak the corn husks.* In a heat-proof bowl, pour boiling water over the corn husks. Lay a plate on the top to keep the husks submerged. Let then rehydrate for a couple of hours until pliable.

2. *Prepare the batter.* In a food processor, puree the beans. Measure the lard (or shortening), baking powder and *2 teaspoons* salt into the bowl of an electric mixer. Using the paddle attachment if there is one, beat on medium-high until light in texture, about a minute. In three additions, add the fresh or reconstituted *masa*, fully incorporating each addition before adding the next. Scrape in the black beans and beat to incorporate. Reduce the speed to medium-low, and slowly dribble in enough of the reserved bean cooking liquid, chicken broth or water (usually about ⅓ cup) to give the mixture the consistency of cake batter. Raise the speed to medium-high again and beat for another minute. The mixture has been beaten enough when it's so fluffy that a ½ teaspoon dollop floats in a cup of cold water. If time allows, refrigerate the batter for 1 hour to firm it up for an optional second beating.

3. *Prepare the filling, set up the steamer for tamales.* Break the goat cheese into small pieces, each about the size of a small marble. Pour 1½ inches of water in the bottom of your steamer: you'll use it to steam 15 tamales later; best if it's at least 10 inches in diameter with 6 inches of depth for standing up the tamales, like a small Mexican *tamal* steamer, large vegetable steamer or deep Chinese steamer. Drain the husks, then choose 15 of the largest, most pliable ones—they should be at least 6 inches long and 6 inches wide (at the widest end). If there aren't enough large husks, you can overlap smaller ones. Use several of the longest remaining corn husks to tear into ¼-inch strips for tying the tamales. Line the steamer basket with some of the remaining corn husks.

4. *Make the tamales.* For the lightest tamales, re-beat the refrigerated batter, slowly adding an extra ¼ cup bean cooking liquid, water or chicken broth. (For this to be effective, the batter will need at least an hour's refrigeration to firm up, allowing for the broth's addition without becoming too soft.)

One at a time, form the tamales: On the wide end of one of the large husks, spread ¼ cup of the batter into a 4-inch square, leaving 1½ inches uncovered on the narrow end and at least ¾ inch on each of the long sides. Lay a portion of the goat cheese pieces down the center of the batter. Pick up the two long sides of the husk and bring them together, encasing the filling with the batter. Roll the two long sides you're holding around the *tamal* in the same direction. (If the husk is small, feel free to roll the whole thing in another husk.) Fold up the empty 1½ inches to form a "bottom" on which the *tamal* will stand while steaming; tie it in place with one of the corn husk strips. Stand each of the tamales in the steamer while you form the remaining tamales. Lay extra husks over the open tops of the tamales (don't worry about covering them completely—they won't get soggy as they steam).

5. *Steam the tamales.* Cover the steamer and set over high heat. When the steam comes puffing out, reduce the heat to medium and cook until the batter comes free from the husk, about 1½ hours. (Remove a *tamal* from the steamer to test it. Even when done, the *tamal* itself will seem very soft.) Make sure that the water doesn't boil away; if it becomes necessary to replenish the water, add *boiling* water.

Turn off the heat under the steamer and let stand, covered, about 15 minutes for the tamales to firm up.

Mexican Fresh Cheese
Queso Fresco Mexicano

MAKES ABOUT 1 POUND

1   gallon whole or 2% milk—prefer-
    ably from a small local dairy with
    grass-fed cows; the richer the
    flavor, the better the cheese

2   cups buttermilk

1   teaspoon citric acid (aka sour
    salt, available in the kosher
    section of well-stocked grocery
    stores)

    OR 1 cup fresh lime juice

1   teaspoon salt (pure fine-ground
    sea salt works best here)

MEXICAN FRESH CHEESE

Making cheese sounds like such a stretch for home cooks, doesn't it? That's exactly what I thought until I was motivated to try it by the lack of truly fresh Mexican fresh cheese—queso fresco—most places in the United States. Plus I'd fallen in love with Farmer's Creamery milk—a local brand of unhomogenized, batch-pasteurized organic milk from grass-fed cows—and I wanted to celebrate its true-milk flavor everywhere I could. And I found this type of cheesemaking not very difficult. All you need is a reliable thermometer that goes as low as room temperature; check it for accuracy by testing it in boiling water (212 degrees).

To create the richer flavor of artisanal Mexican queso fresco, I culture the milk for several hours using buttermilk as a starter. When time is of the essence, feel free to skip the culturing step. Which I regularly do when I'm turning out a batch of fresh cheese along with dinner, to serve as dessert with a drizzle of honey and fresh figs or raspberries. (I don't salt fresh cheese when serving it for dessert.)

Working Ahead: Once the cheese is finished, it needs to chill for an hour or so to firm up. Covered and refrigerated the cheese will last 5 days or so.

1. *Culture the milk.* Pour the milk into a large (at least 8-quart) pot—I typically use an 8-quart enameled cast iron Dutch oven or a stainless steel 12-quart stock pot. Stir in the buttermilk, attach an accurate thermometer that registers temperatures as low as 75 degrees and set the pot over medium heat. When the temperature reaches 75 degrees, turn off the heat, cover the pot and let stand 3 or 4 hours.

2. *Set the curd.* If using citric acid, stir it into ¼ cup cool water, continuing to stir until dissolved. Uncover the pot, set over medium heat and stir in the dissolved citric acid or the fresh lime juice. You will immediately see small curds start to form. Every couple of minutes, stir slowly, gently and thoroughly over the entire bottom of the pot until the milk reaches 195 degrees—it'll take about 20 minutes. At this point the curds will very obviously be floating in the milky-transparent whey.

Remove from the heat and let stand 5 minutes without stirring for all the curd to rise to the top.

3. *Drain the curd from the whey.* Wet a large piece of cheesecloth and drape it into a large colander. Set the colander in the sink. Using a large slotted spoon or a fine-mesh skimmer, carefully ladle all of the curd into the colander. Gather the cheesecloth up around the curd and gently squeeze to expel a bit more whey. Unwrap the curd onto a plate, break it up and sprinkle with *1 teaspoon* of the salt. Work in the salt with a spoon or your fingers.

4. *Finish the cheese.* Gather the cheese curds into a 1-inch-thick disk, transfer to a plate, cover and refrigerate until thoroughly chilled.

SEPARATING FRESH CHEESE CURDS FROM WHEY   STRAINING EXCESS WHEY FROM CURDS

Yucatecan "Pudding" Tamales with *Achiote* and Chicken
Tamales Colados

MAKES ABOUT 10 LARGE TAMALES

1   pound banana leaves, defrosted if frozen

½   small white onion, thinly sliced

3   sprigs of *epazote* (or a handful of cilantro if *epazote* can't be found), plus extra leaves to use when forming the tamales

    Salt

2   large (about 1¼ pounds) chicken breast halves with bone and skin intact

2   teaspoons store-bought *achiote* paste

1½ pounds (about 3 cups) fresh corn *masa* for tortillas

    OR 2¼ cups dried *masa harina* for tortillas

1   medium-large ripe tomato

3½ cups chicken broth

4   ounces (½ cup) rich-tasting pork lard or vegetable shortening (we've had pretty good luck using Spectrum Organic All Vegetable Shortening)

    About 1½ cups salsa (the classic for these tamales is the Roasted Tomato–Habanero Salsa, page 218), for serving

These are one of the half-dozen classic styles of tamales in the Yucatan, and they always take first-timers off guard. Their texture is almost pudding-like because the batter—the mixture of corn masa, fat and broth—is cooked on the stovetop, stirred and stirred until it resembles a very fine-textured polenta. As it cools, that batter sets up as polenta does, then gets formed, filled, wrapped and briefly steamed, creating an almost ethereal experience for anyone who puts in a fork. Cooking corn masa on the stovetop is standard operating procedure in the Yucatecan kitchen, and that procedure is used here a second time to thicken the achiote-burnished sauce that binds the chicken filling.

1. *Prepare the leaves.* Unfold the banana leaves and trim the thin hard strip on the side of the leaf (where the leaf connected to the central stalk). Cut into ten 12-inch segments, choosing sections that are relatively unbroken. From the widest of the extra pieces, tear twenty ½-inch-wide strips for tying the tamales; set aside the leftovers for lining the steamer. To make the banana leaf pieces pliable, either steam them for 20 minutes or pass each one briefly over an open flame until it turns from dull and stiff to soft and shiny.

2. *Make the filling.* Measure 4 cups water into a medium-size (3-quart) saucepan, add the onion, *1 sprig* of the *epazote* (or a *third* of the cilantro) and 1 teaspoon salt. Set over medium-high heat. When the liquid comes to a boil, add the chicken breast halves, lower the heat to medium, cover and simmer until just cooked through, 10 to 15 minutes.

Remove the chicken from its cooking liquid and set aside. Strain the liquid (discard the solids), skim off any fat that rises to the top, then measure 2 cups of the liquid into a blender jar. (Save any that's left over for another preparation.) Set the pan aside.

Add the *achiote* and ½ cup of the fresh *masa* or dried *masa harina* to the blender jar. Blend until smooth, then strain through a medium-mesh strainer into the saucepan used for cooking the chicken. Whisk constantly over medium heat for several minutes as the rusty-red liquid comes to a simmer and thickens (it'll be a little softer than a just-opened can of cream soup). Taste and season with salt, usually about ¾ teaspoon. Scrape into a bowl to cool, stirring occasionally.

Skin, bone and coarsely shred the chicken breast. Core the tomato and slice into 10 rounds. Pick 10 large leaves from the remaining 2 sprigs of *epazote* (or remaining cilantro).

3. *Make the batter.* If using *masa harina*, mix the remaining *1¾ cups* of it with 1 cup plus 2 tablespoons hot tap water and let stand 10 minutes to reconstitute

Place *half* of the remaining *masa* (reconstituted or fresh) in your blender, along with *1¾ cups* of the broth. Blend until smooth, then strain through a medium-mesh strainer into a large (4-quart) saucepan. Repeat with the remaining *masa* and broth. Set the saucepan with the *masa* mixture over medium heat, add the lard (or vegetable shortening), then whisk constantly for several minutes as the mixture comes to a boil and thickens enough to hold its shape well in a spoon. Remove from the heat, taste and season with salt, usually 1½ teaspoons. Cool completely, stirring occasionally.

4. *Form and steam the tamales.* Set up a steamer (a Mexican *tamal* steamer, large vegetable steamer or deep Chinese steamer will give you the greatest surface over which to distribute the tamales) with water in the bottom and the steaming compartment lined with some of the leftover banana leaves. One by one form the tamales: Spread ½ cup of the corn *masa* on a banana leaf piece (shiny side up) in a 4 x 8-inch rectangle that extends from the center of the leaf to one of the sides. Onto the *masa* in the center of the leaf, spoon 2 tablespoons of the *achiote*-flavored sauce, 2 tablespoons chicken, a slice of tomato and leaf of *epazote* (or a few leaves of cilantro). Fold the uncovered *masa* (and its portion of leaf) over the filling, to cover it. Fold the uncovered stretch of banana leaf over the top, creating a long, thin package. Fold the two ends under the *tamal*, then, in each direction, secure the banana-leaf package with a banana-leaf string.

When all are done, arrange the tamales in a single or double layer in the steamer. Top with a few more of the leftover leaves. Set over high heat, and, when steam comes puffing out, reduce the heat to medium or so, to keep the water at steady boil. Steam for 1 to 1½ hours, until the *masa* comes free from the leaf. (Don't be alarmed that the tamales will be soft; they firm as they cool a little.) Make sure the water doesn't boil away; if it becomes necessary to replenish the water, add *boiling* water.

To give your tamales a nice presentation, untie them, fold back the leaves, tucking them under to form a little boat, spoon some salsa over the top and they're ready to go.

Roasted Tomato–Habanero Salsa
Chiltomate
MAKES ABOUT 1½ CUPS

1 pound (2 medium-large round or 6 to 8 plum) ripe tomatoes

1 habanero chile, stemmed

1 small onion, sliced ¼ inch thick

About ½ (loosely packed) cup chopped cilantro (thick bottom stems cut off)

Salt

As a broad generalization, the further south you go in Mexico, the roastier the salsa ingredients become. And though Yucatecan cooking can be light in many aspects, the age-old rustic preparations all seem tinged by the fire, whether it's the charring of chiles for the chilmole seasoning paste or roasting whole onions in the embers to accompany classic pork poc chuc. Or making salsa: in this Yucatan take on central Mexico's mortar-made salsa de molcajete, embers are replaced by a broiler. And, as is classic, the chile is habanero.

   Working Ahead: *This salsa is best made within several hours of serving.*

1. *Roast the tomatoes, chile and onion.* On a rimmed baking sheet, lay out the tomatoes and habanero. Break the onion into rings or pieces and scatter on the sheet. Roast everything about 4 inches below a very hot broiler until the tomatoes are soft and blackened on one side, about 6 minutes. Flip the tomatoes and chile, and stir the onion, turning the pieces as much as possible. Slide back under the broiler and roast until the tomatoes are soft and blackened on the other side (about 5 minutes more). Cool, then pull the blackened peels from the tomatoes.

2. *Finish the salsa.* Transfer the tomatoes (along with the juice on the baking sheet) and chile to a food processor. Pulse until roughly chopped, then run until the mixture is a coarse puree. Scrape into a salsa dish and stir in enough water to give your salsa an easily spoonable consistency, typically about 2 tablespoons. Chop the roasted onion into small pieces and scrape into the salsa along with the cilantro. Taste and season with salt, usually about a scant teaspoon. Salsa's ready.

PORK *PICADILLO* SWEET CORN TAMALES (PAGE 220)

Pork *Picadillo* Sweet Corn Tamales
Tamales de Elote con Picadillo
MAKES ABOUT 12 MEDIUM-SIZE TAMALES

FOR THE PICADILLO *FILLING*

2 tablespoons vegetable oil

1 medium white onion, cut into ¼-inch pieces

1 pound ground pork—best with coarse-ground pork, often called "chili grind" or "stir-fry" pork

4 garlic cloves, peeled and finely chopped

A generous ½ teaspoon EACH ground cinnamon and black pepper

¾ of a 28-ounce can diced tomatoes in juice (preferably fire roasted)

A generous 1 tablespoon vinegar (apple cider vinegar is a good choice)

⅓ cup raisins

⅓ cup coarsely chopped roasted peanuts or toasted almonds

Salt

FOR THE TAMALES

1 1-pound package banana leaves, defrosted if frozen

The kernels cut from 2 large cleaned ears sweet corn (about 2½ cups)

1 pound (about 2 cups) fresh coarse-ground corn *masa* for tamales

OR about 1¾ cups dried *masa harina* for tamales reconstituted with 1 cup plus 2 tablespoons hot water, then allowed to cool

There are first tastes you never forget. The flavor of local strawberries made into shortcake or pasta with homemade pesto or fresh-caught fish cooked on a campfire. For me, one of the most vivid is a fresh corn tamal filled with sweet-and-savory pork picadillo eaten at a market stall in the old downtown Veracruz market. The stall was makeshift and tiny, a few stools crowded in front of a counter that supported a gas burner on top of which was a steamer full of fragrance. Banana leaves, earthy corn, sweet spices. The pudding-like texture of the sweet tamal dough encased the savory spiced pork with raisins and nuts. And I was seduced.

The corn is different here, but that didn't stop me from creating a very close facsimile.

1. *Make the* picadillo. In a very large (12-inch) skillet over medium-high, heat the oil. Add the onion and meat broken into small clumps. Cook, stirring regularly and continuing to break up the meat into smaller clumps, until richly browned, about 15 to 20 minutes. Add the garlic and spices, stir for a minute, then add the tomatoes (and some of their juice), vinegar and raisins. Simmer, stirring regularly, until the mixture is thick enough to hold its shape when scooped up. Remove from the heat, add the peanuts (or almonds) and season with salt, usually about 1½ teaspoons. Cool.

2. *Prepare the banana leaves.* Unfold the leaves and trim off the thin hard strip on the side of each one, where the leaf connected to the central stalk. Cut into twelve 12-inch pieces, choosing sections that are relatively unbroken. From the widest of the extra pieces, tear twenty-four ½-inch-wide strips for tying the tamales; set aside the leftovers for lining the steamer. To make the banana leaf pieces pliable, either steam them for 20 minutes or pass each one briefly over an open flame until it turns from dull and stiff to soft and shiny.

3. *Mix the batter.* Scoop the corn into a food processor and process to a medium-coarse puree. Add the fresh or reconstituted *masa* to the corn, along with the lard (or one of its stand-ins), sugar, salt and baking powder. Pulse the processor several times making sure that all the lumps are broken up, then let it run for 1 minute, until the mixture is light and homogeneous.

4. *Form and steam the tamales.* Set up a steamer (a Mexican *tamal* steamer, large vegetable steamer or deep Chinese steamer will give you the greatest surface over which to distribute the tamales) with water in the bottom and the steaming compartment lined with some of the leftover banana leaves. One by one form the tamales: Spread ⅓ cup of the corn

4 ounces (½ cup) rich-tasting pork lard, vegetable shortening (we've had pretty good luck using Spectrum Organic All Vegetable Shortening) or unsalted butter, cut into ½-inch bits and slightly softened

2 tablespoons sugar

½ teaspoons salt

1½ teaspoons baking powder

masa on a banana leaf piece (shiny side up) in a 4 x 8-inch rectangle that extends from the center of the leaf to one of the sides. Spoon ¼ cup of the filling onto the *masa* that is in the center of the leaf, then fold the uncovered *masa* (and its portion of leaf) over the filling, to cover it. Fold the uncovered stretch of leaf over the top, creating a long, thin package. Fold the two ends under the *tamal*, then, in each direction, secure the banana-leaf package with a banana-leaf string.

When all are done, arrange the tamales in a single or double layer in the steamer. Top with a few more of the leftover leaves. Set over high heat, and, when steam comes puffing out, reduce the heat to medium or so, to keep the water at a nice boil. Steam for 1 to 1½ hours, until the *masa* comes free from the leaf. (Don't be alarmed that the tamales will be soft; they firm as they cool.) Make sure the water doesn't boil away; if it becomes necessary to replenish the water, add *boiling* water.

STEAMING TAMALES

Roasted Garlic Tamales with Ricotta and Swiss Chard
Tamales de Requesón y Acelgas

MAKES ABOUT 24 TAMALES

1   8-ounce package dried corn husks

1   head garlic, cloves broken apart, unpeeled

10   ounces (1¼ cups) fresh, rich-tasting pork lard or vegetable shortening (we've had pretty good luck using Spectrum Organic All Vegetable Shortening), soft but not runny

1   teaspoon baking powder

     Salt

2   pounds (about 4 cups) fresh coarse-ground corn *masa* for tamales

     OR 3½ cups dried *masa harina* for tamales reconstituted with 2¼ cups hot water

1   cup chicken broth, plus an additional ½ cup for the optional second beating

     About 1 pound (an extra-large bunch) Swiss chard

1½   cups (about 12 ounces) ricotta, farmer's cheese or yogurt cheese (see headnote)

These tamales are the perfect combination of traditional and modern: classic, sensual texture, fragrant with earthy-sweet corn and roasty garlic, filled with good-natured ricotta and rancorous chard. Every time I've served these tamales, they command more attention than anything else on the table. For even moister, almost pudding-like tamales, you can replace ½ cup of the broth in the batter with 1 cup ricotta.

I'm referring here to ricotta like they do it in Mexico and Italy—dry, not creamed. Unless I've bought Italian-style (what's often called "hand dipped") ricotta in the States, I usually scoop it into a strainer and press out as much liquid as I can. Or I use yogurt cheese that I make by pouring a quart of plain yogurt into a cheesecloth-lined strainer set over a bowl, covering it and refrigerating for 24 hours.

These are spectacularly delicious served with Creamy Roasted Jalapeño Salsa (page 185).

Working Ahead: *Though these tamales can be made a couple of days ahead, they don't freeze very well because of the cheese and chard. Keep them in the refrigerator well covered, until you're ready to reheat them in the steamer.*

---

1. *Soak the corn husks.* In a heat-proof bowl, pour boiling water over the corn husks. Lay a plate on the top to keep the husks submerged. Let them rehydrate for a couple of hours until pliable.

2. *Prepare the batter.* Roast the unpeeled garlic cloves in an ungreased skillet over medium heat, turning frequently, until soft and blackened in places, 10 to 15 minutes. Let cool, then peel and finely chop. Measure the lard (or shortening), baking powder and *2 teaspoons* salt into the bowl of an electric mixer. Add *half* of the garlic. Using the paddle attachment if there is one, beat on medium-high until light in texture, about a minute. In three additions, add the fresh or reconstituted *masa*, fully incorporating each addition before adding the next. Reduce the speed to medium-low, and slowly dribble in enough broth (usually about 1 cup) to give the mixture the consistency of cake batter. Raise the speed to medium-high again and beat for another minute. The mixture has been beaten enough when it's so fluffy that a ½ teaspoon dollop floats in a cup of cold water. If time allows, refrigerate the batter for 1 hour to firm it up for an optional second beating.

3. *Prepare the filling, set up the steamer for tamales.* Pour 1½ inches of water in the bottom of a steamer: you'll use it to steam 24 tamales later;

best if it's about 10 inches in diameter with 6 inches of depth for standing up the tamales, like a medium-size Mexican *tamal* steamer, large vegetable steamer or deep Chinese steamer. Bring to a boil. Cut out (or pull out) the central rib from each Swiss chard leaf. Cut crosswise into ½-inch strips. In the steamer, steam the chard until barely tender, about 4 minutes, then spread into a thin layer on a plate to cool quickly. Mix with the remaining garlic and sprinkle with salt. Taste and add more salt if you think necessary. Stir a little salt into the ricotta.

Drain the husks, then choose 24 of the largest, most pliable ones—they should be at least 6 inches long and 6 inches wide (at the widest end). If there aren't enough large husks, you can overlap smaller ones. Use several of the longest remaining corn husks to tear into ¼-inch strips for tying the tamales. Line the steamer basket with some of the remaining corn husks.

4. *Make the tamales.* For the lightest tamales, re-beat the refrigerated batter, slowly adding an extra ½ cup broth. (For this to be effective, the batter will need at least an hour's refrigeration to firm up, thus allowing for the broth's addition without becoming too soft.)

One at a time, form the tamales: On the wide end of one of the large husks, spread ¼ cup of the batter into a 4-inch square, leaving 1½ inches uncovered on the narrow end and at least ¾ inch on each of the long sides. Distribute a generous tablespoon of the chard and about 2 teaspoons of ricotta down the center of the batter. Pick up the two long sides of the husk and bring them together, encasing the filling with the batter. Roll the two long sides you're holding around the *tamal* in the same direction. (If the husk is small, feel free to roll the whole thing in another husk.) Fold up the empty 1½ inches to form a "bottom" on which the *tamal* will stand while steaming; tie it in place with one of the corn husk strips. Stand each of the tamales in the steamer while you form the remaining tamales. Lay extra husks over the open tops of the tamales (don't worry about covering them completely—they won't get soggy as they steam).

5. *Steam the tamales.* Cover the steamer and set over high heat. When the steam comes puffing out, reduce the heat to medium and cook until the batter comes free from the husk, about 1¼ hours. (Remove a *tamal* from the steamer to test it. Even when done, the *tamal* itself will seem very soft.) Make sure that the water doesn't boil away; if it becomes necessary to replenish the water, add *boiling* water.

Turn off the heat under the steamer and let stand, covered, about 15 minutes for the tamales to firm up.

Butternut Tamales with Chipotle Chicken
Tamales de Calabaza y Pollo Enchipotlado

MAKES 12 TO 14 TAMALES

1   8-ounce package dried corn husks

5   ounces (a scant ⅔ cup) fresh, rich-tasting pork lard or vegetable shortening (we've also had pretty good luck using Spectrum Organic All Vegetable Shortening), soft but not runny

½   teaspoon baking powder

    Salt

1   pound (about 2 cups) fresh coarse-ground corn *masa* for tamales

    OR 1¾ cups dried *masa harina* for tamales reconstituted with 1 cup plus 2 tablespoons hot water

    About ¾ cup chicken broth for thinning the masa and the optional second beating

2   cups coarsely shredded, peeled butternut squash (you'll need about ½ of a small squash)

1½ cups very coarsely shredded roasted or grilled chicken (thighs, rather than breasts, stay moistest during the long steaming—starting with raw boneless, skinless thighs, you need 4 to 6, about 1 pound)

2   canned chipotle chiles *en adobo*, seeded (if you wish) and finely chopped

2   tablespoons of the chipotle canning sauce

One thing about mixing shredded butternut (or any winter) squash into the dough for tamales: it's guaranteed to add extra moistness, almost giving them a rich, steamed-pudding texture. Of course, butternut adds color as well, and a gentle sweetness that's perfect with the spiciness of chipotle chile in the simple chicken filling.

Working Ahead: *These tamales are perfectly fine when made several days ahead. Cool, wrap tightly and refrigerate. They can be frozen for about a month. Defrost in the refrigerator overnight, then reheat in a steamer.*

1. *Soak the corn husks.* In a heat-proof bowl, pour boiling water over the corn husks. Lay a plate on the top to keep the husks submerged. Let them rehydrate for a couple of hours until pliable.

2. *Prepare the batter.* Measure the lard (or shortening), baking powder and *2 teaspoons* salt into the bowl of an electric mixer. Using the paddle attachment if there is one, beat on medium-high until light in texture, about a minute. In three additions, add the fresh or reconstituted *masa*, fully incorporating each addition before adding the next. Reduce the speed to medium-low, and slowly dribble in enough chicken broth (usually about ½ cup) to give the mixture the consistency of cake batter. Raise the speed to medium-high again and beat for another minute. The mixture has been beaten enough when it's so fluffy that a ½ teaspoon dollop floats in a cup of cold water. Stir in the shredded butternut. If time allows, refrigerate the batter for 1 hour to firm it up for an optional second beating.

3. *Prepare the filling, set up the steamer for the tamales.* In a small bowl, mix together the coarse chicken shreds with the chopped chipotle and its sauce. Pour 1½ inches of water in the bottom of a steamer: it needs to be large enough to hold 14 tamales; best if it's at least 10 inches in diameter with 6 inches of depth for standing up the tamales, like a small Mexican *tamal* steamer, large vegetable steamer or deep Chinese steamer. Drain the husks, then choose 14 of the largest, most pliable ones—they should be at least 6 inches long and 6 inches wide (at the widest end). (If there aren't enough large husks, you can overlap smaller ones.) Use several of the longest remaining corn husks to tear into ¼-inch strips for tying the tamales. Line the steamer basket with some of the remaining corn husks.

4. *Make the tamales.* For the lightest tamales, re-beat the refrigerated batter, slowly adding an extra ¼ cup chicken broth or water. (For this to be effective, the batter will need at least an hour's refrigeration to firm up, allowing for the broth's addition without becoming too soft.)

One at a time, form the tamales: On the wide end of one of the large husks, spread ¼ cup of the batter into a 4-inch square, leaving 1½ inches uncovered on the narrow end and at least ¾ inch on each of the long sides. Lay a portion of the chipotle chicken down the center of the batter. Pick up the two long sides of the husk and bring them together, encasing the filling with the batter. Roll the two long sides you're holding around the *tamal* in the same direction. (If the husk is small, feel free to roll the whole thing in another husk.) Fold up the empty 1½ inches to form a "bottom" on which the *tamal* will stand while steaming; tie it in place with one of the corn husk strips. Stand each *tamal* in the steamer while you form the remaining tamales. Lay extra husks over the open tops of the tamales (don't worry about covering them completely—they won't get soggy as they steam).

5. *Steam the tamales.* Cover the steamer and set over high heat. When the steam comes puffing out, reduce the heat to medium and cook until the batter comes free from the husk, about 1¼ hours. (Remove a *tamal* from the steamer to test it. Even when done, the *tamal* itself will seem very soft.) Make sure that the water doesn't boil away; if it becomes necessary to replenish the water, add *boiling* water.

Turn off the heat under the steamer and let stand, covered, about 15 minutes for the tamales to firm up.

BUTTERNUT TAMALES WITH CHIPOTLE CHICKEN

**A Perfect Fall Party:
Classic Mexican *Mole*
Fiesta for 24**

A Perfect Fall Party: Classic Mexican *Mole* Fiesta for 24

There isn't a Mexican family—or neighborhood or village—that won't suggest *mole* when fiesta plans are brewing. Or *barbacoa* or *pozole* or *carnitas*—though none of those iconic party dishes defines "Mexican fiesta" quite as elementally as *mole*. Mostly, I'd argue, that's because *mole*'s all about the sauce, sauce being the hallmark of Mexico's kitchen. And what a sauce it is: the most brilliantly complex, tightly fused conglomeration of a couple of dozen ingredients—half indigenous, half immigrants—our world has ever known. It's the history of Mexico on a plate, stunning, bold, earthy, native, foreign, all spun together into a unique, solitary flavor that every Mexican describes simply as *"mole."*

At the big fiestas I've been lucky enough to attend in Oaxaca and Guerrero, the *mole* is made by a team of locals who spread the preparations over several days, ending with the evocatively aromatic, day-long simmering in an earthenware *cazuela* the size of an old-fashioned bathtub. The wood fire that burns beneath the gurgling pots adds another layer of rustic earthiness to the experience. I love *mole* fiestas.

Now, a boat-size *cazuela* simmering over an outdoor fire pit with enough to feed a village may be more than some North Americans want to tackle, but a moderate-size *mole* party shouldn't be. Approach it as you would Thanksgiving dinner. Get a good-size pot, give yourself enough time, divide some of the work among other kitchen-friendly comrades and invite a good-size group to share the creation.

Unless you have a whole kitchen task force or are a serious overachiever, I'd kick the party off with a couple of big vegetable platters (think: Mexican crudité) with a *chamoy* dipping sauce, *chamoy* being the sweet-tangy-spicy Mexican phenomenon that's conquered everything from sorbet to grilled fish to fruit roll-ups. For those without confidence in their knife skills, there's a nice thing about fresh vegetable platters: you can order them from many grocery stores or custom-make ones with jícama and radishes and cubed pineapple from the salad bar offerings.

Though the barnyard chicken for small-town *mole* is typically simmered to tenderness (and the broth used to make the sauce), I've taken a more contemporary approach here. The sauce is made first, and a portion of it is used to glaze the chicken while it bakes. Nice-looking and easy for North American cooks to manage for a group.

For dessert at the village *mole* fiestas, plates or baskets of regional candies may be all you get—or a cake, if it's a really special occasion like a wedding or first communion or *quinceañera* (a girl's rite-of-passage fifteenth-birthday celebration). Though a big beautiful cake means party to all of us, tackling one while deep in *mole* creation could move some cooks right past their limit. Even a big caramel-dripping flan to slice like a cake is nerve-racking, requiring a precise baking time and nerves of steel to unmold. But there's another, far easier approach to that caramel custard

classic: individual flans baked in those flexible silicone muffin molds, lined with store-bought *cajeta* (goat milk caramel) instead of wickedly hot caramelized sugar, and filled with a foolproof custard that uses sweetened condensed milk to make baking time and temperature more forgiving. I've even made the whole idea of "dessert and coffee" easier by infusing the custard with the flavors of Mexican *café de olla*, the after-dinner cup of dark coffee, cloves and orange peel.

Fiesta Game Plan

Special Equipment

Mole pot: You need a large pot—8 to 12 quarts is ideal—because cooking *mole* is kind of a full-contact sport, meaning that a larger pot helps keep the *mole* wrestled inside. A heavy-bottom pot is essential—sauces thickened with nuts and seeds tend to stick in thin-bottom pots. My top pot choices: 9½-quart Le Creuset Dutch oven, 12-quart stainless steel All-Clad stockpot or an earthenware Mexican *cazuela* that holds at least 8 quarts. (I bought my favorite Mexican *cazuela* for *mole* from melissaguerra.com; on their site it's called "Mexican Hand Painted Lead Free Large Green Casserole for *Mole*" and it is stunningly beautiful.)

Rice pot: The 9½-quart Le Creuset pot is perfect for rice, too. Because the rice is baked, a tall 12-quart stockpot isn't an option, since most won't fit in home ovens. Many 6- or 8-quart soup pots or stockpots usually work well.

Baking sheets for cooking chicken: To bake all the chicken at once, you need two large rimmed baking sheets.

Flexible silicone muffin molds for flans: There are many brands available, coming in 6- or 12-muffin sizes. Either 6- or 12-muffin size will work for this recipe. Muffin size options are standard or mini; you want standard.

Large pans for water baths for flans: you need two pans, each 2 inches deep and large enough to hold half of the molds. I use two roasting pans or two broiler pans.

Timeline
A week or so ahead:

● Make a shopping list and buy all the basics from your regular grocery store.

● Buy plantains and let them ripen at room temperature, or order black-ripe plantains to be picked up later in the week from a reliable market.

● Lacking a very well stocked grocery, locate at a Mexican market (or order by mail): dried chiles (mulato, ancho, pasilla, canned chipotles), powdered chile (guajillo or ancho), Mexican cinnamon (*canela*), Tamazula hot sauce, Mexican chocolate, Mexican goat milk caramel (*cajeta*). If visiting a Mexican market, you may want to purchase a lot of your less perishable vegetables (especially lime, tomatillos and jícama), medium-grain rice and sesame seeds (they're usually cheaper).

1 to 3 days ahead:

● Make the *mole*. Unless you are cooking in a Mexican *cazuela*, cool the *mole* in the pot set in a sink filled with water and ice. Transfer to storage containers (or if using enameled cast iron or stainless steel, you may store in the vessel), cover and refrigerate.

● Make the *"café de olla"* flans. Cover and refrigerate.

● You may also make the rice. When the rice comes from the oven, scoop it onto two rimmed baking sheets to release steam and stop the cooking. When it's cool, divide among ovenproof serving dishes (I use decorative 13 x 9-inch baking dishes), mix in the plantains and parsley, cover and refrigerate.

● Make the *chamoy* dipping sauce, scoop into a serving dish and refrigerate.

Early on party day:

● Prepare the vegetables and set up the crudité platter. Cover with damp towels and refrigerate until ready to serve.

About 3 hours before the guests arrive:

● Bake the chicken. When it's done, remove from the oven and let cool.

● Cover the rice with foil and heat in the 350-degree oven for about 25 minutes. When it's hot, remove from the oven and let cool, covered.

● Reduce the oven temperature to 170 degrees.

● Warm the *mole* in a large pot on the stovetop. Set out the toasted sesame seeds for garnish.

● Unmold the flans onto a rimmed baking sheet or platter.

● Clean the watercress for garnish.

● Get ice and keep in ice chests.

● Ice (or refrigerate) the Mexican sodas and beers.

● Put the lime juice for the *micheladas* in a pitcher and refrigerate. Set out the hot sauce, Worcestershire sauce, salt and lime in the drink area.

About 1 hour before serving time:

● Place the chicken and rice (still covered) in the low oven.

● Set out Mexican sodas, beer, lime juice and ice in the drink area.

● Heat the tortillas (see page 197) and keep warm in a small ice chest or a large rice cooker.

Serving Strategy

● When the first guests arrive, serve the beverages to welcome them.

● When about half the guests have gathered, set out the crudité platter.

● Just before serving the *mole*, wrap stacks of hot tortillas in heavy napkins or cloths, and distribute them among the tables.

● You can serve the chicken-mole-rice as a buffet or individually plate it—the latter being my first choice, because it's easy and you can get a beautiful balance on each plate. When serving buffet-style, most American cooks will simply pour a little steaming *mole* on and around the warm chicken and set it out for the guests to serve themselves; trouble is, most guests won't get enough *mole*—they'll simply take a piece of chicken, leaving most of the *mole* behind. That's why I take the Mexican cooks' lead and line up a few guests to help make plates for the whole crowd: One puts chicken on the plate, another pours on about ½ cup of *mole*, yet another spoons on some rice, and the last decorates the plate with watercress and sesame. Every plate for every guest looks beautiful—and celebrates the *mole* as the star attraction.

● Desserts stay in the refrigerator until the last moment. One by one slide them off the tray or platter and onto a plate.

Embellishments

● **Serving the *mole*:** A sure-fire showstopper is *mole* gurgling away in a Mexican *cazuela* over an open fire outside. If you get the pot (see "Special Equipment" on page 231), the rest is easy. On a level, fireproof surface build a brick *hornillo* (page 238), light a fire in it, and set the pot on top. Sometimes I set up a grill to the side of my *mole* pot, maintaining a low fire in it to keep the chicken and rice warm as I serve. Even if you didn't cook the *mole* from start to finish on the wood fire, your guests will never forget the rustic atmosphere, the exotic aroma of *mole* blending with the primal draw of a wood fire.

● **Serving sodas and beers:** One of the easiest ways to serve sodas and beer at an outside party is in really big terracotta pots. Upend one, setting it on a level surface where water draining from melting ice will not be a problem. Set a second pot on top of the first and fill it with ice, sodas and beers.

Mexican "Crudité" Platter with *Chamoy* Dipping Sauce

Botana de Verduras y Frutas Crudas con Chamoy

SERVES 24 GENEROUSLY

FOR ABOUT 1 CUP OF THE DIPPING SAUCE

1⅓ cups apricot spread (not jam)

⅔ cup Mexican hot sauce like Tamazula or Valentina (you'll need a couple of small bottles)

6 tablespoons fresh lime juice

FOR THE VEGETABLES AND FRUIT

2 pounds (usually 4) peeled, cored pineapples (available in most well-stocked grocery stores in the produce section)

2 pounds jícama sticks (I get these from the salad bar at my grocery store)

2 pounds cucumber rounds (from the salad bar, too)

2 pounds radishes, cut in half

8 limes, cut into wedges

FOR THE SPRINKLE

2 teaspoons powdered chile (I like guajillo or ancho, because they're not as hot as cayenne or árbol)

2 teaspoons salt (regular table salt mixes in better than coarse salt)

The first place I ran across chamoy was at a raspado stall in Oaxaca, where an energetic young ice shaver offered me a drizzle over the fresh mango syrup I'd ordered on my snow cone. It was spicy and sweet and tangy and salty, shifting the mango from dessert to savory fruit snack. If you've ever had the always popular street-vendor mango sprinkled with tangy chile salt, you understand what I'm talking about.

I've given weights for prepared vegetables (after being peeled, sliced, cut into sticks), so you'll know how much to buy from a salad bar, should you go that way. If you're doing the vegetable prep yourself, buy a little more jícama, cucumber and pineapple than what's called for here.

Working Ahead: For the freshest looking and tasting vegetables, cut them within a few hours of serving; cover with damp towels and keep refrigerated until needed. The dipping sauce can be made several days ahead; cover and refrigerate.

1. *Make the dipping sauce.* Scrape the apricot spread into a food processor and add the hot sauce and lime juice. Process until blended and smooth. Scrape into a small serving bowl.

2. *Arrange the vegetables and fruits.* Set the dipping sauce in the middle of a large round platter. Stand the pineapple on a cutting board and cut it into quarters. Cut the quarters crosswise into ½-inch slices. Arrange the pineapple, jícama, cucumber and radishes into quadrants around the dipping sauce, filling the space between each one with lime wedges.

3. *Serve.* Mix together the powdered chile and salt. Sprinkle it over the fruits and vegetables (it's easiest to sprinkle evenly if you put the mixture in a small shaker). You're ready to serve.

Lacquered Chicken in Classic Red *Mole*
Pollo Asado en Mole Rojo Clásico
SERVES 24 WITH A GENEROUS ¾ GALLON OF *MOLE*

FOR THE MOLE

10 ounces (5 medium) tomatillos, husked and rinsed

1⅓ cups (about 6½ ounces) sesame seeds

1   cup rich-tasting pork lard or vegetable oil, plus a little more if necessary

12 medium (6 ounces total) dried mulato chiles, stemmed, seeded and torn into large flat pieces

6   medium (3 ounces total) dried ancho chiles, stemmed, seeded and torn into large flat pieces

10 medium (3 ounces total) dried pasilla chiles, stemmed, seeded and torn into large flat pieces

8   garlic cloves, peeled

1   cup (about 4 ounces) unskinned almonds

1   cup (about 4 ounces) raisins

1   teaspoon cinnamon, preferably freshly ground Mexican *canela*

½   teaspoon black pepper, preferably freshly ground

½   teaspoon anise, preferably freshly ground

¼   teaspoon cloves, preferably freshly ground

This is the most streamlined—but thoroughly delicious—mole I know. And by "streamlined," I don't mean it's easy-breezy. Easy mole recipes are like crash diets: they promise a lot, but rarely deliver any long-lasting satisfaction. So plan on a good amount of work here, but not as much as some moles require. And if you're really into creating a memorable experience (for you and for your guests), build a brick hornillo (page 238) and cook the mole over a wood fire as they do in many villages in Mexico. Rather than poach the chicken to serve with the mole, as is common in Mexico, I've baked it with a lovely lacquered-looking coat of chocolate-brown mole. Pretty, tasty and easy for a crowd.

1. *Preliminaries.* On a rimmed baking sheet, roast the tomatillos 4 inches below a very hot broiler until splotchy black and thoroughly soft, about 5 minutes per side. Scrape into a large bowl. In a dry skillet over medium heat, toast the sesame seeds, stirringly nearly constantly, until golden, about 5 minutes. Scrape *half* of them in with the tomatillos. Reserve the remainder for sprinkling on the chicken.

2. *Brown other mole ingredients.* Turn on an exhaust fan or open a kitchen door or window. In a very large pot (I typically use a 12-quart stainless steel stockpot, Dutch oven or medium-large Mexican earthenware *cazuela*), heat the lard or oil over medium. When quite hot, fry the chiles, three or four pieces at a time, flipping them nearly constantly with tongs until aromatic and their interior side has lightened in color, 20 or 30 seconds total frying time. Don't toast them so darkly that they begin to smoke—that would make the *mole* bitter. As they're done, remove them to a large bowl, draining as much fat as possible back into the pot. Cover the toasted chiles with hot tap water and let rehydrate 30 minutes, stirring frequently to ensure even soaking.

Remove any stray chile seeds left in the fat. With the pot still over medium heat, fry the garlic and almonds, stirring regularly, until browned (the garlic should be soft), about 5 minutes. With a slotted spoon, remove to the tomatillo bowl, draining as much fat as possible back into the pot.

Add the raisins to the hot pot. Stir for 20 or 30 seconds, until they've puffed and browned slightly. Scoop them out, draining as much fat as possible back into the pot, and add to the tomatillos. Set the pan aside off the heat.

To the tomatillo mixture, add the cinnamon, black pepper, anise, cloves, bread and chocolate. Add 2 cups water and stir to combine.

2 slices firm white bread, darkly toasted and broken into several pieces

2 ounces (about ⅔ of a 3.3-ounce tablet) Mexican chocolate, roughly chopped

3 quarts chicken broth

Salt

⅓ to ½ cup sugar

FOR THE CHICKEN AND PRESENTATION

½ cup agave syrup (I like the full, rich flavor of Wholesome Sweeteners organic raw) or dark corn syrup

24 portions of chicken—24 leg-and-thigh pieces, 24 bone-in chicken breast halves or a mixture of the two

Sprigs of watercress or flat-leaf parsley for garnish

3. *Blend, strain, cook.* Into a large measuring cup, tip off the chiles' soaking liquid. Taste the liquid: if it's not bitter, discard all but 6 cups (if you're short, add water to make up the shortfall). If bitter, pour it out and measure 6 cups water. Scoop half of the chiles into a blender jar, pour in half of the soaking liquid (or water) and blend to a smooth puree. Press through a medium-mesh strainer into a large bowl; discard the bits of skin and seeds that don't pass through the strainer. Repeat with the remaining chiles.

Return the pot or *cazuela* to medium heat. (The bottom should still have a nice coating of lard or oil; if not, add a little more.) When it's quite hot, pour in the chile puree—it should sizzle sharply and, if the pan is sufficiently hot, the mixture should never stop boiling. Stir every couple of minutes until the chile puree has darkened and reduced to the consistency of tomato paste, about 30 minutes. (I find it useful to cover the pot with an inexpensive spatter screen to catch any spattering chile.)

In two batches, blend the tomatillo mixture as smoothly as possible (you may need an extra ½ cup water to keep everything moving through the blades), then strain it into the large bowl that contained the chiles. When the chile paste has reduced, add the tomatillo mixture to the pot and cook, stirring every few minutes until considerably darker and thicker, 15 to 20 minutes. (Again, a spatter screen saves a lot of cleanup.)

4. *Simmer.* Add the broth to the pot and briskly simmer the mixture over medium to medium-low heat for about 2 hours for all the flavors to come

LACQUERED CHICKEN, PLANTAIN RICE AND BABY GREENS

together and mellow. If the *mole* has thickened beyond the consistency of a cream soup, stir in a little water. Taste and season with salt (usually about 4 teaspoons) and the sugar.

5. *Roast the chicken and serve.* Heat the oven to 350 degrees. In a small (2-quart) saucepan, mix together 1 cup of the *mole* with the agave nectar or corn syrup. Simmer over medium heat until glossy and reduced to 1 cup, about 30 minutes. On rimmed baking sheets, lay out the chicken in a single layer. Season generously with salt. Bake for 45 minutes (the chicken should be tender to the bone at this point—the juices at the thickest part of the leg-and-thigh portions should run clear and register 165 degrees on an instant-read thermometer). Raise the oven temperature to 400 degrees. Tip off the juices that have collected around the chicken, then brush the pieces liberally with the glossy *mole* mixture. Sprinkle with the reserved sesame seeds. Bake for 10 minutes to set the glaze. Remove from the oven, let stand at room temperature for 10 minutes, then slide into a very low oven to keep warm until serving time—preferably no longer than 30 minutes. Serve each portion of chicken with about ½ cup of the *mole*, decorated with watercress or flat-leaf parsley.

How to Build a Temporary Brick Fire Pit (*Hornillo*)

To lend a traditional smoky edge to the flavor of *mole* and paella—not to mention creating a fabulous spectacle—construct a simple, crescent-shaped brick fire pit. On a flat, fireproof surface out in the open (away from overhangs and the like), place bricks in a semicircle a little larger than your pan: about seven if cooking paella in a three-foot pan or *mole* in a large *cazuela*). Build the *hornillo*

five or six courses of bricks high, staggering the bricks to create a sturdy lattice-like structure that allows air to feed the fire. Cut four pieces of rebar (or other heavy metal rod that can withstand high heat) to fit across the *hornillo*, allowing a couple of inches over-hang on each side. Lay them in a cross-hatch pattern—nothing will be supporting two of them in the front. Lash the "cross-hatch" of

rebar together with heavy wire; remove from the *hornillo*. Build a fire in the center (though not necessary, I first lay down an old fireplace grate to elevate the fire, allowing more air circulation for a robust fire). When it's very hot, spread out the fire, lay on the rebar support, position the pan or *cazuela* and you're ready to start cooking. Stoke the fire as needed through the opening in the front.

BRICK FIRE PIT FOR COOKING *MOLE*

Mexican White Rice with Sweet Plantains
Arroz Blanco con Plátano Macho Maduro
MAKES ABOUT 20 CUPS, ENOUGH FOR 24

6 cups chicken broth

   Salt

3 cups vegetable oil (I like to use oil that's especially refined for high-heat cooking)

4 large (about 2½ pounds total) soft, black-ripe plantains, peeled and cut into ½-inch cubes

6 cups white rice, preferably medium-grain

2 large (1 pound total) white onions, chopped into ¼-inch pieces

8 garlic cloves, peeled and finely chopped

   About ¾ cup roughly chopped flat-leaf parsley, for garnish

This is a reliable recipe for a traditional Mexican white rice cooked pilaf-style, perfect when you need to make a memorable pot of rice for a crowd . . . without resorting to foolproof but waxy-textured converted rice.

1. *Heat the broth.* Turn on the oven to 350 degrees. Measure the broth into a large (4-quart) saucepan. Add 1 tablespoon of salt if you are using salted broth, 2 tablespoons if you're using unsalted broth. Cover and set over medium-low heat.

2. *Fry the plantains.* In a very large (9-quart) Dutch oven (or comparable soup pot), heat the oil over medium to medium-high. When the oil is quite hot (but not smoking), add the plantains and fry, breaking apart any clumps until the plantains are a rich golden brown, about 20 to 25 minutes. Use a slotted spoon or wire skimmer to remove the plantain cubes to paper towels to drain.

3. *Fry the rice.* Set up a large strainer over a metal bowl; set beside the stove on a heat-resistant surface. With the pan of oil still over the heat, raise the heat to high and add the rice. Stir regularly until it has turned from translucent to milky white (but not begun to brown), about 10 minutes. Immediately (and carefully) pour the rice and oil into the strainer, making sure to get all the rice out of the pan. Clean off any drips on the outside of the pan.

4. *Cook the rice.* Without washing the pan, set it over medium heat. If there isn't a generous coating of oil on the bottom, spoon a little of the strained oil back into the pot. Add the onion and cook, stirring regularly, until soft but not browned, about 5 minutes. Add the garlic and stir for 1 minute. Add the rice and broth. Stir several times through all parts of the pan, making sure to scrape down any rice grains that are clinging to the sides above the liquid. Cover and place in the oven. After 30 minutes uncover and test a grain of rice: if it's still a little chalky in the center and it's clear that all the liquid has been absorbed, drizzle about ¼ cup of water over the rice, re-cover and bake for 5 to 10 minutes longer.

5. *Serve the rice.* When the rice is ready, sprinkle the fried plantains and chopped parsley over the top and gently fold them in—if you're careful and stir all the way to the bottom, you'll release a lot of steam, which will stop the rice from overcooking.

"*Café de Olla*" Flan
Flan Sabor "Café de Olla"
MAKES 24 SMALL FLANS

1½ cups *cajeta*

6 cups milk

4 14-ounce cans sweetened condensed milk

8 2 x 1½-inch strips of orange peel (colored part only)

3-inch cinnamon stick, preferably Mexican *canela*

8 cloves

⅔ cup coarsely ground dark-roast coffee

12 eggs

16 egg yolks

Used to be, the standard-issue, after-dinner coffee in Mexico was café de olla, a pot-brewed concoction with all its ingredients—coffee, dark sugar, spices, water—boiled in an earthenware pot, cowboy style. But those days are gone, the old-fashioned coffee satisfying traditionalists in only a few not-so-modern eateries nowadays. Everyone else wants espresso. Nonetheless, I won't let go of those rich, spicy café de olla flavors. And since they infuse beautifully into custards and ice creams, I can offer my guests a traditional taste of coffee and dessert in a single bite.

This recipe is an unorthodox approach to flan, since the caramelized sugar—a kitchen terrorist if ever I have seen one—is replaced by store-bought cajeta (goat milk caramel) and the custards are baked in flexible silicone muffin molds for easy removal. (You can use disposable aluminum cups, but the edges of the unmolded flans won't be as pretty.)

Working Ahead: The flans can be made several days ahead; cool, cover and refrigerate. They can be unmolded several hours before serving. I unmold them onto rimmed baking sheets, leaving the molds on top to protect them. Refrigerate until ready to serve. Lacking enough molds for 24 flans (you'd have to have four 6-muffin molds or two 12-muffin molds), you can make a set of 12 flans the day before the party, refrigerate them overnight, unmold them then next day and make the second batch.

1. Coat the molds. Set four 6-muffin or two 12-muffin silicon (flexible) muffin molds into two large pans that are at least 2 inches deep (large roasting pans work well). Spoon 1 tablespoon of *cajeta* into the bottom of each mold, tilting the molds so that the *cajeta* completely covers the bottom. Turn on the oven to 325 degrees.

2. Make the custard. In a very large (8-quart) soup pot, combine the milk, sweetened condensed milk, orange peel, cinnamon, cloves and coffee. Heat to a simmer, stirring occasionally, then remove from the heat and cover. Whisk together the eggs and egg yolks in a large bowl. When the coffee mixture has steeped about 10 minutes, strain it into the eggs. Whisk to combine. Divide the mixture among the molds.

3. Bake the flans. Open the oven door, pull out the racks, set a roasting pan on each rack. Pour hot water around the molds in one of the pans, filling the pan to a depth of about 1 inch. Carefully slide that rack back into the oven, then do the same with the second pan. Bake until the flans are just barely set in the middle, 50 to 60 minutes. Remove from the oven and let cool in the hot water bath, then remove and refrigerate until thoroughly chilled, about 2 hours.

4. *Unmold the flans.* Run a small knife around the edge of each of the flans to release it from the sides of the mold.

Next, flip the molds over onto a rimmed baking sheet or a deep platter; here's the easiest way I know to do that. Set half of the molds on a rimmed baking sheet. Flip a second rimmed baking sheet over on top of them, then, holding the two rimmed baking sheets securely, flip them over.

Shake the molds back and forth and up and down—squeezing the sides of the molds slightly if you need to—to ensure that each flan has dropped. Remove the molds. Scrape any remaining caramel out of the molds and onto the flans. Repeat with the second set of molds.

Using a small metal spatula, transfer each flan to a serving plate. Divide the caramel among them and you're ready to serve.

Beverages

***Micheladas* and Beer:** The *micheladas* are usually made of light, crisp beer (Sol, Tecate and Carta Blanca), since those work well with lime and ice. Besides the *michelada* beer, I would suggest some medium and dark flavored beer as well, like Bohemia and Negra Modelo. I would plan a couple of beers per person, plus ones for the *micheladas*. You know your crowd: you may need to plan more than I'm suggesting; you make the call.

Mexican Sodas—A Nickel Tour: While most of us are attracted to the neon-bright colors of Mexican sodas like those made by Jarritos, I find their flavors very artificial tasting and disappointing. Boing! brand sodas, if you can find them, are more natural tasting because they contain fruit juices; their colors are less dramatic, however. Two other Mexican soda favorites: Cidral Mundet, for its vibrant apple juice flavor, and Sangría Señorial, which is less a nonalcoholic sangría than a fruity version of Dr Pepper.

SETUP FOR *MICHELADAS*

Icy Beer *Micheladas* for a Crowd
Micheladas

MAKES 24 *MICHELADAS*

About 1 quart fresh lime juice

A bottle or two of Mexican hot sauce (Tamazula, Valentina and Búfalo have very traditional flavor)

1   bottle of Worcestershire sauce

A small plateful of coarse (kosher) salt

1   juicy lime

About 4 pounds (6 quarts) ice cubes

24 Mexican beers (the lighter fla-vored beers such as Tecate, Sol, XX Lager and Carta Blanca work really well in this beverage)

1. *Preparations.* Pour the lime juice into a pitcher and refrigerate until serving time. On your beverage table, set out the hot sauce, Worcestershire and the plate of salt with the lime cut in half. Have the ice cubes at the ready and the beers chilled.

2. *Serve.* Transfer the ice to a large bowl or ice bucket. Rub the cut side of a lime over the rims of large (16-ounce) beer glasses or mugs to moisten them. Invert into the salt to coat the rims. As your guests are ready for a *michelada*, half-fill a mug with ice, add 2 tablespoons to ¼ cup of lime juice (depending on how tangy they want it), then fill with a beer. Either encourage guests to add hot sauce and Worcestershire to the mug or do it according to their direction. Stir with a long-handle spoon before taking the first sip.

A Few Off-Beat Albums That Will Bring Your Party Alive

Latin Bitman (DJ Bitman): This is a quirky, funky mash-up of great, groovy party music from one of South America's most talented DJs.

The Very Best of (Lila Downs): Downs sings gorgeous classic Oaxacan ballads interspersed with straight-ahead ranchero songs, and she sings in Spanish, English and an indigenous Oaxa-can language.

Sonidos Gold (Grupo Fantasma): One of my favorites of the Nuevo Cumbia music. You won't be able to sit still: this is Latin dance music, but easy, groovy-funky and fun. Especially if you understand the food-related lyrics in songs like "Arroz con Frijoles" and "Bacalao con Pan."

iTunes Live from Soho (Locos por Juana): The most captivat-ing album from this multicultural group from Miami. Great party music, because they weave together influences from Latin cumbia and salsa (even reggae) with a little urban hip-hop and rock.

Chuntaros Radio Poder (El Gran Silencio): Funky rock, cumbia and rap. The combination really grows on you. Especially the northern-style Mexican radio announcer interludes.

Uniendo Fronteras (Tigres del Norte): A classic album from this definitive northern Mexican band (playing umpa-style *norteño* with snare drums and accordion). Mostly a straight-ahead one-two beat, banging out story-songs called *corridos*.

Aniversario 100 (Mariachi Vargas de Tecatitlan): This is a recording of one of Mexico's best maria-chi groups singing super-classic Mexican songs you've probably heard if you've ever been to Mexico (or even to a Mexican restaurant). Amazing, almost orchestral-sounding.

Live-Fire Cooking, Fast and Slow

hy—just where everyone's expecting the entrée chapter—am I giving you "Live Fire Cooking"? Where is the section of fancy main dishes for dinner parties, for birthdays, for holiday dinners? Why focus the book's crescendo on cooking's most rustic, most primal method of transforming raw ingredients into dinner?

And besides all that, didn't the last chapter already have a detailed recipe for steak tacos, Mexico's most iconic grilled dish?

Okay. Steak tacos are great. I'll readily admit that. But they only take you a short distance into the adventure that licking flames and smoldering coals can offer. Which is why I've put together this chapter of very special dishes, showstoppers in their own ways. Showstoppers despite their lack of decorative flourishes, buttery richness or expensive ingredients. Some may not even seem that complex.

These dishes impress because they employ certain cooking techniques (plus a few distinctive spices) that give them unique flavor, techniques that no one would confuse with the now-ubiquitous "quick and easy" cooking so many Americans say they're in search of. Trouble is, after a while "quick and easy" all starts to taste the same.

Just take the recipe for Grilled Mussels (page 256) as a starting place. Mussels are so darn easy to dump in a pan with a little flavorful liquid and steam until they open; why go through the more tedious process of grilling them? Two words: "flavor" and "show." Mussels turned over the coals until they pop open are captivatingly tinged with the flavors of both smoke and sea. And because mussels are typically done last-minute, the guests get to look on with anticipation, offering a hand in pulling off top shells and spooning on salsa. The experience—from the unexpected scattering of mussels over glowing charcoal to slurping tomatillo-doused mussel meat from charred shells—becomes an experience your friends and family won't soon forget.

For most of us, *achiote*—if we've tasted it at all—is a flavor associated with long cooking: *cochinita pibil*, that banana leaf–wrapped, slow-roasted *achiote* pork from the Yucatan, is one of Mexico's most famous dishes. But a limey *achiote* marinade on shrimp (*Achiote*-Seared Shrimp, page 247) creates a very different flavor when seared on a hot grill—brighter, earthier, more riveting.

Most of us are quite comfortable with traditional uses of the grill to cook something like an inspiring Rack of Lamb with Honey-Pasilla Glaze (page 270), a green-chile crusted "Brava" Steak (page 258), some Chipotle-Glazed Baby Back Ribs (page 261) or even the more adventurous splayed whole-fish preparation, *pescado zarandeado* (page 252) from Mexico's upper west coast, that's smeared with a garlicky marinade and turned over a live fire.

WOOD-BURNING *HORNILLO* FOR COOKING *MOLE* OR PAELLA

But I love to use a grill in unexpected ways. Most of us know that you can cook foods fast directly over the coals (steaks and burgers, for instance), or you can slow-cook foods indirectly by moving them away from heat (chicken works well this way). But what about searing meat and then grill-braising it in a pot. That's a page I took from Mexico's centuries-old pit cooking technique, translated for the American backyard barbecue.

But what most people don't know is digging a pit for traditional Mexican *barbacoa* is not out of reach for an adventurous American cook with a patch of ground, a moderately strong back and access to some bricks. I've detailed the dimensions and specific equipment you'll need for creating a pit that matches that of my Yucatecan pit-master friend, Silvio Campos (page 275). And talk about a showstopper: when your friends experience the unearthing of the lamb or goat or pig from its earthy pit, having cooked for hours in an aromatic blanket of herby leaves, they'll never forget it.

Less of a commitment, but equally remarkable, is a three-foot Paella (page 276) for a crowd, cooked over burning logs surrounded by a temporary brick enclosure called an *hornillo*. It's the same kind of brick-bordered fire pit used across Mexico to support earthenware pots of *mole* that are big enough to feed a small village. Want to know how to tackle *mole* for that party of a lifetime? I've detailed the steps on page 228 . . . as well as those for making a small batch of the absolutely simplest *mole* in the world . . . in your slow-cooker (page 262).

Wood-Grilled Whole Fish (or fillets) Puerto Vallarta Style
Pescado Zarandeado

SERVES 4

4 dried ancho chiles or 8 dried guajillo chiles (2 ounces of chiles total), stemmed, seeded and torn into flat pieces

1 8-ounce can tomato sauce

2 garlic cloves, peeled and roughly chopped

3 tablespoons soy sauce

3 tablespoons Worcestershire sauce

   Salt

1 3-pound whole fish (round fish like snapper, grouper or striped bass work really well), split as described in headnote

   OR 1½ pounds meaty fish fillets

   Oil for brushing or spraying the basket and fish

1 medium, red onion, thinly sliced, for serving

2 limes, cut into wedges, for serving

   Chinese toasted chiles in oil (or your favorite salsa or hot sauce), for serving (optional)

   Corn tortillas, for serving

Along Mexico's west coast, it seems like all the best seafood restaurants are flipping hinged flat baskets of butterflied, marinated fish over wood fires, fragrant with garlic and smoldering branches. And this flipped fish—pescado zarandeado is how that translates into Spanish—is for the locals about as celebratory as a cochinita pibil in the Yucatan or huge pot of mole in central Mexico.

There's strong Asian influence along Mexico's west coast (many Chinese settled there after helping build railroads in the late nineteenth century) and it surfaces here in the use of soy sauce in the marinade and Chinese toasted chiles in oil as a condiment. But I've never quite understood why the marinade at Tino's (the famous Fish Zarandeado place near Puerto Vallarta) starts with achiote, a spice that's used practically nowhere but the kitchens of Yucatan. My marinade echoes Tino's quite accurately, except that I've replaced achiote with red chile puree.

Butterflying a whole fish: In most places, cooks simply lay out a fish (scaled, gills removed) and, holding a butcher's knife parallel to the work surface, cut the fish in half, starting at the lips and cutting straight through the head, then the body, then the tail. Once past the head, the knife typically stays on one side of the backbone, so that the finished fish winds up in two flat half-fish pieces, one with the backbone, the other without. At Tino's, they go one step further, ensuring even cooking and easy eating. They split the

SPLITTING WHOLE FISH

fish in half as I described, but then remove the backbone from the piece that still has it. The two marinated sides (they look like fillets with head and tail still attached, rib bones still in place, backbone removed) get grilled along with the marinated backbone, which Tino's clientele enjoys picking at for the tasty nuggets that cling to the bones. If you're not a wizard with a knife, ask the person behind the fish counter to butterfly your fish as I described (you may remove the head and tail if you wish), making sure to keep the bones to marinate and grill along with the boneless parts.

To make Pescado Zarandeado, you'll need a large, hinged flat grill basket (like Rome's #68 15 x 18-inch Super Grill Basket).

Working Ahead: *The marinade can be made a week or two in advance and refrigerated, covered. It's best to buy the fish the day you're cooking it; if you have to buy it the day before, wrap it well and store it in the coldest part of your refrigerator packed in ice. Marinating the fish for too long can result in oddly textured, "cured" fish, so smear on the seasoning just before you cook the fish. Which should be when everyone is ready to sit down.*

SMEARING MARINADE OVER WHOLE FISH

1. Marinate the fish. In a dry skillet over medium heat, toast the chile pieces a few at a time, pressing them firmly against the hot surface with a metal spatula until they are aromatic, about 10 seconds per side. In a bowl, cover the chiles with hot tap water and let rehydrate for 30 minutes; place a plate on top to keep them submerged.

Use a pair of tongs to transfer the rehydrated chiles to a food processor or blender. Add ½ cup of the soaking liquid, along with the tomato sauce, garlic, soy and Worcestershire. Blend to a smooth puree. Press through a medium-mesh sieve into a bowl. Taste and season *highly* with salt, usually about 2 teaspoons.

Cut ½-inch-deep diagonal slashes along the flesh side of the fish (to promote even cooking and aid in marinade penetration). Sprinkle both sides with salt. Spread or brush about 3 tablespoons of the marinade over both sides of the fish—spread some on the bones as well. (You'll probably have marinade left over for another round of fish. It'll keep for a couple of weeks in the refrigerator.)

GRILLED FISH READY FOR SERVING

2. Grill the fish. Turn on a gas grill to medium or light a charcoal fire and let it burn until the coals are covered with white ash. Lay a grill basket over the fire. When the basket is quite hot, brush or spray it generously with oil. Spray or lightly brush the fish with oil, then lay the oiled side down on the basket; spray or brush the other side. Close the basket and lay it over the fire. Cook, turning every 3 or 4 minutes, until the fish is cooked through but still juicy—a 3-pound snapper typically takes 10 to 15 minutes.

Gently and carefully open the basket and remove the fish to a platter. Serve with the red onion, lime and toasted chiles—and plenty of warm corn tortillas—for making very tasty soft tacos.

Achiote-Seared Shrimp with Quick Habanero-Pickled Onions

Camarónes al Achiote con Cebollas Curtidas al Habanero

SERVES 4

½ of a small (3½-ounce) package prepared *achiote* paste (such as Yucateco, La Anita or Marin brand)

2 garlic cloves, peeled and roughly chopped

½ cup fresh lime juice

¼ cup fresh orange juice

1 tablespoon vinegar (apple cider vinegar works well here)

Salt

1¼ pounds large shrimp, peeled, leaving tail and final shell segment intact and deveined if you like

1 medium red onion, thinly sliced

1 small fresh habanero chile (or other fresh chile), stemmed, seeded and thinly sliced

A little olive or vegetable oil

Roughly chopped cilantro or parsley, for garnish

Achiote, *that earthy-orange seed with the earthy-floral aroma, stains so much food in Mexico's Yucatan peninsula the color of glowing embers and anoints it with a fragrance that reminds me of the limestone beneath the region's shallow soil and tropical flowers and the jungle thicket that protects them. Many are introduced to its uniqueness as the marinade that makes pork pibil the delicious mouthful that it is, or as the stuff that's painted on split-open fish but shielded from direct fire by banana leaves.*

While splitting a fish might be more than some cooks want to tackle, cooking shrimp (or scallops, if those are more appealing to you) is child's play. And with so many Mexican groceries dotting our North American landscape, little boxes of achiote (already ground to a paste with garlic, the typical host of spices, a little something tangy) can be an easy pantry staple. Go ahead: buy a bunch of boxes when you see them (or order them online). They keep well on a pantry shelf for 6 months or longer.

With achiote paste on hand, you can have these very delicious, very Yucatecan-tasting shrimp with spicy, half-pickled onions on the table in jiffy. In the winter, I bring the preparation inside, sautéing the shrimp, rather than grilling.

Working Ahead: The marinade can be made early in the day it's used; marinate the shrimp within an hour of grilling. The onions can be made a day or two ahead.

1. *Marinate the shrimp.* Break the *achiote* paste into a blender jar and add the garlic, *half* of the lime juice, the orange juice, vinegar and ½ teaspoon salt. Blend until smooth. Pour over the shrimp, stirring to coat well, cover and refrigerate 30 minutes.

2. *Prepare the onions.* In a small bowl, combine the onion, habanero (or as much of it as you think you'll like), the *remaining* lime juice and 1 scant teaspoon salt. Cover and let stand until the shrimp is ready. (If working ahead, the onions may be stored in the refrigerator, covered, for several days.)

3. *Grill and serve the shrimp.* Turn on a gas grill to medium-high or light a charcoal grill and let the coals burn until quite hot and covered with white ash.

Thread the shrimp on skewers (if using bamboo skewers, it's best to first soak them in water for a few minutes), leaving most of the marinade in the bowl. Scrape the leftover marinade into a small saucepan, bring to a simmer over medium heat, and stir until darker in color and thickened, about 5 minutes. Stir in enough water to bring the sauce to the consistency of a light cream soup. Taste and season with more salt if you think necessary. Cover and keep warm over low heat.

Spritz or brush the shrimp with oil, then lay on the hot fire and close the grill. After 2 or 3 minutes, when the shrimp are browned on one side, turn the skewers over and cook the other side: it usually takes a minute or so longer, depending on the exact heat of your fire, to cook the shrimp until just the slightest hint of translucency remains in the center of each piece.

Lay the grilled shrimp skewers on a serving platter (or pull the shrimp from skewers before piling on the platter), drizzle with the sauce and sprinkle with chopped cilantro or parsley. Serve with the spicy pickled onions.

Grilled Mussels with Tomatillo Salsa and Cilantro
Mejillones Asados con Salsa Verde y Cilantro
SERVES 8 AS A NIBBLE OR LIGHT APPETIZER

About 48 (1½ pounds) tightly closed mussels, scrubbed, any "beards" pulled off

About ⅔ cup Roasted Tomatillo Salsa (page 208) or store-bought tomatillo salsa

¼ cup (loosely packed) chopped fresh cilantro

In the grilling world, mussels are about as easy as it gets: lay them on the grill, wait for them to open, take them off the grill. You could douse them with garlic-cilantro butter and be done, letting each of the eager eaters around your table get all buttery digging out those smoky morsels. Or, you could do a little-easier-to-eat presentation, breaking off the top shell, releasing the meat from the bottom shell (but leaving the meat in that shell) and spooning on a little salsa. If you have one of those little wood-chip smoker boxes for your gas grill, this would be the perfect place to use it.

You can do this same preparation with medium top neck clams (they'll be about 5 to a pound; buy 24 to 32 pieces). They take longer to open and cook and require more salsa.

Working Ahead: Because these salsa-topped grilled mussels are good at room temperature, feel free to grill the mussels an hour ahead. Serve them at room temperature, spooning on the salsa when you're ready to carry them to your guests.

Turn on a gas grill to medium-high or light a charcoal grill and let the coals burn until quite hot and covered with white ash. Spread the mussels onto the grill grates. As they open—it'll take 2 to 4 minutes for the two sides of the shell to have completely released from each other—remove the mussels to a rimmed baking sheet. When cool enough to handle, break off the empty half of the shell and, using your fingers or a small knife, release the meat from the shell. Lay the meat back in the shell (the "empty" side of the shell is actually prettiest for serving).

Arrange the mussels on a serving platter. Spoon a half teaspoon or so of the salsa on each one, sprinkle with cilantro and you're ready to serve.

"Lazy" Salsa
Salsa Huevona

MAKES 2 ½ CUPS, SERVING 6 GENEROUSLY

1½ pounds (4 medium-small round) ripe tomatoes

1   medium white onion, cut in half

3 or 4 fresh jalapeños, stemmed

4   garlic cloves, unpeeled

    Salt

Okay, I know the name's a little edgy, since many people wouldn't use huevona *around their grandmother. Perhaps I should have translated* salsa huevona *as "lazy-ass salsa," more clearly capturing the sentiment one of our cooks was expressing when he christened this salsa. That was after his cousin put tomatoes, onions and jalapeños on the backyard grill one Sunday afternoon and promptly forgot them until they were nearly throw-away blackened. And then he decided to use them anyway, which actually was to his credit, because something, well, alchemical seemed to happen. Alchemical and quite delicious. Though rustic and a little* huevona.

Working Ahead: This salsa keeps well for 3 or 4 days in the refrigerator, covered.

GRILLING TOMATO, GARLIC, SERRANO CHILES AND ONION FOR SALSA

1. *Char the ingredients.* Light a charcoal fire and let the coals burn until they are covered with gray ash; position the grill grate and let it heat for a couple of minutes. Lay on the tomatoes, onion halves, jalapeños and garlic. (To keep the garlic from dropping through and to make cleanup easy, I typically lay one of those perforated grill pans on the grill grates, heat it up, then lay on the vegetables.) Grill the ingredients, turning occasionally, until they are kind of charred, but not incinerated—about 10 minutes for the garlic, 15 minutes for the chiles and 20 minutes for the tomatoes and onions. As they are done remove to a rimmed baking sheet. Let cool. Peel the garlic. If you wish, you can pull the charred skins off the tomatoes.

2. *Finish the salsa.* In a food processor, combine the garlic and chiles. Pulse until coarsely pureed. Add the tomatoes and any juices that have collected on the baking sheet, and pulse until roughly chopped. Chop the charred onion and place in a bowl. Stir in the tomato mixture, along with a little water (usually about 2 tablespoons), to give the salsa an easily spoonable consistency. Taste and season with salt, usually about 1 teaspoon.

"Brava" Steak
Carne Asada Brava
SERVES 6

6   large garlic cloves, unpeeled

4   fresh serrano or 2 fresh jalapeño chiles, stemmed

¼   cup fresh lime juice

2   tablespoons vegetable or olive oil, plus more for the steaks

    Salt

6   rib-eye steaks about 1 inch thick (they'll weigh about 10 to 12 ounces each)

My directions may sound a little cranky, calling as they do for a charcoal fire with no gas grill alternative. It's just that I'm trying to make a point. Of course you can use a gas grill to cook the meat . . . but those special ingredients you're lavishing on your guests just won't be able to work all their magic. Unless you use charcoal, or wood, or at least throw some pieces of hardwood on your gas grill to conjure those special aromatics. The thrillingly spicy roasted garlic–green chile marinade sears more genuinely into the rib-eye steaks over a smoky fire. And salsa huevona (page 257), should that be your choice to spoon alongside the steak, is decidedly better when the ingredients are blistered and blackened over glowing coals. This is one of the most delicious spicy steak dishes I know.

    Working Ahead: The marinade can be made a day or two ahead. Don't marinate the steaks for more than hour or so, or the meat can lose its color and surface texture. And don't grill the steaks until you're nearly ready to eat. They will hold (in fact, they have better texture when held) for up to 30 minutes in a very low oven on a rack set over a rimmed baking sheet to catch juices.

1. *Marinate the steaks.* In a small ungreased skillet, roast the unpeeled garlic and the chiles over medium heat, turning occasionally, until both are soft and blotchy black in places—5 to 10 minutes for the chiles, 10 to 15 minutes for the garlic. Cool, then peel the garlic. Place both garlic and chiles in a food processor along with the lime juice and oil. Run the machine until the mixture is as smoothly pureed as possible. Season highly with salt, usually about 1½ teaspoons. Smear the mixture over both sides of the steaks, cover and refrigerate for 1 hour.

2. *Grill the steaks.* Light a charcoal fire and let the coals burn until they are covered with gray ash; position the grill grate and let it heat for a couple of minutes. Spray or brush the steaks on both sides with a little oil. Lay on the grill grates and let cook for 3 or 4 minutes, until the grates have nicely seared beautiful grill marks into the meat—don't attempt to move the steaks until you can see nice marking. Flip the steaks and cook until as done as you like (typically about 2 to 3 minutes longer for medium-rare). I like to let the steaks rest for a few minutes (on a cool part of the grill, on a grate suspended over the back of the grill or on a rack over a baking sheet in a very low oven) before serving to allow the meat to reabsorb all the juices. Serve with "Lazy" Salsa (*salsa huevona*, page 257) or another salsa or hot sauce of your liking.

"BRAVA" STEAK

Chipotle-Glazed Baby Back Ribs
Costillas al Chipotle Enmielado
SERVES 8

FOR THE DRY RUB

4 garlic cloves, peeled and roughly chopped

⅓ cup ground ancho chile

4 teaspoons brown sugar

1 teaspoon dried oregano, preferably Mexican

½ teaspoon ground cumin

4 teaspoons ground black pepper

5 teaspoons salt

FOR THE RIBS AND GLAZE

4 large slabs (about 6½ pounds) baby back ribs

1 7.5-ounce can chipotles *en adobo*

¾ cup honey

This is a rather unconventional approach to rib cooking: First, baby back ribs—not the larger spareribs—are showered with a dry rub that's not too far from the one I learned in my parents' barbecue restaurant in Oklahoma City; overnight the rub cures the flesh lightly, ensuring a juicy outcome. Then they're slowly baked until they're juicy-done. And, when all the hungry have assembled, the ribs are grill-singed and slathered with a sticky chipotle chile glaze—smoky, sweet, porky and anything but fainthearted. Richard James, our long-time chef de cuisine in Frontera Grill, developed this take on ribs— reliable, manageable, crowd pleasing—for the Saturday nights when ribs are the special and we serve 400 guests. Which pretty much describes a typical Frontera Saturday night.

Working Ahead: The ribs are best when baked the same day you eat them and grilled within a few minutes of serving. They will hold well in a very low oven for a half hour or so before serving.

1. Season the ribs. Combine all the dry rub ingredients in a food processor and run until thoroughly blended. Sprinkle the mixture on both sides of each slab of ribs, rub it in to ensure even coverage, then cover and refrigerate overnight. You'll probably have a little dry rub left; in a tightly closed jar in the refrigerator it will last several months.

2. First rib cooking. Heat the oven to 300 degrees. Lay the ribs in a single layer on two rimmed baking sheets and bake for about 1¼ hours, until the meat is tender when tested with a fork. (This cooking may be done early in the day you're serving. Cover and refrigerate the cooked ribs until an hour before serving.)

3. Second rib cooking. Turn on a gas grill to medium or light a charcoal grill and let the coals burn until medium-hot and covered with white ash.

In a food processor, blend the can of chipotles with the honey. Scrape into a small bowl and carry to the grill, along with a basting brush.

Lay the ribs on the grill, convex-side down. When hot and well browned, about 3 minutes, flip them over and brush liberally with the chipotle glaze. Cover the grill and cook about 7 minutes for the glaze to set and begin to brown a little. There will likely be leftover glaze, which can be covered and refrigerated for a week or two.

Cut the ribs apart (that's my preference) and serve right away.

"Easy" Slow-Cooker *Mole* with Grilled Chicken
Mole "Fácil" con Pollo Asado a las Brasas

SERVES 12 WITH ABOUT 2 QUARTS OF SAUCE (YOU'LL HAVE LEFTOVERS)

½ cup rich-tasting pork lard or vegetable oil, plus a little more if necessary

6 medium (about 3 ounces total) dried mulato chiles, stemmed, seeded and cut into roughly 1-inch pieces

3 medium (about 1½ ounces total) dried ancho chiles, stemmed, seeded and cut into roughly 1-inch pieces

5 medium (about 1½ ounces total) dried pasilla chiles, stemmed, seeded and cut into roughly 1-inch pieces

4 garlic cloves, peeled

¾ cup (about 3 ounces) whole almonds—with or without skins

½ cup (about 2 ounces) raisins

1 15-ounce can diced tomatoes in juice (preferably fire roasted)

½ teaspoon cinnamon, preferably freshly ground Mexican *canela*

¼ teaspoon black pepper, preferably freshly ground

¼ teaspoon anise, preferably freshly ground (optional)

A scant ⅛ teaspoon cloves, preferably freshly ground

1 ounce (about ⅓ of a 3.3-ounce tablet) Mexican chocolate, roughly chopped

"Easy," in the context of mole, *certainly has a different connotation than when read alongside, say, "fettuccine." Meaning an "easy mole" is more akin to an easy Thanksgiving dinner, requiring several hours rather than several days, fewer pots and pans, less painstaking precision. But satisfying nonetheless.*

In the last thirty years, I've learned a lot about mole *making from some of Mexico's—the world's?—best cooks. And from their teachings I've gleaned two very important truths. First, for a good* mole *it's important to toast or brown all the basic ingredients thoroughly. But no one said that for a relatively small amount, those ingredients can't be toasted together—which is what I've done here, saving an enormous amount of time and energy. And second, nothing can replace a* mole's *long, mellowing simmer. But how about giving them that mellowing simmer while the ingredients are unblended, helping soften them for easier blending later? And how about an untended slow-cooker to make the whole process worry-free?*

Is this easy mole *the best* mole *you'll likely ever taste? Maybe not, but it's great—certainly a great place to start. And to tell you the truth, when I've been stuck with few resources, I've made this* mole *with all dried ancho chiles (instead of the mixture of ancho, mulato and pasilla); while the* mole's *a little less complex, it's still very good. Partly because all the remaining host of ingredients are in place, especially the good proportion of almonds, which add a luxurious richness. Many in Mexico would call this a* mole almendrado.

You'll need a large (6-quart) slow-cooker to make this mole *comfortably; one with a removable, stovetop cooking crock means one less pot to wash. Without a slow-cooker, I'd use a Dutch oven, cover it and bake the whole affair in a 225 degree oven for the 6 hours; then I'd blend, strain and simmer the* mole *on the stovetop.*

Unless you have all the measured, prepped ingredients at easy reach when you start cooking, you'll wind up feeling frazzled.

1. *Preparing the* **mole** *base.* If your slow-cooker has a removable cooking crock that can be placed directly on the heat, measure in the lard or oil and set it over medium heat. Otherwise, heat the lard or oil in a very large (7- to 8-quart) pot or Dutch oven. When hot, add the chiles, garlic, almonds and raisins. Stir slowly and continually until the chiles are thoroughly toasted (the interior of each piece will become lighter in color) and the almonds have taken on a creamy color and toasty aroma—about 5 minutes.

Add the tomatoes (with their juice), spices, chocolate and bread. Cook until the tomato juices are reduced and quite thick, about 2 minutes. Add

1   slice firm white bread, darkly
    toasted and broken into several
    pieces

¼   cup sugar (plus a little more if
    needed)

    Salt

    About 2 quarts chicken broth

12 good-size pieces of chicken—
    bone-in chicken breast halves or
    leg-and-thigh pieces—trimmed of
    excess fat

⅓   cup sesame seeds

2 cups water, the sugar and 1½ teaspoons salt. Stir to combine. When the liquid comes to a simmer, transfer the crock to the slow-cooker (or scrape the mixture into your slow-cooker). Cook on low for 6 hours. After 6 hours most of the liquid will be reduced to a glaze. The mixture can hold for several hours on the slow-cooker's "warm" setting.

2. *Finish the* mole. Scrape every bit of the *mole* base into a bowl, then scoop *half* of it into a blender jar. Add 2 cups of the chicken broth, cover and blend until as smooth as possible—for most household blenders this will take 4 to 5 minutes. Set a medium-mesh strainer over the slow-cooker's cooking crock and press the *mole* base through it. Repeat with the remainder of the *mole* base. Stir in 3 cups more chicken broth. Simmer in the slow-cooker for 2 hours or so on high. If the sauce has thickened past the consistency of a cream soup, stir in a little more of the broth. Taste and season with additional salt (usually about 1 teaspoon) and sugar (usually 2 to 3 tablespoons).

3. *Grill the chicken.* Light a gas grill, setting the temperature at medium on the sides, off in the center; or light a charcoal fire, letting the coals burn until they're covered with white ash and medium hot, then banking them to the sides. Sprinkle both sides of the chicken pieces liberally with salt, then lay them, skin side up, in the center of the grill. Cover and cook until the chicken is done (160 degrees on an instant-read thermometer or a small knife inserted into the thickest part of the thigh draws clear—not rosy—juices), 35 to 45 minutes. With this method of chicken grilling, there's no need to turn the chicken, only to move pieces on the edge around if they are browning more quickly than those in the middle. The internal temperature of the grill should stay at about 325 degrees.

4. *Serve.* In a small skillet over medium heat, toast the sesame seeds, stirring nearly constantly, until lightly browned and aromatic, about 4 minutes.

Lay a piece of grilled chicken on each dinner plate. Pour a generous ½ cup of sauce on and around the chicken, then sprinkle with a generous shower of sesame seeds. Serve right away.

Grill-Braised Short Ribs with Árbol Chiles, White Beans, Mushrooms and Beer

Costillas de Res Guisadas con Chiles de Árbol, Alubias, Hongos y Cerveza

SERVES 8

4 pounds (8 good-size pieces) bone-in beef short ribs

Salt

Black pepper, preferably freshly ground

8 dried árbol chiles

2 tablespoons olive or vegetable oil

1 large white onion, cut into ½-inch pieces

8 ounces full-flavored mushrooms (think wild ones here, or maybe shiitakes), stemmed and quartered

2 cups full-flavored beer (I like Bohemia)

2 cups beef broth

1 head garlic, cut in half across the center, unpeeled

3 sprigs of fresh thyme

1 15-ounce can diced tomatoes in juice (preferably fire-roasted)

4 cups cooked white beans (home-made or canned—you'll need 3 15-ounce cans), drained

Here's a tasty intersection of modern and traditional. The rich smokiness of grill-braised beef short ribs with roasted tomatoes, a little hot chile, woodland mushrooms, white beans, hoppy beer—all the ingredients that make our eyes light up these days, ingredients that have been staples in Mexican kitchens for ages. Even grill-braising sounds modern, though, to be truthful, the basic technique of cooking a pot of something over embers in a closed environment (an accurate description of the pit cooking used for barbacoa) dates back millennia in Mexico. In a nutshell, this dish is a great way to thoroughly satisfy both traditionalists and trend-seekers at the same table.

Oven Alternative: This dish can be made very successfully in the oven. In the Dutch oven in a little oil, brown the meat, then braise everything together, covered, for about 2½ hours at 325 degrees.

Working Ahead: The whole dish can be made a day or so ahead, cooled, covered and refrigerated. When making the dish ahead, I like to remove the meat to a separate container to ensure that its juices don't overwhelm the other flavors of the dish. Reheat, covered with foil, in a 350-degree oven for 30 to 45 minutes.

1. Sear the meat. Turn on a gas grill to medium-high or light a charcoal grill and let the coals burn until quite hot and covered with white ash.

Generously sprinkle the meat on all sides with salt and pepper. Lay the short ribs on the grill and sear on all sides, until richly browned, 4 or 5 minutes total depending on the heat of your fire. Remove to a rimmed baking sheet.

2. Flavor the short ribs. Break the stems off the chiles, then roll them between your fingers to loosen the seeds. Break the chiles in half and shake out all the seeds that come free easily. Set a large (7- to 8-quart) Dutch oven over medium-high heat. When the pot is hot, pour in the oil. Add the chiles and stir for 10 to 15 seconds, until they are noticeably darker and aromatic. Remove to a small plate, draining as much oil as possible back into the pan.

Add the onion to the pot and cook, stirring regularly, until golden, about 7 minutes, then stir in the mushrooms and cook another couple of minutes. Add the beer, broth, garlic, thyme, tomatoes, beans, toasted chiles, 1½ teaspoons salt and a generous ½ teaspoon black pepper.

Add the short ribs (and any juices that have collected around them) to the pot, nestling them into the liquid.

3. *Grill-braise the short ribs.* Either turn the grill burner(s) in the center to medium-low or bank the coals to the sides for indirect cooking. Set the pot in the center of the grill and cook until the short ribs are fork-tender, 2 to 2½ hours. As necessary add additional charcoal to keep the fire medium-hot.

4. *Serve.* Carefully remove the short ribs to a deep serving platter. Discard the garlic and thyme sprigs from the braising liquid. Using a slotted spoon, spoon the beans and mushrooms around the short ribs. If a lot of fat has rendered from the short ribs, ladle it from the top of the sauce. Taste the sauce and season with additional salt if you think necessary, then ladle it over the ribs and beans. You're ready to serve.

Chile-Roasted Pork on the Grill, Chiapas Style
Cochito Chiapaneco
SERVES 6

2 medium (about 1 ounce total) dried ancho chiles, stemmed and seeded

4 medium (about 1 ounce total) dried guajillo chiles, stemmed and seeded

2 whole cloves

8 allspice berries

2 bay leaves

1 teaspoon mixed dried herbs (such as marjoram, thyme and oregano)

2 tablespoons fruity vinegar (apple cider is my choice here)

2 garlic cloves, peeled and roughly chopped

1 small white onion

1½ tablespoons fresh, rich-tasting pork lard or vegetable oil

Salt

4 pounds bone-in pork shoulder roast (or a 3-pound boneless roast, if that's all you can find)

OR 4½ pounds fresh picnic ham, preferably with the skin still on

A 1-pound package of banana leaves, defrosted if frozen

6 to 8 romaine lettuce leaves, for garnish

2 radishes, thinly sliced, for garnish

Thirty years ago, when I lived in Mexico and canvassed the thirty-one states in a chartreuse VW van with blue-and-green-striped curtains, I traversed the 175-mile pass from Tabasco to Chiapas, from sea level to 6,500 feet and back down, a trip that would seem generously a six-hour endeavor were it not for the intermittent landslides and hundreds—maybe thousands—of switchbacks. But when you settle into Chiapas, there's a feeling that things are different. Less Mexican somehow, more alien, more distant in time and custom. Yet, at roadside stands on Sunday afternoons, my wife and I found comfort in smoky roast pigs painted with ancho chile, swathed in banana leaves, served according to the old-fashioned custom with ensalada of romaine leaves, radishes and onions. Cochito Chiapaneco they call it, part Yucatecan cochinita pibil with its leaf wrapping, part Oaxacan carne adobada all covered in red chile paste. A big pot of this aromatic meat is, for me, one of the most evocative dishes in Mexico's cookbook.

It's good even without the banana leaves, so don't worry if you can't find them. As available as they've become in grocery stores (and Asian and Mexican markets), that won't be often. They do add character, as well as a subtle, but distinguishable, herbal flavor. And since the cooking is long and slow, not toasting the chiles goes without notice.

Oven Alternative: This dish can be made very successfully in the oven at 325 degrees for 2 to 3 hours.

Working Ahead: The red chile marinade can be made ahead, as can the entire dish. Let everything cool, remove the meat from the juices, and discard the leaves, leaving behind as much liquid as possible. Store meat and juices separately. Reheat the meat, juices spooned on top, in a 325-degree oven for 30 minutes or so, everything laid on a new slice of banana leaf if you want the greatest aromatic impact.

---

1. *Make the chile marinade.* Place the chiles in a small bowl, cover with hot tap water, weight with a plate to keep them submerged, and rehydrate for 30 minutes. Drain, reserving ⅔ cup of the soaking liquid; transfer chiles and reserved liquid to a blender jar. Pulverize the cloves, allspice and bay leaves in a spice grinder or mortar. Add to the blender, along with the mixed herbs, vinegar and garlic. Cut the onion in half. Roughly chop one half and add to the blender; slice the other half and set aside to use as garnish. Blend the chile mixture until smooth, then strain through a medium-mesh sieve.

Set a large Dutch oven over medium-high heat and add the lard or oil. When it's hot enough to make a drop of the puree really sizzle, add the puree all at once. Stir constantly as the puree sears and darkens into a thick paste, 4 or 5 minutes. Remove from the heat, scrape into a bowl, stir in ½ cup water and season highly with salt, usually a generous 2 teaspoons. Set the pot aside without washing.

2. *Season and grill-roast the meat.* Turn on a gas grill to medium or light a charcoal grill and let the coals burn until medium-hot and covered with white ash. When ready, either turn the grill burner(s) in the center to medium-low or bank the coals to the sides for indirect cooking.

If you are using pork shoulder, cut it into 2-inch slabs; leave a picnic ham whole, but make 1-inch-deep incisions every few inches all over the meat.

Line the chile-cooking pot or a roasting pan with a double layer of banana leaves (if using), then lay in the meat. Spoon the chile marinade over the meat. Cover with another double layer of banana leaves, then pour a cup of water over the leaves. Lastly, cover lightly with a piece of foil (just to keep the top banana leaves from drying out too much). Set the Dutch oven or roasting pan in the center of the grill and cook until the pork is fork-tender, 2 to 3 hours. (The grill temperature should remain between 300 and 325 degrees.) From time to time, I typically remove the foil and upper banana leaves and baste the meat with the pan juices. If, at any point, the liquid completely evaporates, add a little bit more: you want some easily spoonable pan juices for serving.

3. *Serve.* Line a large platter with the romaine leaves. Uncover the pork, discarding the banana leaves. Cut or tear off large pieces of the meat and lay them over the romaine. Taste and season the juices with additional salt if you think they need it; if there is a lot of fat floating on top, feel free to spoon it off. Spoon the juices over the meat, then garnish with the reserved onion and the radish slices.

Slivered Ancho "Salsa"
Salsa de Tijeras

MAKES ABOUT 1½ CUPS

8   medium (about 4 ounces total) dried ancho chiles, stemmed and seeded

1½ tablespoons vegetable or olive oil

½   medium white onion, sliced ⅛ inch thick

2   garlic cloves, peeled and finely chopped

A generous tablespoon cider vinegar, plus a little more if needed

¼   teaspoon dried thyme

¼   teaspoon dried marjoram

Salt

3   tablespoons Mexican *crema* (page 200), whipping cream or *crème fraîche*

1 or 2 tablespoons of finely crumbled Mexican *queso añejo* or Parmesan (optional)

This salsa—one that's found rather infrequently in Mexico—has an interesting texture. It's thickish, almost a little chewy from the dried anchos that are sliced and toasted and moistened. It has some crunchy browned onion to play against the sweet earthiness of the chiles and the splash of vinegar tang. And, of course, there's the cream's richness. A salsa you just have to try to appreciate its full beauty. Words aren't adequate.

Working Ahead: The salsa may be made an hour or so ahead of time but don't add the cream and cheese until you're ready to serve

---

1. *The chiles.* Turn on the oven to 325 degrees. With a pair of kitchen scissors or a sharp knife, cut the chiles into ⅛-inch slices. (I think it's best to work with scissors, because the chile skins are quite tough and will require a fair amount of pressure from your knife—which can be a little dangerous.) Spread on a baking sheet and toast in the oven for about 5 minutes, until very aromatic. Transfer to a bowl, cover with hot water, and let rehydrate, stirring frequently for 10 minutes—no more, since you want them to retain an appealing, slightly chewy texture. Drain and discard the water.

2. *Finish the salsa.* In a large (10-inch) skillet, heat the oil over medium-high. Add the onion to the pan and cook until nicely browned but still a little crunchy, about 5 minutes. Add the drained chiles, garlic, vinegar, herbs and ½ teaspoon salt, and remove from the heat. Stir in the cream, taste and season with additional salt, if you think it needs more, and cool to room temperature. If the salsa seems too thick to spoon easily, stir in a little water. Scrape into a salsa dish. If using the cheese, sprinkle it over the salsa.

GRILLED RACK OF LAMB WITH HONEY-PASILLA GLAZE
(PAGE 270)

Grilled Rack of Lamb with Honey-Pasilla Glaze
Rack de Borrego al Pasilla

SERVES 4

6 garlic cloves, unpeeled

6 (about 2 ounces total) dried pasilla chiles, stemmed, seeded and torn into flat pieces

1 teaspoon dried oregano, preferably Mexican

¼ teaspoon black pepper, preferably freshly ground

⅛ teaspoon cumin, preferably freshly ground

¼ cup honey (a dark one goes well with pasilla chiles)

2 tablespoons vinegar (I prefer balsamic here)

Salt

2 lamb racks (each should have 8 rib bones and weigh about 1¾ to 2 pounds), trimmed of excess surface fat and rib bones scraped clean ("frenched") if you wish

Olive or vegetable oil to brush or spray on the racks

1 small red onion, finely chopped

About ¼ cup grated Mexican *queso añejo* or another garnishing cheese like Romano or Parmesan

Flat-leaf parsley leaves, for garnish

It all started on a Sunday afternoon at Restaurante Arroyo in Tlalpan, south of Mexico City, with a plate of pit-cooked lamb barbacoa, seasoned with rock salt and cooked in a cloak of huge agave "spears" and aromatic avocado leaves. And served with dark borracha salsa of toasted pasilla chiles, garlic, beery pulque and crumbled dried leaves of Mexican oregano. The sweet gaminess of the lamb smack dab against the ocean-deep richness of those dark chiles left an indelible mark on my palate, on my understanding of flavor's potential.

As the spirit of that dish emerged in various dishes I created for Frontera Grill and Topolobampo, a perennial favorite is grilled rack of lamb—we cook it over a wood fire—with a salsa that features pasilla chile's robust baritone brightened with a little vinegar and mellowed with a bit of honey. At home, I occasionally grill a boneless butterflied lamb leg instead of lamb racks. Over a medium-hot fire, an average-size leg takes 25 to 35 minutes to cook to medium.

1. *Make the pasilla marinade.* Roast the unpeeled garlic on one side of a large skillet over medium heat, turning occasionally, until soft and blackened in spots, about 15 minutes; cool and peel. While the garlic is roasting, toast the chile pieces a few at a time on the other side of the skillet, pressing them down firmly with a spatula for a few seconds until they release a toasty aroma, then flipping them, and pressing down the other side. Scoop the chiles into a small bowl, cover with hot tap water and let rehydrate 30 minutes. Drain, reserving ⅓ cup of the soaking water.

In a food processor or blender, combine the chiles, the reserved soaking liquid, garlic, oregano, pepper, cumin, honey, vinegar and 1 teaspoon salt. Blend to a smooth puree, scraping down and stirring frequently. Press through a medium-mesh strainer into a small bowl.

2. *Marinate the meat.* Lay the meat in a baking dish. Smear both sides of the racks with about ⅓ of the marinade. Cover and refrigerate for several hours, if time permits.

3. *Make the salsa.* Stir enough water into the remaining marinade to give it drizzleable consistency—it usually takes at least ¼ cup. Cover and set aside at room temperature (or refrigerate if not using within a couple of hours).

4. *Grill the meat.* Light a gas grill, setting the temperature at medium-high on one side, medium-low on the other; or light a charcoal fire, letting the coals burn until they're covered with white ash but still very hot, then banking them to one side. Using the side of a spoon, scrape the marinade off the meat, reserving it for basting later. Brush or spray the lamb racks with oil and lay them, meaty "cap" side down, on the hottest part of the grill. When they are well seared ("marked" with the grill grate pattern, as we say in the restaurant kitchen), about 2 minutes, flip them over and sear on the bony underside. Baste the tops with the reserved marinade, then move them to the cooler part of the grill and let them cook until as done as you like, usually about 5 minutes for medium-rare.

5. *Serve.* It's best to let the meat rest for a few minutes on a very cool part of the grill or in a very low oven, to reabsorb the meat's tasty juices. Then slice the chops between the bones. Drizzle a little of the salsa on each of four warm dinner plates and sprinkle with the onion. Arrange the meat over the top and sprinkle with the cheese and parsley leaves. Serve right away.

GRILLED LAMB RACKS READY FOR SLICING

SLICED RACK OF LAMB

Oaxacan-Style Lamb Pit Barbecue
Barbacoa de Borrego, Estilo Oaxaqueño

SERVES 25 TO 30, WITH ABOUT 6 QUARTS OF CONSOMMÉ

Most of you will chuckle as you read through this recipe, not really believing that I included it here. It's a little like the now-cliché tale of the fellow who requested the recipe for the delicious rabbit dish he was eating. "First, you catch the rabbit," started the cook's instructions. In like manner, my first instructions here are to dig a traditional Mexican barbacoa pit, line it with bricks and heat it with a wood fire for at least 24 hours before you lower in your whole lamb (see page 275). Definitely not cooking for the quick-and-easy crowd, or for those who feel more comfortable with meat that comes neatly shrink-wrapped.

Barbacoa is as celebratory as food gets—the mariachi band and fireworks of the culinary crowd. It's live-fire cooking at its earthiest, most elemental—which means that it will appeal to a primal streak that runs through a bunch of us. And I suggest you pull together a group of those people to help pull this off. After all, camaraderie around a few shovels, the fire and a whole animal is just about as important as the deliciously slow-cooked, smoke-tinged barbacoa that you'll be serving to the crowd that collects to devour it.

Barbacoa is the centerpiece of important festivities all over Mexico. In central Mexico, it's typically made with lamb that they season with coarse salt, top with a few avocado leaves, wrap in flame-softened sections of agave "leaves" (known as pencas in Spanish), and pit-cook. In Oaxaca, which is the inspiration for this recipe, the lamb (or often, goat) is slathered with bright-and-tangy red chile marinade and the agave is replaced by branches of those aromatic leaves from the wild avocado tree. So many branches, in fact, that an exact replica is pretty much out of the question for anyone north of the border. My suggestion: use a big handful of the wild avocado leaves for their anisey flavor (they're available from Mexgrocer.com, Gourmetsleuth.com and at many Mexican groceries) and protect the meat from drying out by wrapping it in the easier-to-find banana leaves—just like cooks do in Yucatan when making pork pibil, another of Mexico's great pit-cooked delicacies.

One of my favorite parts of a barbacoa feast is the herby vegetable soup—what they call the consomé—that cooks under the lamb in the pit, catching all its delicious drippings. (In central Mexico, they add garbanzos to the pot, making the soup more substantial.) And then there's the fall-off-the-bone-tender meat, which cries out for fresh corn tortillas and a rustic salsa like Oaxacan Pasilla Salsa (page 203) or the "Drunken" Salsa (page 184). Plus a spoon of black beans (preferably cooked with epazote and rich lard) and some fresh-made guacamole. Honestly, food can get fancier, but it doesn't get much better.

1½ heads garlic, cloves broken apart but not peeled (divided use)

⅓ cup vegetable oil

6 ounces (about 24) dried guajillo chiles, stemmed, seeded, deveined (if you wish) and torn into large flat pieces

⅔ cup apple cider vinegar

1 teaspoon cinnamon, preferably freshly ground Mexican *canela*

1 teaspoon fresh black pepper, preferably freshly ground

½ teaspoon cloves, preferably freshly ground

¼ cup salt

2 tablespoons sugar

FOR FINISHING THE BARBACOA

1 small lamb (about 30 pounds dressed weight), separated into large (primal) cuts

3 pounds (about 6 large) white onions, cut into ½-inch pieces

3 pounds (about 12 medium) carrots, peeled (if you wish) and cut into ½-inch pieces

10 bay leaves

A handful of fresh thyme sprigs (or 1½ teaspoons dried)

A handful of fresh marjoram sprigs (or 1½ teaspoons dried)

4 2-foot lengths of banana leaf, if available

About 4 ounces dried avocado leaves

Coarse salt for serving

Now for a little friendly advice: as rustic and imprecise as cooking in a hole in the ground sounds, it's not. Your pit needs to be close to the size I've outlined or too much heat will disperse, leaving the food undercooked. And the bricks that line the pit need to be heated to somewhere near 800 degrees before you lower in the lamb or, yes, the lamb may not get done. But you're cooking with residual heat here—not the fire itself—so you have to carefully seal the edges of your pit cover with dirt to cut off all oxygen and suffocate any live embers. Otherwise, the fire may continue to flame and you risk burning the lamb. And finally: though it's not absolutely necessary, I highly recommend that you buy the pan I recommend on page 275. It's sturdy and just the right size for the lamb and the soup.

For 30 people, plan about a quart of salsa, about 1¼ gallons of beans, and guacamole made from 12 to 15 avocados.

---

1. *The pit.* Dig the pit and line it with bricks as directed on page 275. Build a fire the night before you're going make the *barbacoa* to preheat the bricks and earth that surrounds them. Build a rip-roaring fire—keep it going for about 3 hours—then let it burn out and cover the pit to trap residual heat.

Early on the morning of your party, uncover the pit and build another huge fire in it. Keep adding wood so that the fire stays very hot (700 to 800 degrees) for at least 3 or 4 hours.

2. *Make the* adobo. Roast *6 cloves* of the garlic in a large dry skillet over medium heat, turning regularly, until soft and blotchy black in spots, 10 to 15 minutes. Meanwhile, heat the oil in another large skillet over medium-high. A few at a time, oil-toast the chiles for a few seconds on each side, until noticeably darker and toasty smelling—certainly not smoking and blackened. Remove the chiles to a large bowl, pour on 3 cups of hot tap water and weight with a plate to keep them submerged. Soak 20 minutes.

Peel the roasted garlic and place in a blender along with the chiles (and their soaking liquid), vinegar, spices, salt and sugar. Blend to a smooth puree. Press through a medium-mesh strainer (to strain seeds and unblended skin) set over a large bowl.

3. *Marinate the lamb and set up the roasting pan.* Smear the red chile marinade over the lamb. Set four 3- to 5-inch heat-proof supports (empty tin cans, custard cups or ramekins) near the four corners of your huge braising pan. Peel the remaining garlic, roughly chop it and scatter it over the bottom of the pan, along with the onions, carrots and herbs. If you have the innards (heart, kidney and liver) add them to the pan as well. Set a rack on the supports (an oven rack, grill grate or large cooling rack are good choices). Cover with 2 of the banana leaves and half of the avocado leaves. Lay in the pieces of marinated lamb, keeping them in as close to a single layer as possible. Cover with the remaining avocado leaves and 2 pieces of banana leaves. Carry to the pit.

4. *Cook the lamb.* The fire should be burning very, very hot just before you lower in the lamb. Use a shovel or fireplace tongs to remove all the burning logs (but not the coals) from the pit. (The temperature of the pit should be about 800 degrees—the temperature of a traditional pizza oven—though without professional equipment, the temperature will be hard to measure.) Pour ½ gallon water around the edges of the lamb. With the help of another (strong) person wearing oven mitts, lower the braising pan of meat onto the coals in the very hot pit. Immediately cover the pit. Transfer the smoldering logs to the middle of the cover. Shovel enough dirt around the edges of the cover to completely seal the pit (when complete, you should see no smoke or steam escaping). Shovel more dirt (around the smoldering logs) over the cover to a depth of about 2 inches, to trap the heat.

Let the lamb cook for about 6 hours. If everything's gone right, after 6 hours, the temperature of the cover, once you've swept the dirt back with your hand, will be about 175 degrees—so hot that you can only touch it for a few seconds.

5. *Unearth the lamb and serve.* Shovel and sweep all the dirt off the cover (I shovel it into a garbage can that I cover and store until the next time I use the pit). Uncover and lift out the braising pan. Remove and discard the top set of leaves. Transfer the meat to large serving platters or roasting pans, pulling off and discarding the bones (and the fat and skin, if you're so inclined) as you go. Keep warm in a low oven.

Discard the leaves that were below the meat. Remove the rack and supports. Ladle the soup into a large soup pot. Fish out the garlic and herbs and discard. (Fish out and cut up the pieces of innards if you used them, then return them to the soup.) Let stand a few minutes for the fat to rise to the top, then skim it off. Taste and season the soup with salt, usually about 1½ tablespoons. Keep warm over low heat.

When you're ready to serve, ladle the soup into small bowls for your guests to enjoy as a first course. Then, sprinkle the meat with coarse salt and set it out for everyone to enjoy with warm corn tortillas, salsa, guacamole and black beans.

Building a Pit

FOR THE PIT

Tape measure, stakes and string for mapping out the pit area

Shovel (and lots of energy)

Bricks

A steel or corrugated metal sheet to cover the pit

1. Dig the pit. The day before, find a flat area in your backyard that's not too near your neighbors, with no low-hanging tree branches.

Measure and stake out an area that is about 8 inches larger all around than the pan you are planning to use, and about 8 inches deeper. For this recipe, the roasting pan I use is a heavy gauge aluminum roaster that measures about 21 x 17½ x 17 inches; it's made by Vollrath and can be purchased at most restaurant supply companies. If your pan matches mine, you'll be measuring and staking out a rectangular pit that's 37 x 33 inches. Dig the pit to an even depth of 16 inches, working to keep the sides straight and even all the way down. Keep the excavated dirt in a pile beside the pit.

Next, line the bottom of the pit with bricks, fitting them tightly together, then line the sides up to the top, packing the bricks tightly against the earthen sides.

2. Build the fire(s). To warm up the bricks and ground around them (and also to "season" a newly dug pit), build a bonfire in the pit for 7 hours or so the day before you cook the *barbacoa*.

Early on the day of cooking, build another huge fire in the pit and let it burn for about 5 hours, adding logs regularly to keep the temperature up at around 700 or 800 degrees. (If you put your hand near the edge of the fire, it should be so hot that you'll have to withdraw it instantly.) Set the steel or corrugated metal sheet beside the pit.

Mexican Paella for a Crowd with Shrimp, Mussels and Chorizo

Paella Mexicana con Camarónes, Mejillones y Chorizo

SERVES 30 GENEROUSLY

There are some dishes—it's good to recognize this—that simply assume the role of honored guest wherever they show up, catching every gaze, captivating imaginations, creating a party out of a mere gathering in a way that's rare and remarkable. Paella is one of them. True paella, that is, the kind cooked in a pan that's bigger than a manhole cover, cooked over a wood fire. Paellas like the hundred or so that are toiled over on a late summer afternoon at Mexico's huge Vendimia Festival—the wine harvest festival in Mexico's Baja peninsula, just east of Ensanada, south of Tecate. Or paellas like they make on the beach all summer long in Valencia, across the Atlantic.

Paella has long been a special dish in Mexico—it was a Sunday special in many of the family-owned little restaurants that dotted the downtown Mexico City neighborhood I lived in several decades ago. But there, it's often expressed with classic Mexican ingredients like fresh, tangy chorizo instead of the cured, smoked variety of Spain, like roasted green poblanos instead of red pimientos. But the captivation of its dramatic creation remains intact.

SEARING CHICKEN FOR PAELLA

All you need is a huge pan—mine is 32 inches in diameter. And my first glimpse of that pan, in a store in California, was love at first sight. I had to have it, to have it shipped to Chicago, where I stored it in the garage rafters waiting for an occasion worthy of its debut.

Finally, the event: my daughter's quinceañera, her blow-out fifteenth birthday party, complete with mariachis and a tower of chocolate cupcakes. Though I'd purchased the huge gas burner to fire my paella, a wood fire—the kind I'd seen on the Valencia beach—seemed like it'd be more thrilling. Smoky and rustic, framed by a wrestling match with burning logs. I knew it would feel monumental enough to capture the joy and importance of the day.

Here's the recipe for the paella I created for my daughter's party, classic in its approach, thoroughly Mexican in its flavor. You can purchase your own 32-inch paellera (and the burner, if a wood fire isn't your thing) from Tienda. com and SpanishTable.com; 32 inches is approximately 80 cm. Because it's live-fire cooking, I have described the state of the fire and the cooking times as clearly as I can. Just know that yours may vary. And should you build an hornillo (page 238) to cook your paella, start the fire an hour early to thoroughly warm up the bricks.

Working Ahead: I always do the preparations through Step 1 before the guests arrive; occasionally I do the browning of the chicken (Step 2) as well, either in the paella pan or in skillet(s) on the stove. Once you start Step 3, you've triggered the countdown to serving. Recently, at the wedding of one of our chefs, I carried the finished paella to a buffet table, supported it on 5-inch-tall glass bricks and kept it warm for an hour with 8 tea lights underneath.

1 gallon plus 1 quart chicken broth

¼ cup salt (⅓ cup if you're using low-sodium broth, ½ cup if using unsalted broth), plus more for the chicken

3 pounds red-ripe tomatoes

OR 2 28-ounce cans diced tomatoes in juice (preferably fire roasted), undrained

10 large fresh poblano chiles

30 chicken thighs (with bones and skin intact)

1¼ cups good-quality olive oil

3 large (about 1½ pounds total) white onions, cut into ½-inch pieces (about 5 cups)

3 pounds fresh Mexican chorizo sausage, casing removed

2 heads garlic, peeled and finely chopped

8 pounds medium-grain rice

4 pounds medium-large (21 to 25 count per pound) shrimp, peeled (leaving the tail and final joint intact, if you wish) and deveined

7 pounds mussels, scrubbed, any "beards" pulled off

1½ pounds frozen peas, defrosted

1 cup chopped flat-leaf parsley

⅔ cup silver tequila (optional)

A note about portions: *If paella is the only main dish, this quantity will serve 30 generously. If there is a lot of other food, especially other entrees, I've stretched this to be a nice tasting portion for 120 or so.*

1. *The broth and flavorings.* In a large (12-quart) stock pot, combine the broth and salt. Measure in 1 gallon plus 2 cups of water, cover the pot and set over medium-low heat.

If using fresh tomatoes, roast them on a rimmed baking sheet 4 inches below a very hot broiler until blackened and blistered, about 6 minutes per side. Cool, then peel (if you wish). Scoop the tomatoes (fresh roasted or canned roasted) into a blender or food processor, along with all their juices. Puree and set aside.

Roast the poblanos over a gas flame or 4 inches below a very hot broiler, turning frequently, until blackened all over, about 5 minutes for the open flame, 10 minutes under the broiler. Collect in a bowl and cover with a kitchen towel. When cool, rub off the blackened skin and pull out the stem and seed pod, then tear the chiles open, scrape out the seeds and rinse briefly under cold water to remove stray bits of skin and seeds. Cut into ½-inch pieces.

2. *Brown the chicken.* If using an *hornillo*, build a wood fire in it. Sprinkle the skin side of the chicken thighs with salt. Set the paella pan over the wood fire or a paella burner—the burner set on medium-high, the wood fire stoked to a pretty impressive blaze. Give the pan a minute or so to heat up, then add the olive oil. Tip the pan to distribute the oil, then immediately start laying in the chicken, skin side down. Sprinkle with salt. Fry—move the pieces around as necessary to ensure they're not sticking and that they are cooking evenly—until the skin is deeply golden, about 10 minutes. Turn the chicken thighs over (I like to do this with a pair of tongs), and fry until

START PAELLA COOKING

browned and cooked through (juices from a small cut at the thickest part will run clear), 8 to 10 minutes longer. Remove to a rimmed baking sheet.

3. *Cook the flavorings.* Immediately add the onions and chorizo to the pan. Stir (I use a long-handled grilling spatula), breaking up lumps of chorizo, until the chorizo is cooked through and the onion is beginning to brown, about 10 minutes. Add the garlic and stir for a couple of minutes longer. Add the tomatoes and poblanos, and cook, stirring nearly constantly, until the mixture is very thick and the oil has started to separate from it, 7 or 8 minutes.

COOKING CHORIZO FOR PAELLA

4. *Start cooking the rice.* If using wood, make sure your fire is still stoked to burn very hot. Add the rice to the flavorings, stir to combine, and keep stirring for 4 or 5 minutes, until a good portion of the rice has turned from translucent to milky white. Pour in the hot broth mixture—if your temperature is right, the broth should come to a boil in less than a minute. Set a timer for 12 minutes. Stir your paella only once a minute, slowly and thoroughly scraping across the bottom of the pan and moving the rice from edges into the center. At 12 minutes, the rice should have absorbed enough liquid to look like risotto. Check a kernel of rice: it should be getting soft, but still have a tiny bit of chalkiness at the center. If the rice doesn't look or taste ready, let it cook another minute or two.

ADDING RICE TO PAELLA
SAUTÉING RICE FOR PAELLA

REMOVING LOGS FROM *HORNILLO*
FOR FINAL COOKING OF PAELLA

5. *Add the chicken and shellfish.* Working quickly (I usually ask a friend to help), nestle the chicken thighs into the center of the rice, lay the shrimp in a ring around the chicken and arrange the mussels in the rice around the edge of the pan. Cover the pan with two pieces of heavy duty foil (it's typically 18 inches wide) or with a folded-up tablecloth. Turn the burner to its lowest setting or remove the burning logs from under the paella (but leave the embers). Let stand for 10 minutes to cook the shrimp and mussels and finish cooking the rice.

6. *Serve the paella.* Uncover the paella and sprinkle with the peas, parsley, and, if you're using it, the tequila. Using a large serving spoon, gently fluff the mussels and shrimp into the rice mixture. (You can do the same thing with the chicken, but it's more difficult.) You can breathe a sigh of relief. You're ready to serve.

ADDING PEAS AND HERBS TO FINISHED PAELLA

FINISHED PAELLA

Mexican Paella for Six
Paella Mexicana para Seis
SERVES 6

3¼ cups chicken broth

1   teaspoon salt (1½ teaspoons for low-sodium broth, 2 teaspoons for unsalted)

1   large poblano pepper

1   15-ounce can diced tomatoes in juice (preferably fire roasted), undrained

¼   cup olive oil

6   chicken thighs (bones and skin intact)

½   medium onion, chopped into ¼-inch pieces

½   cup (4 ounces) fresh Mexican chorizo sausage, casing removed

3   garlic cloves, peeled and finely chopped

2   cups medium-grain rice

½   pound medium-large shrimp, peeled (leaving the tail and final joint intact, if you wish) and deveined

1   pound mussels, scrubbed, any "beards" pulled off

1   cup frozen peas, defrosted

    A couple of tablespoons chopped flat-leaf parsley

2   tablespoons silver tequila (optional)

Making a small paella isn't much of a challenge at all, especially when compared with the rather daunting expanse of a 3-foot-wide pan and the expectations of a hungry horde. I make it all the time in a deep 12-inch cast-iron skillet (I don't even bother with a real paella pan, though I have nothing against using one) and set the hearty-looking dinner in the middle of the table for everyone to dig into, fishing for shrimp or mussels or another spoon of rice.

Working Ahead: All your set-up can be done ahead (on occasion, I've taken the prep through Step 2). Finish the dish when the guests have gathered: it doesn't hold very well.

1. *Preliminaries.* Measure the broth into a medium (3-quart) saucepan, add the salt, cover and set over low heat.

Roast the poblano over a gas flame or 4 inches below a very hot broiler, turning frequently, until blackened all over, about 5 minutes for the open flame, 10 minutes under the broiler. Cool under a kitchen towel until handleable, then pull off the skin, pull out the stem and seed pod, then scrape out the seeds and rinse briefly. Cut into ½-inch pieces. Pour the undrained tomatoes into a blender or food processor. Puree and set aside.

Turn on the oven to 325 degrees.

2. *Brown the chicken.* Set a deep, heavy 12-inch skillet or paella pan over medium-high heat and pour in the olive oil. Sprinkle the skin side of the chicken thighs with salt, then lay them into the hot oil skin side down. Sprinkle with salt. Fry until the skin is deeply golden, about 10 minutes. Turn and cook until browned and cooked through (juices from a small cut at the thickest part will run clear), about 10 minutes longer. Remove to a rimmed baking sheet.

3. *Cook the flavorings.* Reduce the heat under the pan to medium and add the onion and chorizo. Cook, stirring to break up lumps of chorizo, until the chorizo is cooked through and the onion is beginning to brown, about 10 minutes. Add the garlic and stir for a minute longer. Add the tomatoes and poblanos, and cook, stirring nearly constantly, until the mixture is very thick and the oil has started to separate from it, about 5 minutes.

4. *Start cooking the rice.* Add the rice to the flavorings and stir for 4 to 5 minutes, until a good portion of the rice has turned from translucent to milky white. Pour in the hot broth mixture, stir once to ensure everything is evenly mixed; scrape down any rice kernels sticking to the sides. Cook without stirring for 12 minutes, at which point the rice should have absorbed enough liquid to look like risotto. Check a kernel of rice: it should be getting soft, but still have a tiny bit of chalkiness at the center. If the rice doesn't look or taste ready, let it cook another minute or two.

5. *Add the chicken and shellfish.* Nestle the chicken thighs into the center of the rice, lay the shrimp in a ring around the chicken and arrange the mussels in the rice around the edge of the pan. Cover the pan with a piece of foil, slide into the oven and bake for 15 minutes.

6. *Serve the paella.* Uncover the paella and sprinkle with the peas, parsley, and, if you're using it, the tequila. Using a large serving spoon, gently fluff the mussels and shrimp into the rice mixture. Re-cover and let stand 10 minutes to finish cooking the rice and shellfish. You're ready to serve.

Sweet Inspirations from Street Stalls, Bakeries and Ice Cream Shops

Once you get past flan and a *tres leches* cake, Mexican sweets are, for most American cooks, uncharted territory. Maybe on a Mexican beach vacation, you've had unexpectedly good ice creams, rustic sorbet-like ices or what may have struck you as oddly flavored ice pops (I'm thinking flavors like mango with chile). Those frozen treats can be such good dessert choices for casual get-togethers that I've included recipes for a slew of modern interpretations—everything from modern Dark Chocolate–Chile Ice Cream (page 308) to sweet-soothing Cucumber-Lime Ice (page 317) and "Mojito" Fruit Ice Pops (page 318).

Of course, you can't go wrong with an iconic flan for dessert, and you probably have a favorite recipe already. Even though I've published a score of favorites over the last 25 years, I have a new and easy production twist to share, one that can be employed with any flan recipe: For a big party, I use bottled *cajeta*—the goat milk caramel I buy at my Mexican grocery—instead of hot caramelized sugar to coat the bottom of individual flan molds. But I'm not thinking custard cups here. Instead, I use flexible silicone muffin molds. The custardy flan mixture goes in right over the *cajeta*, the filled muffin molds are baked in roasting pans with about an inch of water in the bottom, then the baked flans are chilled to firm. Finally, I flip the molds over and massage each cup gently until the flan plops out. These individual flans are perfect drizzled with a little more *cajeta*.

That *cajeta*-for-caramelized-sugar substitute is employed in the making of Impossible Cake (page 290)—truly a delicious culinary oddity. A large *cajeta*-coated mold is spread with chocolate cake batter, then topped with flan mixture and slid into the oven. During baking, the cake and flan reverse (honestly!), resulting in a nice chocolate cake on top, *cajeta*-glazed custard underneath. Unmold it onto a platter and present your fused cake-flan creation. A real showstopper.

As is, of course, any *tres leches* cake. But *tres leches* can be a little tricky for a party, especially my favorite version, which is frosted with whipped cream. So I've devised Chocolate *Tres Leches* Parfaits (page 302)—think of it as ultra-moist *tres leches* cake meets chocolatey tiramisu. Do-ahead, impressive, crowd-pleasing.

A Fresh Corn Cake (page 304) may sound more savory than sweet to American ears, but Mexican cooks have long seen many sweet possibilities in the golden ear. Blend some fresh kernels with a little cinnamon, some sweetened condensed milk and a dollop of butter, and you've created the enticingly moist cake that's a classic throughout much of Mexico. Perfect with a scoop of Cointreau-infused Sweet Corn Ice Cream (page 313) and a handful of fresh berries.

Okay. So now we've tread into the side of Mexican sweets that may seem puzzling to some American cooks. Truth is, I'm in love with them. And I think you will be, too, if you just take a bite. And I love the traditional Mexi-can candies—the Milk Fudge with Fruit and Nuts (page 324), the Pumpkin

Seed Brittle (page 323), the Golden Fresh Coconut Candies (page 326). And all those street pastries, from the famous golden churros to the crispy, paper-thin *buñuelos* (page 298) and their flaky molded cousins (page 296). And what about those melt-in-your-mouth cookies called *polvorones* (pages 320 and 322). They're all so delicious. And come to think of it, they can be the perfect sweet send-off for a celebration.

IMPOSSIBLE CAKE (PAGE 290)

Impossible Cake
Pastel Imposible (aka Chocoflan)
SERVES 12 GENEROUSLY

FOR THE CAKE PAN

A little softened butter and some flour

1   cup homemade or store-bought *cajeta* (goat milk caramel)—store-bought Coronado brand *Cajeta Envinada* in the squeeze bottle works well here

FOR THE CAKE

5   ounces (1 stick plus 2 table-spoons) butter, slightly softened

1   cup sugar

1   egg

2   tablespoons espresso powder dissolved in 1½ tablespoons hot water

OR 3 tablespoons espresso

¾   cup all-purpose flour

1   cup cake flour

¾   teaspoon baking powder

¾   teaspoon baking soda

⅓   cup plus 1 tablespoon cocoa powder (I like the more commonly available—not Dutch process—cocoa best here)

1   cup plus 2 tablespoons buttermilk

FOR THE FLAN

1   12-ounce can evaporated milk

1   14-ounce can sweetened con-densed milk

4   eggs

1   teaspoon pure vanilla extract, preferably Mexican vanilla

I guess I'm really a kid at heart, because I can't stifle a streak of unbridled glee every single time I watch the improbable reversal of cake and custard as this "impossible" cake makes its tour though the hot oven. Even more than the ascent of a soufflé or the ballooning of cream puffs, there's remarkable culinary wizardry going on here. A cake pan gets coated with the Mexican caramel called cajeta, spread with chocolate cake batter, topped with liquidy custard and slid into the oven. Whereupon the cake batter starts puffing, as you'd expect from any self-respecting batter as it warms, making it lighter than the not-yet-set custard. Glob by glob, you can watch the batter break through the liquidy layer, reuniting into a solid cap of cake at about the same time the custard sets. See what I mean? A tasty little science lesson that turns out a creamy caramel custard "impossibly" fused to a dense, choco-latey chocolate cake—double appeal.

Working Ahead: *The cake can be made 2 or 3 days ahead, cooled, tightly covered with plastic—still in the pan—and refrigerated. Unmold the cake a couple of hours before serving and leave it at room temperature.*

1. *Prepare the cake pan.* Turn on the oven to 350 degrees and position the rack in the middle. Generously butter the bottom and sides of a 10-inch round cake pan (you need one that's 3 inches deep), sprinkle with flour, tip the pan, tapping on the side of the counter several times, to evenly distribute the flour over the bottom and sides, then shake out the excess. Microwave the *cajeta* for 30 seconds to soften it, then pour over the bottom of the pan, tilting the pan to coat the bottom evenly. Place a kettle of water over medium-low heat. Set out a deep pan that's larger than your cake pan (a roasting pan works well) that can serve as a water bath during baking.

2. *Make the cake batter.* With an electric mixer (use the flat beater, if yours has a choice), beat the butter and sugar at medium-high speed until light in color and texture. Scrape the bowl. Beat in the egg and espresso. Sift together the all-purpose and cake flour, baking powder, baking soda and cocoa. With the mixer on medium-low, beat in about ½ of the flour mixture, followed by ½ of the buttermilk. Repeat. Scrape the bowl, then raise the speed to medium-high and beat for 1 minute.

3. *Make the flan mixture.* In a blender, combine the two milks, the eggs and the vanilla. Blend until smooth.

4. *Layer and bake.* Scrape the cake batter into the prepared cake pan and spread level. Slowly, pour the flan mixture over the cake batter. (I find it

easiest to pour the mixture into a small ladle, letting it run over onto the batter.) Don't be alarmed if some of the cake batter begins to float up through the custard—it'll come out fine in the end. Pull out the oven rack, set the cake into the large pan, then set both pans on the rack. Pour hot water around the cake to a depth of 1 inch. Carefully slide the pans into the oven, and bake about 50 to 55 minutes, until a toothpick inserted into the cake comes out dry. Remove from the water bath and cool to room temperature, about 1 hour. For easiest unmolding, I like to refrigerate the cake for several hours or overnight.

5. *Serve.* Carefully run a thin-bladed knife around the edge of the cake/flan to free the edges. Invert a rimmed serving platter over the cake pan, grasp the two tightly together, then turn them upside down. Gently jiggle the pan back and forth several times to ensure that the cake/flan has dropped. Remove the pan, scraping any remaining *cajeta* from the pan onto the cake.

Flaky Turnovers with Various Fillings
Empanadas de Rellenos Surtidos

MAKES TWENTY-FOUR 3-INCH TURNOVERS

FOR THE DOUGH

3¼ cups (1 pound) all-purpose flour, plus a little more for rolling the dough

A generous ½ teaspoon salt

2 teaspoons sugar

1 cup (8 ounces) well-chilled lard

OR 1 cup (8 ounces) chilled vegetable shortening (we've had good luck using Spectrum Organic All Vegetable Shortening)

OR 1½ sticks (6 ounces) unsalted butter plus ½ cup vegetable shortening or lard

About ⅔ cup ice water

FOR THE FILLING

Choose one of the fillings on page 295

FOR GLAZING THE TURNOVERS

1 egg beaten with 1 tablespoon milk or cream

I've never made my way through the shelves of a self-service Mexican bakery without coming across at least one tray of turnovers—pumpkin or sweet potato, pineapple or apple pie filling, tuna or bacalao if it's Friday or Lent, shrimp if you're on Mexico's west coast, beef if you're in the north—all encased in short pastry, puff pastry, yeast dough, biscuit dough, what have you. As nice as they may be, they have none of the beauty or delicacy of empanadas I visited regularly several decades ago in the rather remote town of Chilapa, Guerrero. The Sunday morning market there spreads over the downtown streets, across the plaza and up to the entrance to the market building, where a gaggle of bread vendors collects, with wide, shallow baskets full of turnovers—just big enough to lay in the palm of your hand, made fat with pumpkin or purple-skin sweet potato filling and twisted beautifully into a decorative rope edge. The dough is the simplest lard pastry, and there is nothing like it for lightness and flakiness. Very different from the dough for the fried, triangular, shrimp-filled empanadas available in every little seafood restaurant in Mexico City.

These small turnovers are beautiful on a dessert table, to offer as a snack with hot chocolate or café con leche or to put out at a picnic. I frequently use them as appetizers with savory fillings—even filling them with my own concoctions like roasted red peppers and poblanos or with shiitake mushrooms cooked in ancho chile and roasted garlic.

Working Ahead: The dough and filling(s) can be made a couple of days ahead and stored in the refrigerator, covered. The finished empanadas can be frozen in single layers uncovered on parchment-lined baking sheets, and, when completely frozen, transferred to a freezer bag for longer storage; frozen empanadas should be baked from their frozen state. Empanadas are best served within a few hours of being baked.

1. *Make the dough using a food processor:* Measure the flour, salt and sugar into a large food processor, and stir the salt and sugar into the flour. Cut the lard, shortening and/or butter into ½-inch bits and scatter them over the flour. Cover and pulse eight times (1-second pulses), until the fat is cut into tiny bits. Uncover, sprinkle ⅓ cup of the ice water over the top, re-cover and pulse three times. Uncover, sprinkle on another ⅓ cup of ice water, re-cover and pulse a few more times, until the mixture starts to come together. (If, after four or five pulses, the mixture doesn't start to clump, sprinkle in a little more water and pulse again.) Uncover, dump the dough onto a work surface, gather into a ball, wrap in plastic and refrigerate for at least 1 hour.

Without a food processor: Measure the flour, salt and sugar into a large bowl, stir to mix well, then distribute the fat over the top. Use your fingers or a pastry blender to cut the fat into the flour until it is in tiny bits. Dribble in ⅓ cup of the ice water, working it in with fingertips or a fork; repeat with another ⅓ cup of ice water, stopping when the mixture can be collected into a mass (it shouldn't feel wet, but be moist enough to hold together without crumbling). Wrap in plastic and refrigerate for at least 1 hour.

2. *Make the filling.* Choose the filling you'll be using (page 295), prepare it and, if necessary, cool to room temperature.

3. *Form the empanadas.* Cut the dough in half; re-wrap half and return it to the refrigerator. On a lightly floured board, roll the remaining half into a thin rectangle 12 x 16 inches. Cut out twelve 3½- to 4-inch circles. Brush the edges very lightly with water, then spoon a portion of the filling in the center of each circle: about a scant tablespoon of pumpkin or cheese-*ate* mixture, or a one-teaspoon smear of the pumpkin seed paste, almond paste or Nutella topped with 2 teaspoons of the apples. Fold the dough carefully over the filling and press the edges together to seal. Put a final seal on the empanadas by pressing the two edges together with the tines of a fork or by making the decorative rope edge described on page 294.

Transfer the empanadas to an ungreased baking sheet and prick each one in two places. Cover and refrigerate.

Make empanadas from the second piece of dough, then cover and refrigerate (or, better, freeze) about an hour before baking. (If you wish, you can gather up the scraps of dough, re-roll, cut into circles and fill. Re-rolled dough, however, rarely turns out as tender as the original.)

4. *Bake the empanadas.* Heat the oven to 425 degrees. Bake the refrigerated or frozen empanadas for 15 minutes (20 minutes if frozen), until beginning to color, then remove and brush lightly with the egg-milk glaze. Return to the oven about 5 minutes longer, until nicely browned. Cool a little and they're ready to serve.

Creating a Decorative Rope Edge for Empanadas

Hold an empanada in one hand. With the thumb and first finger of the other hand, pinch out a ½-inch section of the dough on the nearest end, flattening it so that it extends out ¼ inch beyond the rest of the edge. With your thumb, curl over the top half of the pinched-out section of dough (it should look like a wave breaking), then gently press it down to secure it. Now pinch out the next ½-inch section of dough, curl the top side over (another wave breaking), and press it down. Continue until you reach the other end. Fold the last pinched-out section back on itself, finishing the seal.

FLAKY TURNOVERS WITH VARIOUS FILLINGS (PAGE 292)

Three Empanada Fillings

Pumpkin with Raw Sugar and Mexican Cinnamon

2   cups pureed cooked pumpkin
    (canned is fine here)

⅔   cup chopped *piloncillo* (Mexican
    raw sugar in cone form) or lightly
    packed dark brown sugar

1½ teaspoon ground cinnamon, pref-
    erably Mexican *canela*

½   teaspoon salt

Combine all the ingredients in a small (2-quart) saucepan; cover and set over medium-low heat. Stir every few minutes until the sugar is completely melted, then uncover and simmer until very thick, about 15 minutes. Scrape into a small bowl and cool to room temperature. If you're planning to freeze empanadas made with pumpkin filling, they'll turn out watery if your filling isn't very dry.

Cream (or Goat) Cheese with Quince or Guava *Ate*

1   pound cream cheese or fresh goat
    cheese

⅓   cup granulated sugar

    A little finely grated lime zest
    (colored rind only)

4   ounces jelled quince or guava
    paste (*ate*), cut into ¼-inch cubes
    (you'll have about ½ cup)

Lacking ate, smear a little tropical fruit jam (guava, mango, whatever's available) into the center of each dough round, top with a small spoonful of cream or goat cheese and fold up.

In a small bowl, mix together the cream or goat cheese with the sugar and lime zest until malleable. Stir in the *ate*.

Caramelized Apple with Pumpkin Seed or Almond Paste (or Nutella)

4   tablespoons (½ stick) butter (plus
    an additional 5 tablespoons if
    using pumpkin seeds)

6   medium (2½ pounds) apples
    (Honeycrisp and Gala hold their
    shape when cooked), peeled,
    cored and cut into ½-inch cubes

6   tablespoons sugar

1   cup toasted, salted pumpkin
    seeds (like the ones you find with
    the salty snacks)

    OR one 8-ounce can almond paste

    OR ¾ cup Nutella

In a large (10-inch) skillet, melt the butter over medium-high heat. When it begins to brown, add the apples and sprinkle with the sugar. Stir nearly constantly until the apples are tender and richly caramelized. Scoop into a shallow bowl and cool to room temperature. Into a food processor, scoop the pumpkin seeds or break up the almond paste. For pumpkin seeds, add the additional 5 tablespoons butter; for almond paste, add 2 tablespoons water. Process until smooth, dribbling in a little water to achieve a spreadable consistency. If using the almond paste, add a little salt. If using Nutella, simply stir in a little salt.

Paper-Thin Fritters with Spiced Syrup
Buñuelos

MAKES EIGHTEEN 10-INCH FRITTERS

During one summer back in the '70s, while visiting Oaxaca for the first time, I asked around for the famous Oaxacan paper-thin fritters called buñuelos. *They laughed:* buñuelos *are only for Christmas. Then I traveled to Morelia—known for lots that is good to eat but not necessarily* buñuelos—*and there they were, sitting in proud high stacks in the late afternoon summer sun, ready for the evening's customers at the food plaza. When the crisp, paper-thin fritters are broken up and briefly dunked into a cazuela of bubbling dark syrup, they are fun to eat with your fingers, as I learned that night.*

A couple of years later, Deann and I went out to Coyoacán in southern Mexico City to see an open air pastorela (those medieval Christmas tales still popular in Mexico), when we discovered a string of identical, brightly lit stands, all manned by Oaxacans and all making buñuelos a la vista *("buñuelos in front of your eyes"), like a* buñuelo *cooking class. We sat on a bench in front of the nicest-looking one, ordered our pastries and cups of masa-thickened atole and saw the dough go from golf ball–size spheres to 14-inch sheets of near transparency. The young man rolled a piece with a dowel, then laid it on a cloth-covered, upside-down earthenware bean pot, stretched it gently out to a foot, then held it up and spun it to the thinness of phyllo. His mother took the thin sheet from him and eased it into an inch or so of hot oil, prodding it with pointed chopsticks to keep it submerged until it was golden and crisp. Next, it passed to her daughter, who broke it into thirds, gave it a quick dunk in hot molasses-y syrup, laid it on a bright-colored plastic plate and passed it our way.*

It was only a week later that we were having Christmas buñuelos *every night on the square in Oaxaca, not made* a la vista, *but just as enjoyable because each customer got to keep the flawed earthenware bowl in which the* buñuelo *was served—a bowl to make a wish over, then smash on the pavement. The more pieces, they say, the more likely you'll see your wish fulfilled.*

Off season, I've enjoyed countless glazed (not dunked) buñuelos *at the sweet shop Dulcería de Celaya in Mexico City and from bakeries and street vendors in Guadalajara (where they are called* muéganos). *But in Vera-cruz . . . well,* buñuelos *there are a kind of fried cream puff, or what we called a cruller when I was young.*

Buñuelos *are very special and I think they're fun to make—worth at least the once-a-year Christmas endeavor. For a dressier presentation at Frontera Grill, we make* buñuelos *the size of small tortillas and sandwich them with a scoop of ice cream: a little* buñuelo–*ice cream tower.*

FOR THE BUÑUELOS

½ cup warm (110-degree) water

1 package active dry yeast—instant is okay

1 teaspoon sugar

1 pound (about 3¼ cups) all-purpose flour

2 tablespoons unsalted butter, slightly softened, or vegetable shortening (we've had good luck with Spectrum Organic All Vegetable Shortening)

4 large eggs, at room temperature

1 teaspoon salt

Oil to a depth of 1 inch in a wide skillet, for frying

FOR THE SYRUP

¾ pound *piloncillo* (cone sizes very widely; note weight on package), roughly chopped

OR 1½ cups packed dark brown sugar plus ¼ cup molasses

¼ teaspoon anise seeds, coarsely crushed (optional)

1-inch cinnamon stick, preferably Mexican *canela*

2 whole cloves

2-inch strip orange zest (colored part only), removed with a vegetable peeler

The recipe that follows relies on Josefina Velázquez de León's dough from her book Cocina oaxaqueña, *forming and frying instructions from the Coyoacán vendors and a glazing a la Dulcería de Celaya. To make the dunked variety, double the sauce but simmer it only 20 minutes. Split sugar cane and little* tejocotes *(Mexican hawthorn) or guavas are popular flavoring additions to the light syrup. Just before serving, break a* buñuelo *into two or three large pieces, lay in a deep plate and douse with a generous amount of warm syrup (and fruit, if you've used it).*

A note about the mold for stretching *buñuelos: In Mexico,* buñuelos *are stretched over a cloth-covered* olla, *a round-bottom earthenware pot used frequently for cooking beans. Lacking a bean pot, use a deep upturned bowl.*

Working Ahead: *Once the dough is rolled into balls, it can be refrigerated for up to 2 days. Fry the* buñuelos *as they're rolled and stretched, then serve them within a few hours.*

---

1. *Prepare the "sponge."* In a small bowl, stir together the warm water, yeast and sugar; let stand 10 minutes. If the mixture isn't foamy, the yeast isn't active: throw it out and start again with new yeast. Measure the flour into a large bowl. Scoop out ½ cup of the flour and stir it into the yeast mixture. Cover and set in a warm place for an hour—the longer, the fuller the flavor. In fact, I typically let the sponge rest for an hour, then refrigerate it until the next day for maximum flavor development.

2. *Make and portion the dough.* Make a well in the center of the flour that's still in the large bowl, pour in the sponge and add the butter or shortening. Beat the eggs with the salt and pour them into the well, too. With a large spoon, thoroughly mix the mixture in the well, then stir in a wider circle to slowly incorporate the surrounding flour. When the mixture becomes too thick to stir, turn it out onto your work surface, along with all the unincorporated flour.

Knead until smooth and elastic, about 10 minutes, adding as much of the flour as necessary to produce a medium-soft consistency dough (but not sticky). Lay the dough in a very lightly greased bowl, flip over, cover with plastic wrap or a towel, and let the dough rise to double in bulk, about 1½ hours.

Scoop out the dough onto a lightly floured work surface, lightly flour the top and press it into a rectangle. Cut into 18 pieces. Pat into disks and place on a baking sheet lined with a floured towel. Cover with a second floured towel. (Laying another damp towel over the top will prevent the dough from getting crusty.)

3. *Stretch and fry the dough.* Cover a round-topped mold (see headnote) with a kitchen towel, making large, even pleats. Secure it at the bottom with a string or rubberband and rub flour thoroughly into the surface.

Roll a disk of dough into a 7-inch circle. Lay over the mold and stretch into a nearly paper-thin 9- to 10-inch circle: Slip your fingers under the dough, thumbs still on the outside, and gently stretch the dough downward between thumb and fingers, letting it slip slowly through your grasp. Rotate the mold and gently stretch the dough again, continuing the process until you have a round that's about 9 inches across, thin enough to read a newspaper through. The edge will be thicker, so make a pass around the dough, stretching short sections with both hands, to gently thin the edge. (When finished it will hang in ruffles around the mold.) Make ¼-inch cuts through the dough at 6 places, to allow steam to escape during frying.

In a very large (10- to 12-inch), heavy, deep skillet, heat the oil to 375 degrees; use a deep-fry thermometer and regulate the heat to keep the oil temperature as constant as possible. Carefully lay the stretched dough across the surface of the hot oil. Continually press it down with a pair of tongs, to expel the air and encourage hot oil to flow over the edges. After 30 seconds, flip it and fry for 30 to 45 seconds longer, until thoroughly browned and crisp. Remove and drain on paper towels, preferably standing on edge to allow all the oil to drain off.

Stretch and fry the remaining disks of dough in the same fashion.

STRETCHING *BUÑUELO* DOUGH OVER ROUND-BOTTOM POT
MAKING SMALL SLITS IN DOUGH TO KEEP *BUÑUELO* FROM PUFFING TOO MUCH DURING FRYING
FRYING *BUÑUELOS*

4. *Prepare the syrup and finish the* **buñuelos.** In a medium (3-quart) saucepan, combine 3 cups of water and the rest of the syrup ingredients. Boil over medium-high heat, stirring from time to time, until reduced to 1½ cups, about 30 minutes. (The syrup should be as thick as honey at this point—thick enough to cool to a glossy-looking, not-at-all-sticky coating. Brush some on a plate, let it cool and touch it to make sure it's not sticky.)

Brush the hot syrup in a thin coating over each *buñuelo*. Let dry in a single layer until no longer very sticky, then stack the fritters on a tray— they are ready to serve.

DRAINING JUST-FRIED *BUÑUELOS*

Chocolate *Tres Leches* Parfaits
"Tres Leches" de Chocolate en Parfait
SERVES 6

A little softened butter and some flour

¾ cup cake flour

1 teaspoon baking powder

6 large eggs, room temperature

½ cup plus 2 tablespoons sugar

1 teaspoon pure vanilla extract

1 cup milk

7 ounces good-quality semisweet chocolate, chopped

1 cup canned evaporated milk (not sweetened condensed milk)

¾ cup bottled *cajeta* (goat milk caramel)—I like the Coronado brand called *Cajeta Envinada*, sold in squeeze bottles

1½ cups (12 ounces) mascarpone cheese, at room temperature

About 1 cup whipped cream, for garnish

Grated semisweet or Mexican chocolate, for garnish

Turning out a beautiful cream-covered, dripping-moist tres leches cake is a challenge for some cooks. First you have to make a spongy cake that will soak up just the right amount of the delicious milky mix of evaporated, sweetened condensed and whole—the right amount to stave off dryness, yet not so much as to risk sodden collapse. And then there's the choice of frostings (whipped cream or meringue) and the question of frosting strategy for your special cake.

While the making of a tres leches cake might not be welcomed by every cook, these parfaits deliver the satisfying tres leches experience more-or-less stress free—and with a nice amount of chocolate. After you've cut rounds of thin sponge cake, you layer them in tumblers with a little mascarpone, dousing the whole thing with my chocolate version of the "three milks": whole, evaporated, and cajeta (goat milk caramel). An impressive, up-to-date, easy-to-serve, make-ahead dessert rooted in Mexican tradition.

Working Ahead: The cake, "milks" and mascarpone mixture can be made several days ahead; refrigerate everything separately, well wrapped. (The cake can be frozen for up to a month.) The finished desserts will keep for a day or two in the refrigerator; careful covering is a must to avoid off flavors.

1. *Make the cake.* Turn on the oven to 350 degrees. Butter and flour a 17 x 12-inch half sheet pan. Lightly butter the pan, then line with parchment paper; butter and flour the paper. Sift together the flour and baking powder. Separate the eggs: In the large bowl of an electric mixer, place the 6 yolks; in another bowl, place 4 of the whites (refrigerate or freeze the remaining 2 whites for another preparation). To the yolks, add ½ *cup* of the sugar, the vanilla and 3 tablespoons hot water, then beat at medium-high speed for 5 full minutes, until light in color and texture. Using a whisk or rubber spatula, gently fold in the flour mixture in two additions. If you have only one mixer bowl, scrape the egg-flour mixture into a large bowl, wash the mixer bowl and beaters or whisk attachment and transfer the whites to the mixer bowl.

Immediately beat the whites at medium speed until they hold soft peaks. Add *1 tablespoon* of the remaining sugar; beat for 1 minute, then add the *remaining 1 tablespoon* sugar and beat a minute or so longer, until the whites hold nearly firm shiny peaks. Fold into the batter in three additions.

Gently spread the batter in an even layer onto the prepared pan. Bake until golden brown and springy to the touch, about 15 minutes. Cool 10 minutes on a cooling rack, then turn out onto the rack and carefully peel off the paper. Cool completely.

2. *Combine the "milks."* In a small saucepan over medium heat, combine the milk and chopped chocolate. Stir until the chocolate has melted, then add the evaporated milk and the *cajeta*. Stir until smooth, then let cool.

3. *Prepare the mascarpone.* In a small bowl, stir ⅓ *cup* of the cooled chocolate "milks" into the mascarpone. Cover and set aside.

4. *Finish the desserts.* Set up six glass tumblers for layering the parfaits (mine are 10-ounce tumblers with a diameter of 3 inches and a height of 3½ inches). Cut the sponge cake into rounds that fit the tumblers—you will need 18 cake rounds. Lay the cake rounds onto a parchment-lined baking pan.

Pour *1 cup* of the "milks" in a small bowl and set aside.

Spoon *half* of the remaining "milks" over the cake rounds, soaking them evenly, then flip them over with a small metal spatula and soak the other side with the rest of the "milks."

Place a small dollop of the flavored mascarpone in the bottom of each tumbler, and top with a layer of cake. Spoon on another dollop of mascarpone, then add a second layer of cake. Spoon on a final dollop of mascarpone, then add the third layer of cake. Press lightly to compress. Divide the reserved *1 cup* of "milks" equally among the 6 glasses, pouring over the cake layers. Cover tightly and refrigerate for at least 4 hours for the textures to meld.

Right before serving, top each glass with a dollop of whipped cream and a sprinkling of grated chocolate.

Fresh Corn Cake, Veracruz Style
Torta de Elote a la Veracruzana

SERVES 8 TO 10

4   ears fresh sweet corn, husk and silk removed

6   ounces (1½ sticks) unsalted butter, cut into 6 pieces, softened to room temperature

3   large eggs

1   14-ounce can sweetened condensed milk

¼   cup white corn meal (preferably coarse-ground, polenta style)

½   teaspoon cinnamon, preferably freshly ground Mexican *canela*

1½ teaspoons baking powder

If you've ever sat at a table on the patio of the famous old Gran Parroquia coffee shop overlooking the Veracruz wharf, you've likely snacked on torta de elote as you sipped your tall glass of café con leche, the milk for which streamed steaming from a huge kettle just moments before. A bite of the rough-textured, sweetish denseness takes you to a new appreciation of corn. Or at least a different one: torta de elote in Mexico is made from milk-stage (often called "green") field corn—the starchy grain corn that's grown for drying and grinding into corn meal. Some Americans don't like it, smitten as we are with super-sweet, super-tender varieties of corn. Which is exactly what most Mexicans say the first time they taste our favorite sweet varieties. But the torta is really good—worth translating north of the border, worth working into a sweet corn version that captures some of the rustic textures of the original. Here's my take, based on an original recipe from Veracruzana Doña Hilda, the mother of Patricia Madrid, a long-time server in my restaurant, Topolobampo.

Torta de elote is one of those Mexican desserts that typically combines sweet and salty—classically served with a drizzling of Mexican crema (tangy like crème fraîche; page 200) and salty fresh cheese (queso fresco). Serve with Blueberry-Tequila Ice Cream (page 316) or Sweet Corn Ice Cream (page 313) with a little blueberry sauce.

Production notes: If you use a Vitamix blender, you'll get the smoothest texture, and the size of the blender jar will allow you add the condensed milk, corn meal, baking powder and cinnamon and use the machine to mix them in. The torta is easiest to cut when it has cooled completely (has even been refrigerated); if the torta is at room temperature, we cut it with a knife heated under hot tap water.

Working Ahead: The finished cake keeps in the refrigerator, well wrapped, for several days. Bring to room temperature or warm it in a 350-degree oven before serving.

1. *Prepare the batter.* Turn on the oven to 350 degrees and position the rack in the middle. Cut the corn kernels from the cob, measure 3 cups and scoop into a blender or food processor. Add the butter and eggs. Process until smooth, then scrape into a large bowl. Measure in 1 cup of the sweetened condensed milk, along with the corn meal, cinnamon and baking powder. Whisk to combine.

2. *Bake the cake.* Butter (or spray with oil) the bottom and sides of a 9-inch cake pan. Cut a circle of parchment to fit the bottom and press it firmly in place. Pour the batter into the pan (it will be full to the top) and slide into the oven. Bake until richly golden and set (no longer jiggly) in the middle, 45 to 50 minutes.

Remove from the oven, let cool 10 minutes, then turn out on a rack. Immediately flip the cake over (the top is the prettiest side) and let cool completely.

Chocolate-Pecan Ice Cream
Helado de Choconuez
MAKES 1½ QUARTS, SERVING 10 TO 12

6   ounces (about 1½ cups) pecan
     halves or pieces

4   ounces Mexican chocolate,
     roughly chopped (about ¾ cup)

4   ounces bittersweet chocolate,
     roughly chopped (about ¾ cup)

½   teaspoon cinnamon, preferably
     freshly ground Mexican *canela*

1   quart half-and-half

4   egg yolks

½   cup sugar

1½   tablespoons rum

I think of choconuez *as a Mexican version of the favorite Italian chocolate-hazelnut ice cream called* gianduja—*a version that features pecans rather than hazelnuts and embraces a rustic, cinnamon-infused chocolate profile. And it shares all of* gianduja's *popularity.*

1. *Make the chocolate-nut milk.* Heat the oven to 325 degrees. Spread the pecans on a baking sheet and toast until very aromatic, about 10 minutes. Cool, then transfer to a food processor along with the Mexican chocolate. Pulse until both nuts and chocolate are quite fine, then run the machine for a minute or so until the mixture resembles nut butter. Scrape into a medium (3-quart) heavy-bottom saucepan. Add the bittersweet chocolate, cinnamon and half-and-half. Set over medium heat and, when steaming, whisk thoroughly. Turn off the heat, cover and let stand 20 minutes.

2. *Set up a double boiler.* Set up a 4-quart saucepan with 1 inch of water. Choose a 3-quart stainless steel bowl that you can nestle into the pan without touching the water. Bring the pot of water to a boil over high heat while you're preparing the custard base.

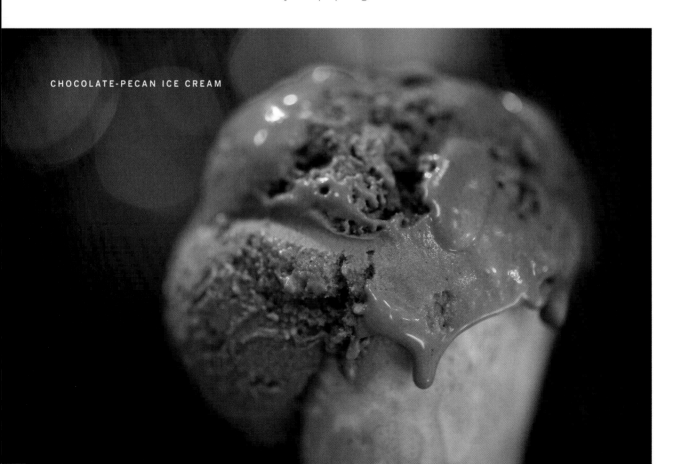

CHOCOLATE-PECAN ICE CREAM

3. *Cook the base.* In the stainless steel bowl, whisk together the egg yolks and sugar until thoroughly combined, then whisk the warm chocolate-nut mixture into the egg-sugar mixture. Reduce the temperature under the pot of boiling water to maintain a gentle simmer. Set the bowl of custard base over the simmering water (reduce the heat to maintain a gentle simmer) and whisk frequently, scraping down the sides of the bowl regularly with a rubber spatula, until the mixture thickens noticeably, about 5 minutes. The custard is sufficiently cooked when it reaches 180 degrees on an instant-read thermometer. (You can also test it by dipping a wooden spoon into the custard, then running your finger through the custard: if the line holds clearly, the custard has thickened sufficiently.) For the finest texture, pour the custard through a fine-mesh strainer into a similar-size stainless steel bowl.

4. *Freeze the ice cream.* Fill a large bowl halfway with ice. Nestle the custard into the ice and whisk regularly until completely cool. Stir in the rum and freeze in an ice cream maker according to the manufacturer's directions. Scrape into a freezer container and freeze for several hours to firm.

Dark Chocolate–Chile Ice Cream
Helado de Chocolate y Chile Pasilla

MAKES 1 QUART, SERVING 6 TO 8

1   large dried pasilla negro chile,
    stemmed, seeded and, if you
    wish, deveined

1⅓ cups half-and-half

4   ounces bittersweet (preferably
    70%) chocolate, chopped into
    small pieces

½   cup sugar

4   egg yolks

1⅓ cups heavy cream

1½ teaspoons vanilla extract, prefer-
    ably Mexican vanilla

2   tablespoons Kahlúa or other
    coffee liqueur

Though in the United States it's popular to think of chocolate and chile as a classic Mexican combination, it's not. In fact, the combination is more popular north of the Rio Grande than south. Not that it's bad. Not that it wasn't a well-known combination back in Aztec times. It's just not top-of-mind in twenty-first-century Mexico.

Dark pasilla negro chiles echo the savory, sharp character of bitter chocolate, making this very chocolatey ice cream a beautiful example of contemporary cuisine's celebration of sweet-and-savory desserts. And it's not really spicy—just radiantly infused with chile flavor and this chile's gentle glow. Ancho chile works here too and has even less spiciness.

Working Ahead: *The base can be made several days ahead and refrigerated, covered. The finished ice cream is best served within a day or two of being frozen.*

1. *Make the chile infusion.* In a small skillet heated over medium, toast the chile, pressing it flat against the skillet with a metal spatula until it is very aromatic—about 10 seconds per side. Place in a small saucepan, add the half-and-half and heat over medium until steaming (but not boiling). Cover and let steep for 10 minutes, then pour into a blender jar and process until the chile is smooth. Press the mixture through a medium-mesh strainer back into the saucepan.

2. *Set up a double boiler.* Set up a 4-quart saucepan with 1 inch of water. Choose a 3-quart stainless steel bowl that you can nestle into the pan without touching the water. Bring the pot of water to a boil over high heat while you're preparing the custard base.

3. *Cook the base.* Reheat the half-and-half mixture just until it begins to steam. Spread the chocolate into a thin layer over the bottom of a bowl. Pour the warm chile-infused mixture over the chocolate and stir until the chocolate has begun to melt. In the stainless steel bowl, whisk together the sugar and egg yolks until thoroughly combined, then whisk in the chocolate mixture. Reduce the temperature under the pot of boiling water to maintain a gentle simmer. Set the bowl of custard base over the simmering water and whisk frequently, scraping down the sides of the bowl regularly with a rubber spatula, until the mixture thickens noticeably, about 5 minutes. The custard is sufficiently cooked when it reaches 180 degrees on an instant-read thermometer. (You can also test it by dipping a wooden spoon into the custard, then running your finger through the custard: if the line holds clearly, the custard has thickened sufficiently.) For the finest texture, pour the custard through a fine-mesh strainer into a similar-size stainless steel bowl.

4. *Cool the base.* Fill a large bowl halfway with ice. Nestle the custard into the ice and whisk regularly until completely cool. Refrigerate if not using immediately.

5. *Finish the base, freeze the ice cream.* Stir the heavy cream, vanilla and Kahlúa into the base. Freeze in an ice cream maker according to the manufacturer's directions. Scrape into a freezer container and freeze for several hours to firm.

White Chocolate–Mezcal Ice Cream
Helado de Chocolate Blanco y Mezcal

MAKES 1 QUART, SERVING 6 TO 8

1 cup half-and-half

4 ounces pure white chocolate, chopped into ¼-inch pieces (we like Scharffen Berger)

4 egg yolks

½ cup sugar

1⅓ cups heavy cream

2 tablespoons Oaxacan mezcal (Del Maguey is quite widely available and really delicious)

1 teaspoon vanilla extract, preferably Mexican vanilla

Some flavors—like people—just get along, even when you wouldn't have predicted it. White chocolate, never one of my favorites, comes alive in the presence of smoky Oaxacan mezcal, transforming them both with near-alchemical wizardry. I grow a stand of anise hyssop in my garden every year; steeping a few leaves with the half-and-half adds a magical hint of anise.

Working Ahead: The base can be made a day or two ahead and refrigerated, covered. The finished ice cream is best served within a day or two of being frozen.

1. *Set up a double boiler.* Set up a 4-quart saucepan with 1 inch of water. Choose a 3-quart stainless steel bowl that you can nestle into the pan without touching the water. Bring the pot of water to a boil over high heat while you're preparing the custard base.

2. *Cook the base.* In a small saucepan over medium heat, warm the half-and-half until it steams. Spread the chocolate into a thin layer over the bottom of a bowl, then pour on the warm half-and-half. Stir until the white chocolate has begun to melt. In the stainless steel bowl that is part of your double boiler, whisk together the egg yolks and sugar until thoroughly combined, then whisk in the chocolate mixture. Reduce the temperature under the pot of water to maintain a gentle simmer. Set the bowl of custard base over the simmering water and whisk frequently, scraping down the sides of the bowl regularly with a rubber spatula, until the mixture thickens noticeably, about 5 minutes. The custard is sufficiently cooked when it reaches 180 degrees on an instant-read thermometer. (You can also test it by dipping a wooden spoon into the custard, then running your finger through the custard: if the line holds clearly, the custard has thickened sufficiently.) For the finest texture, pour the custard through a fine-mesh strainer into a similar-size stainless steel bowl.

3. *Cool the base.* Fill a large bowl halfway with ice. Nestle the custard into the ice and whisk regularly until completely cool. Refrigerate if not using immediately.

4. *Finish the base, freeze the ice cream.* Stir the heavy cream, mezcal and vanilla into the base. Freeze in an ice cream maker according to the manufacturer's directions. Scrape into a freezer container and freeze for several hours to firm.

Cream Cheese Ice Cream with *Ate*
Helado de Ate con Queso

MAKES A GENEROUS 5 CUPS, SERVING 8 TO 10

1   8-ounce package cream cheese, softened to room temperature

1   quart premium vanilla ice cream

4   ounces fruit paste (*ate*), finely diced (my favorite is guava but quince is more available)

Solid bricks of jelled fruit pastes cooked down over hours from temperate quince and tropical guava, what are known as ates in Mexico, are available all over the Republic and in most Stateside Mexican grocery stores. Ate is typically sliced up by those who take it home to serve for dessert, either solo or paired with slices of milky, salty fresh cheese.

The stuff keeps for months, wrapped and refrigerated. So buy it when you find it, then make this delicious concoction at a moment's notice: mix cream cheese with your favorite vanilla ice cream, then stir in ate cubes. It tastes like something you've worked on for days.

Working Ahead: The ice cream can be finished a couple of days before you serve it.

In an electric mixer using the paddle attachment if available, beat the softened cream cheese until light and fluffy. Scrape down the bowl.

Remove the ice cream from its container and cut into thin slices. Add the slices to the mixing bowl and beat on medium-high until the mixture is combined and the consistency of soft-serve ice cream. Stir in the diced fruit paste. Transfer the ice cream into a container and let it firm up for several hours in the freezer.

Blueberry-Tequila Ice Cream
Helado de Mora Azul y Tequila

MAKES ABOUT 1 QUART, SERVING 6 TO 8

4   egg yolks

½   cup plus ⅓ cup sugar

1   cup half-and-half

2   cups (10 ounces) blueberries

⅓   cup sugar

1   cup heavy cream

    Grated zest of 1 lime

2   tablespoons fresh lime juice

2½ tablespoons *blanco* (silver) tequila

There's something about the deep-blue flavor of blueberries that gets transformed with a little lime and tequila. It's the truth, though not what they teach in western Michigan where all our restaurant's blueberries come from.

Working Ahead: The base can be made a day or two ahead, covered and refrigerated. Because the ice cream has no emulsifiers or stabilizers, it's best eaten within 24 hours of being frozen.

1. *Set up a double boiler.* Set up a 4-quart saucepan with 1 inch of water. Choose a 3-quart stainless steel bowl that you can nestle into the pan without touching the water. Bring the pot of water to a boil over high heat while you're preparing the custard base.

2. *Cook the base.* In the stainless steel bowl, whisk together the egg yolks and sugar until thoroughly combined, then whisk in the half-and-half. Reduce the temperature under the pot to maintain a gentle simmer. Set the bowl of custard base over the simmering water, and whisk frequently, scraping down the sides of the bowl regularly with a rubber spatula, until the mixture thickens noticeably, about 5 minutes. The custard is sufficiently cooked when it reaches 180 degrees on an instant-read thermometer. (You can also test it by dipping a wooden spoon into the custard, then running your finger through the custard: if the line holds clearly, the custard has thickened sufficiently.) For the finest texture, pour the custard through a fine-mesh strainer into a similar-size stainless steel bowl.

3. *Cool the base.* Fill a large bowl halfway with ice. Nestle the custard into the ice and whisk regularly until completely cool. Refrigerate if not using immediately.

4. *Make the blueberry infusion, freeze the ice cream.* In a small saucepan, combine the blueberries and sugar. Stir over medium heat until the berries have released their juices, about 3 minutes. In a *loosely covered* blender, combine the warm berries, cream, lime zest, lime juice and tequila. Blend until smooth. Cool completely, then add to the cooled custard base. Freeze in an ice cream maker according to the manufacturer's directions. Scrape into a freezer container and freeze for several hours to firm.

Sweet Corn Ice Cream
Nieve de Elote

MAKES 1½ QUARTS, SERVING 10 TO 12

2 to 3 ears fresh sweet corn

1½ cups half-and-half

4 egg yolks

¾ cup plus 2 tablespoons sugar

1⅓ cups heavy cream

⅓ cup evaporated milk (not sweetened condensed milk)

A scant ½ teaspoon cinnamon, preferably freshly ground Mexican *canela*

2 tablespoons orange liqueur, preferably Gran Torres

1 tablespoon fresh lime juice

If you were raised in Mexico, "corn" uttered alongside "ice cream" would feel ordinary, everyday. In the States, it sounds about as foreign as cauliflower soft-serve or sweet pea gelato. Flavor-wise, though, sweet corn makes sense in an ice cream context, living up to its namesake sweetness and pairing famously with dairy. Mix in a little sugar, a dash of cinnamon and a splash of orange liqueur and you too will become a convert. Now, before you skip the evaporated milk in favor of additional half-and-half, let me explain its purpose: evaporated milk has a unique long-simmered sweetness that adds depth here.

Working Ahead: *The base can be prepared a day or two ahead. Because the ice cream has no emulsifiers or stabilizers, it is best within a day or two of freezing.*

1. *Set up a double boiler.* Set up a 4-quart saucepan with 1 inch of water. Choose a 3-quart stainless steel bowl that you can nestle into the pan without touching the water. Bring the pot of water to a boil over high heat while you're preparing the custard base.

2. *Cook the base.* Husk the corn and pull off all the silk. Cut the kernels from the ears and measure 2 cups. Scoop into a blender and add the half-and-half. Blend until smooth. In the 3-quart stainless steel bowl, stir together the egg yolks and sugar until thoroughly combined. Add the corn mixture and whisk to combine thoroughly. Reduce the temperature under the pot of boiling water to maintain a gentle simmer. Set the bowl of custard base over the simmering water and whisk frequently, until the mixture thickens noticeably, about 20 minutes. The custard is sufficiently cooked when it reaches 180 degrees on an instant-read thermometer. (You can also test it by dipping a wooden spoon into the custard, then running your finger through the custard: if the line holds clearly, the custard has thickened sufficiently.) Pour the base through a medium-mesh strainer into another bowl (preferably stainless steel for quick cooling).

3. *Cool the base.* Fill a large bowl halfway with ice. Nestle the custard into the ice and whisk regularly until completely cool. Refrigerate if not using immediately.

4. *Finish the base, freeze the ice cream.* Stir the heavy cream, evaporated milk, cinnamon, orange liqueur and lime juice into the base. Freeze in an ice cream freezer according to the manufacturer's directions. Scrape into a freezer container and freeze for several hours to firm.

Pomegranate Ice Cream
Helado de Granada
MAKES 1 QUART, SERVING 6 TO 8

3   large (about 2½ pounds) pomegranates

½   cup sour cream

½   cup half-and-half

1   cup heavy cream

2   tablespoons orange liqueur

¾   cup sugar

This pomegranate ice cream is rich, with a tart edge and a deep, winey, cranberry-cherry undercurrent. And, yes, you can make it with store-bought pomegranate juice, but I'll warn you that neither the color nor the flavor will be as vibrant. So my recommendation is to go for the gold; I mean, how often are you going to make pomegranate ice cream?

Working Ahead: *The base can be made a day or two ahead. Because the ice cream has no emulsifiers or stabilizers, I recommend serving it within 24 hours of freezing.*

1. *Make the pomegranate juice.* Dislodge the seeds from the pomegranates: One easy way to do this is to cut a generous ¼ inch off the crown and flower ends of the pomegranates, then score the rind from top to bottom at 1½-inch intervals, cutting about ¼ inch deep. Fill a large bowl with water. Holding a pomegranate under the water, break it apart into sections, then use your fingers to dislodge the seeds. Get rid of the peel. The white membrane connecting the seeds will float to the top of the water and can be easily scooped off and discarded. The seeds will sink to the bottom. (And in the process, no clothes, walls or countertops will get spattered with the staining crimson of random broken seeds.) Pour the seeds into a colander to drain: you should have 4 cups. Scoop the seeds into a food processor. Pulse to create a coarse puree, releasing the juice but not chopping up the white seeds. (When it's ready, you'll see that the white seeds are separate from the pulp.) Press through a medium-mesh strainer to extract as much liquid as possible. Pour the juice into a small saucepan (you should have 1½ cups), set over medium-high heat and boil, stirring frequently, until reduced to 1 cup, about 8 minutes. Cool.

2. *Make the ice cream base.* In a large bowl, whisk the sour cream until smooth. Whisk in the cooled pomegranate juice, then all the remaining ingredients.

3. *Freeze the ice cream.* Freeze in your ice cream machine, according to the manufacturer's directions. Scrape into a freezer container and freeze for several hours to firm.

DARK CHOCOLATE-CHILE ICE CREAM (PAGE 308)
AND POMEGRANATE ICE CREAM (PAGE 314)

Watermelon-Raspberry Ice
Raspado de Sandía y Frambuesa
MAKES ABOUT 3 QUARTS, SERVING ABOUT 20

7 to 8 pounds of seedless watermelon

1½ cups bottled or freshly extracted
pomegranate juice

1   cup fresh raspberries

Leaves from a few sprigs of mint

¼   cup fresh lime juice (you'll need
about 2 large limes)

1   cup sugar

A plain-old watermelon ice or shaved ice or granita or raspado—whatever you want to call it—is one of the simplest, lightest, most refreshing desserts I know. And easy, too, since it is still-frozen in a baking dish, no special ice cream freezer is needed. Add raspberries to the basic mix, plus a little pomegranate juice for tartness and fresh mint for aroma, and the simple edges toward sublime.

Quarter the watermelon, then cut the flesh from the rind and cut the flesh into 1-inch pieces; you should have about 8 cups (3 pounds). In batches, scoop the watermelon into a blender along with some of the pomegranate juice, raspberries and mint, process to a smooth puree and pour into a large bowl. Add the lime juice and sugar, stirring until the sugar dissolves. Taste for sweet-tart balance, adding more lime or sugar if you think necessary. Pour the mixture into a 9 x 13-inch pan (a metal one works best) and set in the freezer. After 45 minutes, thoroughly stir the mixture, breaking up the large crystals that have formed. Return to the freezer for another 15 minutes, then stir it again. Repeat the freezing-stirring process every 15 minutes until you have a panful of large, fluffy crystals. (The whole process takes about 2 hours.) Scrape the finished *raspado* into a freezer container, cover and freeze until you are ready to serve.

WATERMELON-RASPBERRY ICE

Cucumber-Lime Ice
Nieve de Pepino y Limón

MAKES 5 CUPS, SERVING 8 TO 10

¾ cup fresh lime juice (you'll need 5 or 6 large limes)

1 cup sugar

⅓ cup light corn syrup

1 medium seedless cucumber, peeled and roughly chopped (you'll have about 2 cups)

Odd as a sweet limey cucumber dessert may sound to some, it's a classic flavor in Mexican ice pops and in ices, too, the ones called nieves—*think sorbets with a refreshingly lighter, slightly icier texture. Really, the flavor's not too far from what we already know: cucumbers are closely related to melons, and it's that cooling expression of cucumber's melony flavor that's profiled here.*

Working Ahead: Because there are no stabilizers in the ice, it's best eaten within 24 hours of being frozen.

Grate the zest (colored part only) from two of the limes and scrape into a blender jar or food processor. Juice the limes, measure ¾ cup and pour it in with the zest. Add the sugar, corn syrup, cucumber and 1⅓ cups water. Process until smooth. Pour the mixture through a fine strainer into your ice cream maker and freeze according to the manufacturer's directions. The ice will have the best texture if you scoop it from the ice cream maker into a container and let it firm up for several hours in the freezer.

"Mojito" Fruit Ice Pops
Paletas de Frutas, Sabor a "Mojito"

MAKES 20 POPS

¾ cup sugar

2 tablespoons coarsely chopped fesh mint leaves

⅔ cup fresh lime juice

2 cups sparkling water

2 10-ounce bags frozen fruit pieces (choose raspberries, blueberries or diced mango or melon—or practically any fruit that suits your fancy)

All summer long in Chicago, just as in Mexico and other U.S. cities, the jangle of paleteros' jingle-bell carts ricochets through parks and neighborhood streets. My favorite flavor of the Mexican frozen fruit pops they sell is sweet cucumber-lime, either with spicy red chile or without. Unless it's the mango (sweet or spicy) or the guanabana or fresh coconut. Or guava—did I mention guava?

A few summers ago I was hosting our restaurant staff for a huge party—150 co-workers and their families in my backyard—and I contracted a local paletero to bring his fully loaded cart into the yard, where he jingled those bells and delighted the kids and their parents for hours with sweet, cooling delight.

They're easy to make in big quantities, too. Two ten-pop molds turn out dessert for a crowd in no time. And you can customize them, since basically you're making a limeade base, which can embrace practically any berries or cubed fruit. A little sparkling water and some fresh mint gives your pops a sophisticated "mojito" flair.

Measure the sugar into a food processor. Add the mint and pulse until the mint is finely chopped. Scrape the sugar into a large bowl and add the lime juice and sparkling water, stirring until the sugar is dissolved.

Divide the frozen fruit pieces among 20 ice pop molds, then fill with the lime mixture, leaving about ¼-inch head space for expansion. Secure the lids, insert the sticks through the holes, making sure that they're straight and that 1½ to 2 inches remains exposed (for easy grasping). Slide the molds into the freezer.

When the ice pops are firmly set—this will take a couple of hours in most freezers—they're ready to serve. Remove the lids from the molds, then either squeeze the sides of each mold to free the pops or run the mold under warm water to release them.

MEXICAN *PALETAS* (FRUIT POPS)

Seville-Style "Sandy" Shortbread Cookies
Polvorones Sevillanos

MAKES ABOUT 4 DOZEN 1½-INCH COOKIES

3½ cups (1 pound) all-purpose flour (divided use)

2 cups (8 ounces) powdered sugar, plus a cup or more for coating the finished cookies

3 scant tablespoons cinnamon, preferably fresh ground Mexican *canela*

1 cup fresh pork lard, at cool room temperature

These polvorones are the real deal—soul-satisfying flavor poised elegantly on the cusp of sweet and savory, delivered in the most remarkable, meltingly rich, farinaceous texture. Think of them as the most delicate shortbread you've ever put in your mouth. They're so fragile, in fact, that they're always individually wrapped like tiny gifts, which is exactly what they are to me. Learning the intricacies of making them was a gift, too, as I watched Gabriela Bojalil turn out hundreds of them one December afternoon in Puebla.

Judging by how diligently you have to search for them nowadays in Mexico, however, not just anyone is tackling their old-fashioned preparation. I think it's the ingredients, the toasted flour and the fresh pork lard. Both stop most American cooks in their tracks—the flour simply because of its oddity, the lard because, well, because it's lard, and for five or six decades now we've bought the bunk that food made with lard will taste, ipso facto, a little off, greasy for sure, maybe, dare I say, even morally inferior to lardless preparations. Butter's where it's at, we've been schooled. Which is a little narrow, don't you think, when there's no arguable reason for it? Fresh lard contributes a pure, clean-tasting richness; greasiness is just the result of bad cooking; and that moral stuff, well, that's just cultural prejudice. Bad nutrition, then? The scientific community has even determined that lard's actually less harmful than butter. So what are you waiting for? Oh, maybe you're waiting to encounter fresh lard, which seems to have been so marginalized that even well-stocked groceries aren't carrying it—or they're only carrying the tasteless, couldn't-be-worse-for-you hydrogenated cubes distributed by large meat companies. The real fresh lard comes from butchers who render it or from ethnic markets that have connections to those who do. Or you can render cubed pork fat yourself in a 325-degree oven. It's a no-tend process that takes about an hour. Before using your fresh lard, be sure to strain out the browned bits. They're delicious added to beans.

Working Ahead: Polvorones can be made a couple of weeks ahead. Store them in airtight containers.

---

1. *Toast the flour.* Heat the oven to 350 degrees. Measure 1¾ cups flour into a large skillet, set over medium-high heat and stir regularly until the color is uniformly creamy-beige and the flour smells toasty, about 8 minutes. Cool, then sift through a medium-mesh strainer onto your work surface.

2. *Make the dough.* Sift the remaining flour, the powdered sugar and the cinnamon on top of the toasted flour. Using your fingers, mix the dry ingredients until the mixture has a uniform color. Make a well in the middle, then scoop in the lard. Use your fingers to work the flour mixture into the lard, creating a uniform—but somewhat crumbly—dough. Work quickly so as not to melt the lard.

3. *Cut and bake the cookies.* Press half of the dough into a ½-inch-thick round. (The dough will crack a little around the edges.) Use a 1½-inch cutter or Mexican shot glass (*caballito*) to cut out cookies, transferring them to an ungreased cookie sheet as you go. Repeat with the remaining dough. Bake for about 14 minutes to set the cookies (they will not brown, but will develop a slight skin of tiny bubbles on top that will stick to your fingertip when touched.) When you think the cookies are done, break one open and (carefully) taste it: they shouldn't have baked so long that they developed a crisp crust (they should melt in your mouth), the texture should be noticeably less pasty than the raw dough, and the flavor more integrated. Cool for an hour or more, to ensure that the cookies are completely set.

4. *Sugar the cookies.* Spread powdered sugar into a pie pan or small baking dish. One by one, turn the cookies in the sugar, coating them completely. Set them on a serving dish or wrap each one in tissue paper *a la mexicana*.

ICE CREAM, FRESH FRUIT SALSA, PECAN "SANDY"
SHORTBREAD COOKIES (PAGE 322)

Pecan "Sandy" Shortbread Cookies
Polvorones de Nuez

MAKES ABOUT 4 DOZEN COOKIES

6   ounces (about 1¾ cups) pecan halves

3¼ cups all-purpose flour

1   teaspoon salt

1½ teaspoons cinnamon, preferably freshly ground Mexican *canela*

11 ounces (2¾ sticks) unsalted butter, at room temperature

1   cup sugar

2   teaspoons pure vanilla extract

About a cup powdered sugar for coating the finished cookies

For those wanting an easier recipe for sturdier, nutty polvorones—akin to what are called Mexican wedding cakes/cookies in the United States—that are made with butter rather than lard, this one will satisfy you very nicely, I think.

1. *Toast the pecans.* In a 350-degree oven, toast the pecans in a single layer on a rimmed baking sheet for about 10 minutes, until they fill the kitchen with their toasty-nut aroma. Remove from the oven and reduce the oven temperature to 325 degrees.

2. *Make the dough.* Scoop the cooled pecans into a food processor and pulse until finely ground. Scrape into a large bowl along with the flour, salt and cinnamon. Stir to combine.

Using a mixer (fitted with a paddle beater, if available), cream the butter and sugar at medium speed until light and fluffy. Add the vanilla and the flour-pecan mixture, and mix on low speed until thoroughly blended.

3. *Bake the cookies.* Roll the dough into 1-tablespoon-size balls and arrange them on ungreased cookie sheets, leaving 2 inches between each one. Bake for 18 to 20 minutes, until lightly brown. Immediately transfer to a cooling rack. When cool, spread the powdered sugar onto a deep plate and roll each cookie in it to coat all sides. Store in an airtight container until you're ready to serve.

Pumpkin Seed Brittle
Pepitorias

MAKES 18 PIECES OF BRITTLE, EACH ABOUT 1 X 2 INCHES

1   cup (5 ounces) shelled, untoasted pumpkin seeds (*pepitas*)

¾   cup sugar

¼   teaspoon salt

¼   cup water

I offer this recipe for crunchy caramel brittle thick with pumpkin seeds, but in Mexico, pumpkin seeds are only one of the options candy makers think of: this very common street sweet is made just as often with roasted peanuts or toasted sesame seeds or a combo of peanuts, sesame and pumpkin seeds. Upon arriving anywhere in Mexico, after changing dollars to pesos, I typically make pepitorias *one of my first purchases. They're incredibly satisfying, packed with nuts or seeds, sweetened with a hint of hard caramel and easy to tote around on a trip.*

I've given directions for toasting pumpkin seeds, but if toasted ones are available in the snack aisle of your grocery store, I'd use those. The bit of additional salt they add will be welcome.

Working Ahead: As long as it's stored in an air tight container, your pepitorias *will keep for weeks.*

1. *Preliminaries.* Pour the pumpkin seeds into a large (10-inch) skillet and set over medium-low heat. When the first one pops, stir until all have toasted and popped into a round shape—the whole process takes about 5 minutes. Cool. Lightly grease a baking sheet and an offset spatula or a wide-bladed knife.

2. *Cook and mold the candy.* Measure the sugar and salt into a small (2-quart) heavy saucepan, drizzle a little of the water around the sides, then pour the remainder over the center. Bring to a boil, stirring to dissolve the sugar, then wash down the sides of the pan with a brush dipped in water. Boil over medium heat without stirring until the mixture begins to turn amber, about 10 minutes, then begin swirling the pan over the heat until it is a deep amber. Remove the pan from the heat, add the pumpkin seeds and stir to evenly coat them with the amber syrup.

Immediately scrape onto the greased baking sheet. With the greased offset spatula or knife, mold and press the mixture into a compact square that's about 7 x 7 inches and 3/8 inch thick. Use a serrated knife to lightly score the square 6 across by 3 down, scoring what will eventually be cut into 1 x 2-inch rectangles. Let cool at least an hour.

3. *Cut the candy.* Carefully remove the square of candy from the baking sheet, sliding an offset spatula or thin knife underneath to free it, and place on a cutting board. With a serrated knife, cut it into rectangles following the score marks you made, sawing gently back and forth. Store in an airtight container until ready to serve.

Milk Fudge with Fruit and Nuts
Jamoncillo de Frutas y Nueces

MAKES FORTY-NINE 1-INCH SQUARES

1 quart whole milk

2¾ cups (1¼ pounds) sugar

¼ teaspoon baking soda

1½ cups (6 ounces) toasted chopped nuts (pecans, walnuts, pine nuts—singly or in combination), cut into about ¼-inch pieces (if appropriate)

About 1 cup dried or crystallized (or highest-quality candied) fruit, cut into ¼-inch pieces

When I was a kid—before the days of microwave-quick, no-beat fudge—my mom prided herself on having mastered honest, laborious Christmas fudge, knowing when it had been cooked to the right temperature and when it had been beaten—slowly, painstakingly beaten—to the perfect stage of firmness, never crumbly-crystally, never runny. That's the mastery you'll develop here, too, since this recipe turns out the original old-fashioned fudge, fudge as it was made before we chocoholic Americans added cocoa to it, fudge the way they still like it in Mexico. But, unlike my mother, you won't face all the trial-and-error, all the forearm fatigue: you can employ an instant-read thermometer and an electric mixer.

Along with jelled fruit pastes (ates) and nut brittles, this caramely-tasting milk fudge is the stuff that makes eyes twinkle all over Mexico every day, especially when it's studded with nuts and fruit.

Working Ahead: *Because this homemade jamoncillo isn't made with invert sugar or other additives that inhibit further crystallization, the candy's texture is best within a few days of when it's made.*

1. *Cook the candy.* In a large (6-quart) heavy pot, whisk together the milk and sugar. Dissolve the soda in 1 tablespoon of water, then whisk it into the milk mixture. Set the pot over medium heat and bring to a simmer. Regulate the heat so that the mixture simmers briskly, but doesn't risk boiling over. Stir regularly as the mixture cooks to 238 degrees, which takes from 45 minutes to 1 hour; stir frequently, especially as the mixture thickens and darkens toward the end of the cooking. (At 238 degrees, a small amount of the hot mixture will firm to a still-pliable ball when dropped into cold water.)

2. *Beat the candy.* Pour the mixture into an electric mixer (fitted with a paddle if available); don't scrape the pan. Turn on to the *slowest* speed.

While the candy is beating, lightly oil a baking sheet (or line it with parchment or a silicone baking mat). After the candy has been beating for about 15 minutes, the mixture will have cooled to about 150 degrees and the candy will have turned from glossy to satiny and begun to separate from the side of the pan. Turn off the mixer, disconnect the beater, stir the nuts and fruit into the bowl—I use the beater to do this, scraping the mixture from the sides of the bowl and blending everything—including the softer center—thoroughly.

3. *Finish the candy.* Immediately scoop the mixture onto the prepared baking sheet and press it into a neat 7-inch square. Let cool for several hours (in order to firm completely) before cutting into small squares to serve. Store your *jamoncillo* in an airtight container if not serving right away.

FROM TOP: PUMPKIN SEED BRITTLE (PAGE 323), GOLDEN FRESH COCONUT CANDIES (PAGE 326) AND MILK FUDGE WITH FRUIT AND NUTS (PAGE 324)

Golden Fresh Coconut Candies
Cocadas Horneadas
MAKES ABOUT TWELVE 2-INCH CANDIES

1   medium (about 2 pounds) fresh coconut, with plenty of water inside

OR 10 ounces dried unsweetened coconut flakes

¾   cup sugar if using fresh coconut

OR ½ cup sugar if using dried coconut

1   tablespoon light corn syrup

1-inch cinnamon stick

2   tablespoons milk

3   large egg yolks

If you're a big coconut fan, you'll want to go the extra mile and make these classic Mexican street sweets with freshly grated coconut. Dried coconut works fine . . . but, oh, the texture and light natural sweetness of the fresh stuff is unforgettable. Once the coconut question has been resolved, the preparation is pretty straightforward: coconut is simmered to plumpness in a light syrup (that's why dried coconut can work here), then thickened with egg yolk for creamy richness, formed into mounds and baked until the outside is golden and crisp.

Working Ahead: *These candies can be made several days before you want to serve them. Store in an airtight container to keep them from softening too much.*

1. *Prepare the coconut.* For fresh coconut, turn on the oven to 325 degrees. Twist a corkscrew (or drive an ice pick) into two of the "eyes" of the coconut (the dark indentations on one end), then drain the trapped liquid into a cup (strain if it contains any bits of coconut shell) and set the liquid aside. Place the coconut in the preheated oven for 15 minutes to help loosen the flesh from the shell. With a hammer, crack the coconut into several pieces, then use a small knife or screwdriver to pry the flesh from the shell. Use a small knife or a vegetable peeler to peel away the dark skin from the coconut flesh. In a food processor (or, with determination and stamina, using a four-sided grater) grate the coconut into medium-fine shreds.

If you are using dried coconut, measure it out.

2. *Cook the coconut.* Combine the sugar, corn syrup and cinnamon stick in a medium (3-quart), heavy saucepan. If you have coconut water, add enough water to bring the volume to 1 cup; for dry coconut, measure 1 cup water. Stir into the sugar mixture, bring to a boil and wash down the sides of the pan with a brush dipped in water.

Add the coconut and cook over medium to medium-low heat, stirring frequently, just until *all* the liquid has been absorbed or evaporated (do not let it brown)—about 20 minutes for dried coconut, longer for fresh. Remove from the heat and pick out the cinnamon stick.

Mix together the milk and egg yolks, stir in a few spoonfuls of the hot coconut, then stir the yolk mixture into the pan. Set over medium-low and cook, stirring constantly, until the yolk mixture has thickened and been absorbed, about 5 minutes. (The liquid *will* come to a simmer: if heated gently, it will NOT curdle.) Remove from the heat, scrape out on a tray or baking dish and cool to room temperature.

3. *Bake the coconut candies.* Preheat the oven to 325 degrees and line a large baking sheet with a silicone baking mat or parchment paper (or heavily grease and flour the baking sheet). Scoop up about 2 tablespoons of the cooled coconut mixture, form into a 2-inch cake (about ½ inch thick) and lay on the baking sheet; form the remaining coconut mixture into patties in the same manner.

Bake for 20 to 25 minutes, until richly browned. Let cool on the baking sheet, then remove, freeing any that stick by sliding a knife underneath and twisting the blade to pop them free. Let the candies stand upside down for an hour or so, for the bottoms to firm and harden, then store in an airtight container.

Index

Note: Page numbers in *italic* type refer to photographs.

A

F

farmer's cheese:
    in roasted garlic tamales with ricotta and Swiss chard, 222–23
    in roasted tomatillo salsa, 144–45
    savory bean-sauced tortillas with, 196–97
fiestas, 13–14. *See also* parties
fire pit, brick, temporary, 249
    building, 238, *239*
fish. *See also* halibut; salmon; tuna
    for ceviche, 94
    cured, fruity "gazpacho Moreliano" with, 101
    in Frontera Grill's now-classic ceviche, 92
    in herb green ceviche with cucumber, 98–99, *100*
    in salt-and-pepper ceviche, 93
    wood-grilled, whole (or fillets), Puerto Vallarta style, *251*, 252–53
flan, "café de olla," 242–43
flan, sabor "café de olla," 242–43
frambuesa, raspado de sandía y, 316, *316*
fresh cheese:
    "almost Oaxacan" grilled tostadas with chorizo, tangy guacamole and, 202–3
    in fruity "gazpacho Moreliano" with crab or cured fish, 101
    Mexican, 214–15
    in roasted tomatillo salsa, 144–45
    savory bean-sauced tortillas with, 196–97
frijoles negros:
    panuchos fáciles Yucatecos con pollo en escabeche y, 204–5
    tamal de, con queso de cabra, 212–13
fritters, paper-thin, with spiced syrup, *297*, 298–301
fruit. *See also specific fruits*
    "gazpacho Moreliano" with crab or cured fish, 101
    in Mexican "crudité" platter with *chamoy* dipping sauce, 234
    milk fudge with nuts and, 324–25, *325*
    "mojito" fruit ice pops, 318, *319*
    spicy jícama and cucumber skewers, 154, *155*
fruit paste, in cream cheese ice cream with *ate,* 311
fruta(s):
    agua fresca de, 69

    alambritos de jícama y pepino y, con chile y limón, 154, *155*
    crudas, botana de, con chamoy, 234
    jamoncillo de nueces y, 324–25, *325*
    paletas de, sabor a "mojito," 318, *319*
fudge, milk, with fruit and nuts, 324–25, *325*

G

galletas, saladas, de ajonjolí y pepitas, 42
garlic:
    garlicky black pepper tortilla chips, 40
    grilled, and orange guacamole, 32
    Oaxacan-style peanuts with chile and, 35
    roasted, guacamole, with help-yourself garnishes, *31*, 79
    roasted, tamales with ricotta and Swiss chard, 222–23
gazpacho Moreliano de jaiba o pescado curtido, 101
gazpacho "Moreliano," fruity, with crab or cured fish, 101
ginger, in sizzling mojito, 53
goat cheese:
    empanada filling with quince or guava *ate* and, 295
    fresh, black bean tamales with, 212–13
    in fruity "gazpacho Moreliano" with crab or cured fish, 101
    in roasted tomatillo salsa, 144–45
    savory bean-sauced tortillas with, 196–97
goat milk caramel:
    in "café de olla" flan, 242–43
    in chocolate *tres leches* parfaits, 302–3
    in impossible cake, *289*, 290–91
granada, helado de, 314, *315*
Grand Marnier, about, 49
granita. *See* ice(s)
grapefruit juice, in tropical beach ceviche, 97
greens, creamy chicken with roasted poblano and caramelized onion and, 134–35, *135*
grilled foods:
    achiote-seared shrimp with quick habanero-pickled onions, 254–55
    "brava" steaks, 258, *259*

M

turnips, in roasted vegetable enchiladas with creamy
    tomatillo sauce and melted cheese, *198*, 199
turnovers, flaky, with various fillings, 292–93, *294*

V

vegetables. *See also specific vegetables*
    caramelized, *huitlacoche* filling for crispy tacos with,
        194
    in Mexican "crudité" platter with *chamoy* dipping
        sauce, 234
    pickled, savory tomato broth and, for crispy tacos, 195
    roasted, enchiladas with creamy tomatillo sauce and
        melted cheese, *198*, 199
verduras:
    asadas, enchiladas de, 198, 199
    botana de, con chamoy, 234
    caramalizadas, relleno de huitlacoche para tacos dora-
        dos con, 194
    escabechadas, caldo de jitomate y, para tacos dorados,
        195

W

walnuts, in milk fudge with fruit and nuts, 324–25, *325*
watermelon:
    in fresh fruit cooler, 69
    mojito, 54
    -raspberry ice, 316, *316*
white beans, grill-braised short ribs with árbol chiles,
        mushrooms, beer and, 264–65
white chocolate-mezcal ice cream, 310
white wine, sparkling, in Champagne margarita, 46, *47,*
        84, 85
wild lamb's quarters, in creamy chicken and greens with
        roasted poblano and caramelized onion, 134–35,
        135

Y

yogurt cheese, in roasted garlic tamales with ricotta and
        Swiss chard, 222–23

About the Authors

Rick Bayless is the author of six cookbooks, including *Mexican Everyday*. His product line of prepared foods is sold coast to coast. He owns and operates three award-winning restaurants in Chicago: the casual Frontera Grill, named "Outstanding Restaurant" of the year by the James Beard Foundation; the 4-star fine-dining Topolobampo; and XOCO, a LEED gold-certified quick-serve restaurant that opened in September of last year. Rick won Bravo's *Top Chef Masters* competition and was named National Chef of the Year by the James Beard Foundation.

Deann Groen Bayless has coauthored six books with Rick; co-owns and co-operates Frontera Grill, Topolobampo, and XOCO with him; and feels she's done a pretty good job of nurturing along their teenage daughter, Lanie. She is a former president of Women Chefs and Restaurateurs, a national organization that promotes the education and advancement of women in the restaurant industry, and is the administrator of the Frontera Farmer Foundation.